BEYOND REASON

THE MURDER OF A MOUNTIE

ROBERT KNUCKLE

Kayson Pubishing

Kayson Pubishing

92 Jerome Park Drive
Dundas, Ontario, Canada
L9H 6H3

ISBN 0-9682043-0-9
Printed and bound in Canada

Distributed by
Hushion House Publishing
36 Northline Road, Toronto, Ontario, Canada
M4B 3E2

Layout and cover design by Kerry J. Schooley, Good Service Printing Inc.

Kayson Publishing gratefully acknowledges the assistance of the Ontario Arts Council and the Canada Council.

Canadian Cataloguing in Publication Data

Knuckle, Robert, 1935
    Beyond Reason: the murder of a Mountie

ISBN 0-9682043-0-9

    1. Police murders--Manitoba--Virden.
    2. Fugitives from justice--Manitoba--Oaklake.
    3. Royal Canadian Mounted Police.
    4. Archer, Bruce
    I.Title.

HV6535.C33V57 1997   364.15'23'0971273   C97-900908-1

ACKNOWLEDGEMENTS

I would like to thank the following for their contribution toward the completion of this book:

RCMP S/Sgt. (ret.) William Armstrong, Dundas,ON.

RCMP Cpl. (ret.) Syd Barrie and Vivian Barrie, Kamloops, B.C.

Dr. William Beahen, RCMP Historical, Ottawa, ON.

Kevan Browne, Ancaster ON.

RCMP Sgt. Ken Bullock, Regina, SK.

Police Inspector Peter Copple, Calgary, AB.

Former RCMP Cpl. Gerry Coulter, Ottawa, ON.

RCMP Cpl. Adrian (Jake) Cullins and Joan Cullins, Regina, SK.

Runa Dalik, Brandon, MB.

RCMP Inspector Don Davis, Vancouver, B.C.

Denis Deneau, Toronto, ON.

RCMP Superintendent Jerry Doucette, Regina, ON.

Phil and Roberta Drouillard, Ottawa, ON.

Dan Dutchin, RCMP, Winnipeg, MB.

RCMP S/Sgt. (ret.) Jerry Ferguson, Winnipeg, MB.

Cheryll Fuller, Oak lake, MB.

Andy Garlatti, Windsor, ON.

Glen Gordon, RCMP Historical, Ottawa, ON.

Tim Gordon, General Store Publishing, Burnstown, ON.

Bonnie Griffin, Hamilton, ON.

RCMP Cpl. Jane Hall, Surrey, B.C.

Lloyd and Wilma Hatch, Oak Lake, MB.

Tully and Arlene Hatch, Oak Lake, MB.

RCMP S/Sgt. (ret.) Bart Hawkins, Brandon, MB.

Bonnie Heath, Toronto, ON.

RCMP Sgt. Gerard Hebson, Prince Rupert, B.C.

RCMP Chief Superintendent Dawson Hovey, Ottawa, ON.

RCMP Cst. (ret.) Steve and Simone Howell, Belle River, ON.

Bill Husion, Husion House, Toronto, ON.

Detective Sgt. Al Jones, Hamilton, ON.

Ken Johnson, Dundas, ON.

RCMP Insp. (ret.) Don Klancher, Vancouver, B.C.

Ray and Cathy Levesque, Ottawa, ON.

RCMP Cpl. Brenda MacFarlane, St. Johns, NFLD.

RCMP Cst. (ret.) Debbie MacLean, Thompson, MB.
Former RCMP Cpl. Don and Carol Mahar, Ottawa, ON.
Former RCMP Cst. Ralph and Sonja Mahar, Orleans, ON.
Brian Marshall, the Brandon Sun, Brandon, MB.
Paul Mazza, Hamilton, ON.
Detective Insp. (ret.) Ray McBrien, Calgary, AB.
RCMP S/Sgt. (ret.) Don McDonald, Brandon, MB.
RCMP Sgt. Alex McLean, Vancouver, B.C.
Anna Misiti, Stoney Creek, ON.
RCMP Assistant Commisioner J. D. Moodie, Winnipeg, MB.
Anthony O'Grady, Hamilton, ON.
RCMP Cpl. John O'Ray and Marion O'Ray, Dauphim, MB.
Jerry Onofrey, Winnipeg, MB.
Rose Onofrey, Winnipeg, MB.
RCMP Cpl. Candy Palmer, London, ON.
Corny and Thelma Penner, Virden, MB.
Dave Penny, Virden, MB.
Mark Pigott, Ogilvie and Mather, Calgary, AB.
RCMP Cpl. Louise Pirie, Kamloops, B.C.
Jay Prober, Winnipeg, MB.
Reinhard Purfurst, Moto Photo, Dundas, ON.
RCMP Cpl. Derrick Reilly, Hamilton, ON.
Police Chief (ret.) Ernie Reimer, Calgary, AB.,
Joe Scanlon, Ottawa, ON.
RCMP S/Sgt. Mike Seliske, Regina, SK.
Terry Shaw, Ottawa, ON.
Orville and Eileen Sheane, Virden, MB.,
Photographer John Shoveller, Cayuga, ON.,
RCMP Cst. (ret.) Candace Smith, Vancouver, B.C.
OPP Detective George Snider, Ottawa, ON.
Kim Taylor, Hamilton, ON.
Paula Webber, Vancouver, B.C.
RCMP Cpl. Katie Weigert, London, ON.
RCMP Insp. (ret.) Jack White, Kamloops, B.C.
Hersh Wolch, Winnipeg, MB.
Glenn Wright, RCMP Historical, Ottawa, ON.

Thanks to the Canada Council and the Ontario Arts Council for their assistance.

The information provided by the following institutions was essential:

> The Brandon Sun,
> The Calgary Public Library,
> The Calgary Herald,
> Correctional Services Canada,
> The Dundas Public Library,
> The Globe and Mail,
> The Hamilton Public Library,
> The Hamilton Spectator,
> The McMaster University Library,
> The Toronto Star
> The Virden Empire-Advance,
> The Winnipeg Free Press,

Special thanks and appreciation go to:

> RCMP Cpl. (ret.) Russ Hornseth of Chatsworth, Ontario for his exceptional help through the entire duration of the project,

> Sgt. Joe MacDougall and Elaine MacDougall of Winnipeg for their enthusiastic support, hospitality and tremendous assistance in so many ways,

> Peter Fillman of Toronto, my friend since grade one at St. Angela School in Windsor who drew the diagrams for the book,

> Kerry Schooley of Good Service Printing Inc., Hamilton for his cover design, art work and printing expertise,

> Finally, my most profound appreciation to my editor, John Stevens of Toronto who always knows the best way to make a good story better. His comments and suggestions were invaluable.

Robert Knuckle

**FOR ALL MY FAMILY
ELIZABETH,
RICHARD, LEANNE,
LAURA, BOB,
MARK, SCOTT AND KELLY**

A portion of the proceeds of the sale
of this book will go to support the
Mounted Police Foundation
and community policing in Canada.

TABLE OF CONTENTS

BEYOND REASON
THE MURDER OF A MOUNTIE

FOREWORD

This project began in April, 1986 when I answered an ad in the Toronto Star. A convict named Bruce Archer who was serving a life sentence in Kingston Penitentiary wanted someone to write his story. Once I heard the details, I was intrigued and agreed to do it. That pursuit led me on a long and circuitous path that wound from Kingston and Warkworth Penitentiaries, across western Canada and back and to several libraries along the way. As I travelled, I was fortunate to meet a number of people directly involved in the story who were kind enough to help me. Many of them had suffered at the hands of Mr. Archer. Nevertheless, as I probed into the shadows of their memory, they were willing to answer my questions, even though the pain of their experience was still fresh in their hearts. I came to admire them for that.

After the research and writing were completed, I had a difficult time getting the original manuscript published. In retrospect, I think that was a good thing because that first draft was a dark and forbidding tale written from a perspective that offered few redeeming features. It sat in a drawer for years while I went on to other writing projects. Finally in 1996, because I believed so sincerely in the merit of the story, I decided to do a major re-write of the book, one that focused on the human aspects of the tragedy from the police perspective.

The result is the book you are about to read. It would never have made it into print without the cooperation of the principals mentioned above and the encouragement of a number of my friends and business associates who came to believe in the story as much as I did. To all of them I shall remain extremely grateful.

ONE COLD NIGHT

The town of Virden is a gentle, law-abiding community that sits on the flat prairie land of southwestern Manitoba 160 miles west of Winnipeg and eighteen miles from the Saskatchewan border. Many of its 3,400 residents are retired farmers whose ancestors have lived in this part of the province for generations. Most of the new folks in town are oil workers who moved in during the sixties when oil was found in the area and Virden became known as the oil capital of Manitoba.

The town has a small business section with a municipal building, a co-op supermarket, one movie theatre and two hotels. Three grain elevators look down on the sturdy Victorian train station and the Canadian Pacific Railway mainline that was built in 1882 and still runs across the country from Halifax to Vancouver. There is a detachment office of the Royal Canadian Mounted Police.

If the town itself is quiet, the Trans-Canada Highway is busy. Highway #1, as the locals call it, runs across the town's northern edge and is the main east west artery in the province. Several large gas stations with restaurants serve the highway at Virden. Two motels and a thirty-three bed hospital are located on the frontage road that runs adjacent to the highway and parallel with it.

In this part of the country the weather on the open plains is constant: there is lots of wind and little rain. Living in Virden in the summer, spring and fall can be pleasant. In the winter it can be miserable. The temperature takes a numbing dip and, when the frigid wind comes rolling across the prairies from the west, it can produce a chill factor that is sometimes almost paralyzing. It was on one of those cold nights in January of 1978 that the awful fate of four police officers began to play itself out.

Dennis Onofrey, a dark and handsome twenty-seven-year-old Mountie from the Virden Detachment, was working alone in a police cruiser on the night shift. Earlier he and his wife, Paula and their young son, Corey, had been over to Steve and Simone Howells' place for a Sunday brunch. Steve was a fellow Mountie.

3

He and his wife had become friends with the Onofreys since Dennis and Paula arrived in town three years before. For Paula, going out for dinner was a special treat because she was seven months pregnant and looked forward to getting out of the kitchen and off her feet. Corey was less than two years old and, although Dennis was very good at caring for him, he still demanded a lot of Paula's time and attention.

The Onofreys finished their brunch at the Howells' and were home by 4:00 in the afternoon. By 4:30 Dennis was in his uniform and on his way to the detachment office. Paula kissed him good-bye and Dennis told her gently to get some rest. He would try not to disturb her when he came home, sometime after 1:00 in the morning. He also said he would come by in his cruiser around 11:00 to say good night.

Paula was not disturbed by her husband working as a policeman. Unlike many policemen's wives, she had learned to deal with the anxiety of the job. She started working on that the day he left for his six-month training course at the Royal Canadian Mounted Police Depot Division in Regina. By the time Dennis finished his training and was posted to Virden, Paula had taught herself to think positively. She was determined not to spend her life fretting about his safety every time he went out the door to work. It helped her immensely knowing that Virden had a reputation as a good, safe detachment, one that served a peaceful town and rural area where dangers were minimal. Any policing problems that came to Virden usually came off the highway. Vagrants, transients, and sometimes drugged-up hippies used the highway as a conduit to travel back and forth, primarily between Ontario and British Columbia. When these gypsies got high on booze or drugs, their behaviour could be unpredictable and sometimes dangerous. Most of these problems occurred in the summertime, when the weather was more suitable for travelling. Transients didn't use the highway much in the winter. It was too cold a place to be stranded when their old cars broke down or when they were left in the lurch as hitchhikers. If anything, the Mounties in the Virden Detachment complained that policing here in the winter was boring.

On this Sunday afternoon Dennis was on town duty, the safest job in the detachment. Dennis' shift boss was thirty-year-old

Corporal Russell Hornseth, a reliable veteran of ten years. His four postings with the RCMP had taken him from the sweet life on the Musical Ride to the Friday night fights with the hardrock miners in Flin Flon, northern Manitoba. Rugged looking, broad shouldered and trim with leathery skin and a dark service mustache, he resembled the Marlboro Man in the American cigarette advertisements.

Russ had been promoted to corporal three months previously and, as such, was the night shift operational supervisor. That meant that while he was on duty, he would patrol in his own car but he was also responsible for the safety and supervision of the other detachment members on that shift. On the job, Russ was quiet and reserved, polite and efficient. To his comrades he was straightforward, honest and dependable. He treated people in the community the same way. These qualities made him well liked and respected by almost everybody.

This Sunday night Russ was by himself in a cruiser heading out to Ray Needham's farm ten miles southeast of Virden. Although Ray was Russ' best friend in Virden, it was Ray's son, Dave, whom Russ was looking for. Dave wanted to join the RCMP and had asked Russ to come out to help him fill out the application and answer some of his questions. Dave's biggest problem was that he was a little short of the 5'8" height requirement for the RCMP. Russ had told him to hang from the door by his finger tips to stretch himself out for the day of his RCMP physical.

As Hornseth drove past the snow banks that lined the roadways between the flat white fields, he thought to himself that he'd like to have a place of his own in the country someday. Just a small place for him, his wife Kim and their dog Ralph. Finding a place to suit Ralph was no small consideration. He was a huge, black Newfoundland dog that could easily be mistaken for a furry pony. It was no exaggeration to say that Ralph was a big part of the Hornseth family.

The other two Mounties on duty this shift were Constable John O'Ray and a young rookie named Candy Smith. They were working the detachment's highway patrol, which meant they were responsible for everything on Highway #1 from Griswold in the east to the Saskatchewan border in the west. These responsibilities included speeding tickets, attending at accidents or vehicle breakdowns and road closures.

At twenty-eight years of age John O'Ray was a seven-year veteran of the RCMP. He was a good-looking guy with blond hair and a chubby face. There was a marked dimple in the middle of his rather square jaw. Although he was only 5'8", his chunky shoulders and big upper arms made him look bigger and stronger than his size. John usually wore eyeglasses even though he only needed them for reading.

He came to Virden in June of 1973, which meant that he was the member of longest standing in the Virden office. Prior to Virden, John had served in a small detachment in Cranberry Portage, Manitoba, not far from Flin Flon. He and Hornseth had crossed paths up there on several occasions.

Lately John was a very busy policeman. Besides his duties on the highway, he had the extra responsibility of acting as Candy Smith's trainer. Candy, who was twenty-three, had graduated from Depot Division in Regina just six weeks before. It is standard practice with the RCMP to have a new recruit shadow an experienced member for a period of up to six months so he or she can learn first-hand the practical aspects of detachment policing. As soon as Candy arrived in Virden, Staff Sergeant Fred Westerson, the detachment commander, assigned her to work alongside John. O'Ray was honoured to be chosen and looked forward to his new teaching role. The primer he used for his instruction was the *RCMP Recruit Field Training Manual*. The manual posed a variety of practical problems that a police officer might encounter and stipulated how these situations should be handled.

So far the assignment was working out well for both of them because they got along extremely well. John was friendly and talkative. Candy was inclined to be quiet and shy but she soon learned to be comfortable with John as her teacher. Much of their time together was spent in a cruiser working the highway. A few times they made some calls at farms in the area; on one occasion they visited the Sioux Valley Indian Reserve to the northeast. After training six months with John, or possibly less with John's approval, Candy would be cleared to work on shifts by herself. For now her training had been firmly tethered to John.

There were one or two in the detachment who thought Candy could use all the training time she could get before she was sent out on her own. They perceived her as being too quiet and reserved. They were concerned that she might not be aggressive enough to be an effective investigator. Besides that, Candy was very young looking and there were those who wondered whether she presented a strong enough image to operate by herself on the highway patrol or to function alone when she was handling a domestic dispute somewhere on the back roads.

John O'Ray did not share these concerns. Working side by side with her for six weeks convinced him that, once she finished her training, Candy would be able to handle any aspect of police work by herself. Her size and build and physical aggressiveness were certainly not against her. At 5'7" and a lithe 135 lbs., Candy came to Virden with a solid assessment as a capable ground fighter in her self-defense classes at Depot.

These were the four who made up the shift for this fateful Sunday night: Russ, the supervisor, Dennis in town, John and Candy on highway patrol. There was nothing pressing for any of them to do. Early in the evening O'Ray and Smith spent most of their time working on statements, doing reports and file follow-up. Dennis Onofrey found that sitting in his cruiser weaving his way around town was uneventful, almost tedious. His only consolation was that it was comfortably warm in the car and he had lots of time to think. Now that the New Year had arrived, he had many good things to look forward to. A new Onofrey baby was coming soon. His mother, Rose, whom he loved dearly, would be coming out to stay with them to give Paula a hand when the baby arrived. His work on the recreation room in the basement would soon be done. Then his kids would have a nice place to play and he and Paula would have a spot to hold detachment parties. They could probably have their first party down there sometime in the spring. His mind kept rambling back and forth over these pleasant thoughts.

Outside the cruiser the wind was gusting. As he drove past the warm, little houses in town, wisps of snow wafted down from the roof tops and blew across the frozen banks that lined the driveways.

Dennis was aware that he was very alone. There was nobody out on the streets; no one he recognized or wanted to stop and talk to in the restaurants. Nothing came over the radio of any interest, only the occasional crackle when the dispatcher from Brandon spoke to another policeman about things far away and of little concern to Constable Onofrey.

From time to time during the shift Dennis circled back to the detachment office to see if there were any messages or notices that he should attend to. He stomped into the office in his heavy galoshes and exchanged pleasantries with O'Ray and Smith. After finding nothing that needed his attention, he headed back out to his car and began circling through town again.

John O'Ray and Candy Smith continued working together in the detachment office. He showed her how to fill out some standard reports, then reviewed several items in the Training Manual. Candy had covered some of this material during her training at Depot but was glad for the chance to go over it again. Throughout all their work, the phone never rang once. There was even time for a coffee and some friendly banter between them. They enjoyed working together.

Around 10:30 p.m. that same Sunday night, a solitary truck made its weary way along a lonely stretch of the Trans-Canada Highway and crossed the border from Saskatchewan into the Province of Manitoba. The vehicle was a white, square-backed GMC Magnavan covered with the gray grit of the icy roads. Two big people were in the cab. Forty-two-year-old Bruce Archer was behind the wheel and Dorothy Malette, twenty-nine, was asleep beside him. They had come over 600 miles since leaving Lethbridge, almost seventeen hours before. The trip had been tedious because the roads were slippery and Archer had to drive with caution. Besides that, the truck was a rental vehicle that was long overdue. Not wanting to draw any attention from the police, Archer had made sure to stay well within the speed limit for the entire trip. As he drove, his eyes darted from the road ahead to the rear view mirror. He'd been in trouble on and off for the last four years but this time there was more than just a rental truck or a speeding ticket at stake. If the police found him now, he could be in serious trouble.

All things considered, he was making fairly good time. One by one he had left behind the small western cities with strange sounding Indian names: Medicine Hat, Swift Current, Moose Jaw. Brandon was over an hour's drive straight ahead. Bruce knew exactly where he was. He'd been this way before and he liked travelling like this: the country music on the radio, Dorothy half asleep in the seat beside him and, in the back of the truck, everything they owned. Everything was back there except his two prized rifles, which were in their cases stashed behind Dorothy's seat in the cab.

Before long, they were under the mercury vapour lights that lit up the highway just north of the business section of Virden. Everything was pretty well closed up, except one gas station. When Archer saw the sign indicating the service road, he decided he'd had enough for today and pulled off the highway. Even though he was a big burly man who was used to driving moving vans long haul, he was whipped. He needed to find a place to get a good night's sleep.

Up ahead, he saw the tall sign for the Countryside Inn. It indicated there was a vacancy and it looked like a good place for the two of them to spend the night. When Archer stopped the truck by the motel office, Dorothy woke up. She was a very stout woman, heavy in the hips and thighs. She wore dark-rimmed tinted glasses and, although her face was fleshy, there were pretty features hidden underneath. Her eyes were green and beautiful and her long, silky brown hair fell well below her shoulders. Bruce left the motor running as he went inside to get a room.

While Archer was waiting to register at the motel, Dennis Onofrey was heading for his house on Bennett Crescent. Ironically, after a very slow tour of night duty, he was now in a hurry because he had some assignments to perform before he went off shift. They wouldn't take long but they had to be done. However, first, he wanted to go by his house to say good night to his wife.

At home Paula was having a problem getting Corey to sleep. She was in the process of changing him over from a crib to a bed and Corey was having a difficult time settling down. When he finally drifted off to sleep, she was glad to have a few minutes to herself to watch TV. She liked to watch the CBC news at eleven. Although she was sitting low in Dennis' big comfortable chair, she still was able to see out the window and spot his blue and white cruiser as it pulled up in front of the house. Dennis stopped by every night like this when he was on the late shift. She struggled out of the chair and stood in front of the big front window and watched as Dennis shone the beam of his flashlight at her from inside his car. As he made circles with the beam of his light, Paula smiled and waved back at him. She thought to herself that he must really be busy tonight because usually he came into the house for a minute or two to make sure everything was all right.

But it didn't matter to her that he didn't come in, she was just happy that he had stopped by. She waved again and after a few seconds the flashlight went out and the cruiser began pulling slowly away. The car started gently around the curve of the crescent and the last thing she saw were its red tail lights disappearing into the darkness.

After his visit home, one of Dennis' routine assignments was to go to the two hotels in town and then to the two motels out by the Trans-Canada Highway to record the license plate numbers of the cars parked in their lots. Then he had to return to the detachment office and run the plate numbers through the Canadian Police Information Computer (CPIC) to see if there were any irregularities. This procedure was based on the premise that anyone travelling across Manitoba who was wanted by the law or who was driving a stolen vehicle would likely take the Trans-Canada Highway. If they stopped in Virden, the RCMP could check them out and determine who they were, then confront them in their rooms. To be effective, this procedure had to be done late at night, close to the end of the evening shift. By that time anyone who was on the run from the law would have stopped for the night and be nicely settled in their room. Since it was now after 11:00 p.m., Dennis could start to do his licence checks. He steered for the Central Hotel in downtown Virden.

At the Countryside Inn, Bruce Archer waited while the motel owner, June Bohonis, registered two travelling salesmen. They acknowledged Archer with a nod and were amused when they saw this big stranger in the heavy coat and gray, Russian-style hat, bend down to gently stroke the Bohonis' little dog. After the two men were assigned a room, they left and got into their truck. It was shortly after 11:00 p.m.

Now it was Archer's turn. He stepped up to the desk and proceeded to register for him and his wife. As he filled out the registration form, June Bohonis noticed his right hand was bandaged and he was shaking. It looked as if he was in some pain.

He signed his name very slowly. She asked him about it and Archer explained he had hurt his hand helping his sister move.

To secure his registration, Archer used a credit card in the name of Maurice Crystal. June thanked him and assigned him to room 20 on the west side of the motel. She gave him a room key and their routine transaction was over. As Archer went out and drove his vehicle around the side of the building, June went back into her apartment to catch the rest of the news on television.

Meanwhile at the RCMP detachment office, John O'Ray decided that he and Candy had done enough paperwork inside and said they were going out to patrol the highway for a while.

"I know it's pretty quiet out there," he said, "but we better make a run from one end to the other and see what's happening."

Candy was glad for the chance to get out of the office. Without saying a word, she pulled on her dark blue storm coat, then wiggled on her fur cap and gloves.

"Where are we heading?" she asked.

"We'll head east through Routledge to Griswold and then circle back west as far as Elkhorn. How's that sound?"

"Sounds good to me."

As they left the office, they braced themselves against the bitter cold. The first few minutes in the cruiser were uncomfortable. Both of them shivered and mumbled to themselves in the frigid air while they waited for the engine to warm up and the heater to kick in. Under the light of the bright full moon their breath came out in narrow clouds of vapour.

"Brrrr," John moaned. "I just love these Manitoba winters."

Candy shivered and smiled but said nothing.

Within minutes they were heading down King Street. Then they were pulling out on the long highway that stretches towards Routledge. The heater still wasn't producing much warmth.

At the Countryside Inn, Archer parked a little beyond the front of room 20. Together he and Dorothy took their gear in from the truck. This included a couple of suitcases and a cardboard box containing a variety of snack food. It also contained a substantial number of shells for a 20-gauge shotgun and bullets for a high-powered deer rifle. With this box safely deposited in the room, Bruce went back to the truck for one final trip. Carefully removing his two rifles from behind the front seat, he carried them into the

11

motel room. Then he and Dorothy got ready for a good night's sleep.

In town, Dennis found no vehicles to register at the Central Hotel. There were only a couple of cars he didn't recognize and both of them had Manitoba licence plates. He was only interested in vehicles with out-of-province plates. When Dennis nudged his cruiser over to the Alexander Hotel in the next block, he found there was nothing to record there either. He wasn't surprised. He drove across the CPR tracks, past the curling rink and the arena at the fairgrounds, up Queen Street to the frontage road that runs parallel to the Trans-Canada Highway. All along the way there wasn't a person to be seen anywhere on the streets.

It was much the same for John and Candy on the highway. Their trip to Griswold was uneventful. There were very few cars on the road and none of them seemed to be in a hurry to get where they were going. From Griswold back to Elkhorn was more of the same. They used the time to go over arrest procedures. John would describe a specific crime scenario and ask her how she would handle it. Most of her answers were very good. On some things she needed clarification. As they were driving back towards Virden, John posed another of his hypothetical questions.

"OK, Candy. What would you do if you stopped a couple of underage teenagers with sealed beer in the trunk, heading for the pits on a Sunday night?"

Candy thought for a while, then gave her answer.

John zeroed in on one part of her reply. "What section of the Act gives you the right to seize the beer?"

She answered again.

John acknowledged she was right. Then asked, "What would you do with the beer once you seized it?"

Candy wasn't sure about that.

"Well, you'd take the licence number, initial it with the time and date, hold it in the exhibit locker, give it an exhibit number . . ."

On and on it went. As teacher and pupil, they made a good pair. John knew his stuff and loved to explain things. Candy was an intense listener. She wanted to be ready when they sent her out on her own. Both of them found their discussions a rewarding way to pass the time. Before they knew it, the lights of the service stations outside Virden came into view.

"Well," Candy said, "that didn't take very long, did it?"

"No," John agreed, "just long enough to get the car nice and warm." He turned off the highway and headed down King Street.

Candy yawned and said, "Gee, I wish it were busier. I wish we had something to do."

"Please don't say that," John replied. "Every time I hear you say something like that, I want to touch wood. We got plenty to do as it is. We don't need to go looking for trouble."

Candy nodded her agreement. "I guess this is better than having to investigate a homicide or something."

John pulled the cruiser up beside the detachment office and the two partners stepped out into the mean cold of the night.

As they were walking into the office, Russ Hornseth was driving up Ray Needham's laneway. When he got beside the house, he pulled his cruiser over as close as he could to the side porch. Then he turned up the volume on his police radio and left the motor running.

Once he stepped inside the farmhouse door, he could smell the deer steak that Dave was frying in the kitchen. "Hey, what are you doing in there?" Russ called out.

"Cooking up a midnight snack," Dave answered. "You interested in a nice piece of venison?"

Russ was delighted. "You bet," he said as he took off his hat and started to undo his storm coat. "We can do our talking while we eat. Kinda' kill two birds with one stone." It was seldom an outdoorsman like Russ Hornseth turned down a fresh piece of venison.

While Russ was fixing himself a place at Needham's table, Dennis was driving into the parking lot of the Countryside Inn. This motel was in the shape of a T with the top of the T facing the frontage road, containing the office and the apartment of the owners, Bill and June Bohonis. Behind this section a long column of rooms ran off perpendicular to the office. As Dennis eased his cruiser past the front section of the Countryside Inn, he noticed the lights were still on in the Bohonis' apartment. Even though it was almost midnight, he knew this was normal for them. They were probably watching television.

Slowly he moved along the west side of the motel surveying the column of rooms. Most of them were in darkness. He thought to himself that things were really slow tonight; there were only two vehicles in the parking lot. Dennis could understand why. Who would want to be travelling across the country in this kind of freezing weather? He recorded the plate numbers on the two vehicles. One was a blue truck bearing Alberta licence plate D45686; it seemed to belong to room 17. The lights were on in that room. The other was a white, 1976, GMC box van with the British Columbia plate 7879AK. Dennis noticed that four inch stick-on letters spelling "Exporters" had been used to crudely cover over some painted words on the side of the van. It was parked close to room 20. The lights were on in that room too. All the other rooms showed no signs of life. Once Dennis finished recording the two plate numbers, he drove around the bottom of the motel, circled back to the frontage road and pushed on for the Virden Motel. It was in the next block west of the Countryside Inn. When he got to the Virden Motel, he went through the same procedure copying down the plate numbers for the few cars parked in their lot. After that he cut over to First Avenue, drove past the hospital and headed down King Street to the detachment office.

The office was located in a small building on Hargrave Street. At one time it had been an unpretentious storey and a half family home. The RCMP had bought the house and converted it into a detachment office. A service counter was set up inside the front door and much of what had formerly been the living room/dining room of the house was now the general office area. This space was filled with desks and chairs and filing cabinets with reams of papers and folders piled on all of them. Adjacent to the main office was a communications room that housed the detachment's radio and CPIC equipment. Towards the back of the house there was a washroom and two smaller offices for the non-commissioned officers (NCOs) of the post. One of these offices was used by the detachment commander, Staff Sergeant Fred Westerson; the other was an office that was shared by the three detachment corporals: Russ Hornseth, Syd Barrie and Larry Keyes. There was also a small room off the main office that contained breathalyzer equipment. Upstairs there was one big room that was used as a members' lounge. Here they could eat their lunch or have a coffee and a smoke. In the basement of the building there were two roomy cells used to lock up prisoners on a short-term basis. These cells were seldom used during the week; occasionally they were occupied on the weekends.

When Dennis got back to the detachment, John and Candy were doing paperwork in the main office. They stopped what they were doing and exchanged greetings with him. All three made disparaging remarks about the weather. Dennis peeled off his storm coat and fur hat, took out his notebook and moved toward the CPIC computer. John knew exactly what Dennis was doing. He had performed the same routine many times himself.

"Not much doing out there tonight, I wouldn't think," John commented.

"Nothing in town," Dennis replied over his shoulder. "Couple of cars at both the motels. Two trucks actually at the Countryside."

That was the extent of their conversation. Although Dennis was usually very pleasant with people, he was a task-oriented person and, as such, he was not very chatty, especially when he was working. He went directly into the communications room and began to enter the plate numbers into the computer.

O'Ray and Smith moved into the breathalyzer office to go over some material on its operation. John had just begun his instruction when Dennis called out to them.

"Hey you guys, I've got a hit!"

"Really?" John called back.

"Yeah, a white cube van at the Countryside Motel."

"Is it stolen?" John asked. He immediately went out to join Dennis in the communications room. Candy followed behind him.

"No. But it's overdue from a Surrey B.C. rental agency," Dennis replied. "Long overdue."

"No kidding," John said, looking at the printout over Dennis' shoulder.

As Dennis reread the printout, he felt the slightest hint of adrenaline beginning to flow. He had no idea what the overdue rental was about. It could be anything from bad paperwork by the rental agency to a stolen vehicle. He was well aware that the Trans-Canada was infamous for bringing transients and drifters through their community. Whether that was the case this time, was too early to say. As he tugged on his storm coat, he asked John to check with the Surrey RCMP detachment to confirm that B.C. licence # 7879AK was still outstanding and overdue. John, who was

15

equally concerned but not disturbed by the situation at hand, assented. Candy could sense the tension in the air. She saw the signs of strain on Dennis' face as he tugged on his fur hat. Without saying anything, he hurried out the door.

At 12:39 a.m. O'Ray sent a telex to the Surrey detachment asking for confirmation on the overdue van. As he and Smith waited for a reply, Dennis worked his way back to the Countryside Inn. En route he put out a call on his radio for his corporal, Russ Hornseth.

As Dennis was calling for Russ on the radio, Dave Needham was putting a steaming plate of venison and fried potatoes in front of the wiry corporal. Russ was making his first cut into the steak when he heard some squawking come from the radio in his cruiser outside. He shook his head in disbelief. Then, swearing unintelligibly under his breath, he grudgingly got up and went outside to respond to the call.

When he got into the car, the radio call came through again and he recognized Dennis' voice. Russ clicked on the hand microphone and spoke into it, "What's up, Dennis?"

"I got a hit on a box van at the Countryside Inn. It's long overdue out of Surrey B.C. O'Ray is checking with Surrey to see what the status is on the vehicle. I'm on my way to the motel now."

In a flash Russ remembered another incident when they had an overdue vehicle at one of the Virden motels. That time the car was stolen and all hell had broken loose when they tried to arrest the driver. The guy ended up diving out the bathroom window and it took three Mounties to wrestle him to the ground and get him into a cruiser.

Russ said, "I'm at Ray Needham's place and I'm leaving right now. Don't go near that room until I get there."

"OK," Dennis replied, "I'll meet you at the motel office."

"Countryside Inn, right?"

"Right."

"See you at the office," Russ said. Then he repeated, "Dennis, hold off. I'm coming in."

Back at the detachment office as John O'Ray waited for Surrey to advise on the status of the cube van, he could hear Hornseth and Onofrey over the radio in the communications room.

When Russ went back into the house to get his coat and hat,

Dave Needham was sitting at the table munching on his steak.

"I got to go into town," Russ said.

"Got a problem?" Dave asked between bites.

"Maybe. Hard to know but I got to go."

"OK," Dave replied, "I'll see you when you get back."

"Yeah, I'll be back," Russ said. "Don't throw my meat out, I'll be back as soon as I can."

Then Russ went out the door and climbed in his cruiser. He backed down the laneway and slewed backwards onto the side road. Then he put it in forward and sped away for the motel. Wanting to be as inconspicuous as possible, he decided against activating his flashing roof lights.

At 12:52 a.m. Surrey Detachment confirmed to O'Ray that the cube van B.C. plate 7879AK was still overdue. John got on the radio and twice attempted to contact Dennis in his cruiser. Both times he received no response.

"Why doesn't he answer?" Candy asked.

"I don't know. He might be out of his PC (police cruiser) and talking to someone in the motel office." John could see the concern registered on Candy's face. "It's nothing to worry about. He won't do anything at the motel until Hornseth gets there."

Then O'Ray contacted Hornseth en route and advised him that the van was still overdue. He also told him that he and Candy were heading over to the motel too. Hornseth acknowledged his message and said he would meet O'Ray and Smith with Onofrey at the motel office.

"Do you think it's something serious?" Candy asked John.

"I don't think so," he replied. "But you never know. It could be something, could be nothing. Either way they could use our support. Get your coat on and let's go."

While John and Candy were dressing for the cold, Dennis was out of his cruiser knocking on the office door of the Countryside Inn. Bill and June Bohonis had gone to bed and were just dozing off when they heard the office doorbell ring. This was a common occurrence for them, so Bill got up and put on his pants and robe and went out to the office. He was somewhat surprised at this time of night to see a police officer at the door. As soon as he opened it, he recognized the officer as Dennis Onofrey. Like all of the sixteen Mounties posted in Virden, Dennis was well known around the town.

"Hello, Dennis," Bill said. "What brings you here this time of night?"

"Hi, Bill," Dennis replied. "Just trying to check something out. Can you tell me who's staying in room 20?"

"Sure, c'mon in."

Dennis followed Bill into the office and waited while he went through his registration cards.

"Guy by the name of Maurice Crystal and his wife. What's the problem?"

"I don't know. Might be a stolen truck. Can I have that card for a minute?"

"Sure, help yourself."

"Thanks, I'll be back in a minute." Dennis went out to his cruiser and called Hornseth who, by now, was only minutes away.

"Russ, it's me Dennis."

"Yeah, go ahead."

"I'm outside the office at the Countryside Inn. The people with the overdue van are a guy named Maurice Crystal and his wife."

"OK," Russ replied.

"They're staying in room 20."

"OK, Dennis, stay where you are. Wait for me there."

"Roger. Will do."

As John O'Ray was pulling his cruiser away from the detachment office, he and Candy heard the conversation between Dennis and Russ.

"Did you get that room number?" he asked Candy.

"Yes, room 20 . . . the Countryside Inn," she replied.

"Good for you," John said. "Let's go see what's going on."

As Dennis waited outside the motel, Hornseth, O'Ray and Smith hurried to meet him.

None of them had any idea how this cold winter's night would change their lives forever.

DEPOT DIVISION

Dennis Onofrey, his mother Rose and his older brother, Jerry, were abandoned by the boys' father when they were infants. Rose raised them alone on her modest secretary's income. Although she didn't have much money, Rose made sure her sons had enough to eat, plenty of love and motherly attention. The three of them lived in a one bedroom apartment that was part of a divided house in the toughest section of downtown Winnipeg. For a long time their uncle, Edward, lived with them, sleeping on a couch in the living room. For twenty years Dennis and Jerry shared a Murphy bed that folded out of the wall in that same room. The boys' sleeping arrangements epitomized the closeness they shared all through the years they were home.

Rose, whose maiden name was Kaskiw, was Ukrainian. She spoke the language fluently and cooked the best perogies and cabbage rolls on the block. As a devout Roman Catholic, she never served meat on Friday and took her boys to nine o'clock mass every Sunday at St. Mary's Cathedral in the core of the city. Dennis and Jerry attended St. Mary's Elementary School adjacent to the cathedral. Every day Rose would walk the boys to school and then pick them up from the playground on her way home from work.

Dennis was good in school. His teachers liked him because he was a considerate, reliable boy who always had his work done and never caused any problems in the classroom. Like many of the kids his age, Dennis was industrious. He had a paper route and used his earnings to buy himself a bicycle. When he finished grade eight, Dennis went to St. Paul's High School. He was a spindly kid with glasses who liked sports but was too small and thin to try out for the school teams. Although school had never been a problem for Dennis, he now began to struggle. His marks were passable but Rose could see his heart wasn't in his work. He wasn't happy at St. Paul's and after a year, somewhat against Rose's wishes, Dennis transferred to Daniel McIntyre Public High School. Even with a fresh start, Dennis' performance didn't improve. The energy that he once had applied to his school work was now going to a

19

little rock band called "The House Grannies" that he and his brother were playing in. The band was organized by one of their friends; another buddy played drums; Jerry was on lead guitar; Dennis played bass and sang backup. The band would listen to records by the Beatles and the Rolling Stones and then imitate what they heard. Each tune they learned took them six or seven hours to master. Over a period of time, they built up a reasonable repertoire and began to get jobs playing at local community clubs around Winnipeg. On one occasion they got a job in Shoal Lake about 140 miles west of the city. This was a big deal for Dennis and Jerry. Not only was their band going on the road but Shoal Lake was where their grandmother, Mary Kaskiw, lived. They knew she would be bragging to everyone in town in her thick Ukrainian accent that her two grandsons were coming in with a band to play for the dance at the community hall.

As Dennis got older, Shoal Lake became one of his favourite places. He and his best friend, Ray Levesque, would drive out there to go hunting. It was Ray who taught Dennis how to handle a shotgun. Although Dennis didn't like the idea of shooting things, he loved the physical experience of being outdoors. After spending most of the day tromping through the bush looking for ducks and partridge, they would head for Dennis' grandmother's place for a good Ukrainian meal. When Ray and Dennis weren't hunting at Shoal Lake, they would often go to the Sandy Lake Reserves south of Winnipeg to hunt for game birds.

School remained a problem for Dennis. In the summer holidays after grade ten, he got a job at a Winnipeg printing company and liked it so much that when it came time to return to school he didn't want to go back. Rose was upset because she knew he needed more education than just grade ten. She called the owner of the printing company and told him she didn't want Dennis working there any more; she wanted him in school. The owner said that Dennis was very good at his work and he couldn't fire him; returning to school was entirely up to Dennis. Rose tried her best to persuade Dennis to go back to school but he wouldn't do it. Dennis stayed at the printing shop against his mother's wishes for the next two years.

The job put a little money in his pocket and gave him a chance to help his mother with the household finances. That was typical of Dennis. He was a very caring son. He and his mother both worked downtown so they walked to work together. People would see them strolling along, laughing and talking and couldn't believe they were mother and son. They seemed more like a couple of old friends. Sometimes they went out for lunch together. At night, no matter what time Dennis came home, he would never go to bed with out saying good night to his mother, even if he had to knock on her door and wake her up to do it.

Rose pleaded with him to get his high school diploma but Dennis wasn't interested. He liked the idea of having a few dollars in his pocket and the freedom to pursue new interests, particularly sports. By then he was bigger and stronger so he decided to try out for the junior football team in St. Vital. In his first year he became one of their star linemen. He also played baseball and did some boxing. He and Ray Levesque would go down in Ray's basement, put on the gloves and spar with each other. Since Dennis was much bigger and stronger than Ray, he was always able to beat him but he was careful not to hurt him. Ray, in turn, was smart enough not to antagonize him. He had seen what Dennis was like when he lost his temper. At high school, Dennis had taken on a bully who had been beating up on other kids. Dennis was ferocious that day and the fight was over before any punches were thrown. He slammed the bully up against a locker and warned him to leave other people alone. The fury in Dennis was so intense, the bully was afraid to test it.

Dennis had a passion for fast cars so the second year that he was working, he bought himself a new maroon Barracuda 318 Fastback that could go a hundred miles an hour. This was the first major purchase of his life and, considering the hard circumstances he'd come grown up in, it felt good to splurge on such a luxury.

No matter how contented Dennis was with his working life, Rose never lost sight of her goal to have him return to school. She pestered him every chance she got and, finally, Dennis began to see the value of having a high school diploma.

Partly to please his mother and partly because he knew it was the right thing to do, Dennis enrolled in a night school Adult Education course that would give him his high school equivalency. Rose was delighted when she saw how seriously he applied himself to his school work. Both of them were thrilled at the results he began to bring home. He finished the course and got his diploma in record time with the highest marks in his class. Then in 1970 he met the young woman who would be his wife.

Their first date wasn't very auspicious. Ray Levesque's girlfriend, Cathy, was training as a nurse at Winnipeg General Hospital. Her best friend in the residence was an attractive, dark-haired girl named Paula Bradshaw. At Ray's suggestion, Cathy invited Paula over to her folks' place to meet Dennis. They all sat around Cathy's recreation room munching potato chips and watching television until Dennis and Paula both fell asleep in the middle of the movie. Ray had to wake them up when it was time to go home. Something must have clicked between them because from that time forward they began dating and before long they were going steady.

This was an adjustment for Rose because she was used to having Dennis all to herself. Now he was seeing Paula almost every night. All through their courtship Dennis tried to be sensitive to his mother's needs. He made sure to call her if he was going to be coming home late. He tried to let her know where he was and what he was doing. And he always made sure to phone and wish her good night.

After dating for a year, Dennis and Paula got engaged. Another year later they were married at St. Mary's Cathedral, the same church where Dennis had been baptized and confirmed. Dennis asked his brother to be his best man but Jerry declined because he didn't like the idea of making a speech. Ray Levesque was happy to stand in Jerry's place.

Since Dennis and Paula couldn't afford an expensive honeymoon, they took a room in a downtown Winnipeg hotel on their wedding night. The next morning they happened to meet Rose at mass and they all went to her place for breakfast.

The Onofreys were a typical young couple. They wanted to have fun and enjoy their lives together but they also wanted to save enough money to buy a house. They golfed together, went to dances and house parties, exchanged dinner dates with their friends. Paula, who had only stayed in nursing for a year, took a job with Manitoba Telephone. Dennis put in as many hours as he could with Public Press.

In his relationship with Paula, Dennis was clearly the more

dominant of the two. Although he was a gentle man who seldom raised his voice, he exuded an inner power that gave him an aura of authority. He was more inclined to have unwavering opinions than Paula and he was vocal about them. Paula tended to be quiet and reserved, accepting of his attitudes and decisions.

A year or so after they were married, it became apparent that Dennis was unhappy at his printing job. It wasn't that he disliked the work; he simply felt it was a dead-end occupation with limited prospects for the future. As he became more and more disenchanted, he started talking about becoming a policeman. That was fine with Paula but when Rose heard about it, she was upset.

"Why do you want to be a policeman?" she asked him.

"I've always wanted to be a policeman," Dennis answered. "You know that . . . ever since I was a little kid."

"Oh, Dennis all little boys want to be a policeman when they're young but when they grow up, they change . . . that idea goes away."

"Well, it hasn't gone away with me, Mom. I've been thinking about it more and more. I think I'd like to be a Mountie."

"A Mountie! Oh, Dennis, then you'd have to move away from home. I'd never get to see the two of you."

"Sure you would. You could come and visit us."

"They could send you way up to the Yukon or something."

"No they wouldn't. You have to apply for something like that. They let you stay in your own province now. I could even be stationed right here in Winnipeg."

"Oh, Dennis please think of something else. I don't want you to be a policeman," she told him. "It's too dangerous."

"Mom, don't be so silly. I could just as easily get hurt crossing the street."

Their discussions on this topic always ended in a stalemate. Rose couldn't be convinced; Dennis wouldn't be deterred. So in the spring of 1973, as much as he didn't want to go against his mother's wishes, Dennis applied to join the RCMP. He was turned down, for two reasons. They weren't accepting married men and they weren't accepting applicants who needed glasses for distance. Dennis was disappointed. Rose was delighted. Paula was caught in the middle.

In 1974 the RCMP eased the restrictions that had previously excluded Dennis. There was a projected demand for more RCMP replacements. British Columbia and Newfoundland had contracted the police services of the RCMP in 1950. In two years many of the members in those two provinces having completed twenty-five years of service would be eligible for unpenalized pensions and would leave the Force. The country was also gearing up for the 1976 Olympics in Montreal and a lot of Mounties would be required to serve in security positions for visiting teams, heads of state and their retinues. What's more, these were the Trudeau years and there was a lot of money available for national programs. The RCMP wanted to take advantage of the government's largesse while it lasted.

Dennis, aware of the change in requirements, applied for both the RCMP and the Winnipeg City Police. Other than his eyesight, Dennis was a good candidate. He was bright, well spoken and a fine physical specimen, standing 6'1" and weighing a well-muscled 180 lbs. This time, much to his delight and Rose's consternation, Dennis was accepted into both forces. He chose the Mounties and began the process of being inducted.

Both he and Paula were excited. A new phase in their life's adventure was opening for them. They would probably be moving, maybe somewhere far away. They would be meeting new friends, possibly starting a family. Paula's only concern was that Dennis would be training in Regina for six months with only a few chances to come home for a weekend. Dennis convinced her that was a small price to pay for a secure future, an honourable job and a respected place in a community. Paula knew he was right and made up her mind she could get along without him for six months.

Dennis was to begin his training on December 1, 1974. After he was sworn in as an RCMP constable in Winnipeg, he loaded his suitcases into his Barracuda, kissed Paula and his mom good-bye, and headed west for RCMP Depot Division.

Depot is a sprawling complex of red brick buildings that lies on the western fringe of the City of Regina. Its origin dates back to 1882 when it served as the headquarters of the fledgling North-West Mounted Police that had been sent out by Sir John A. Macdonald to help settle western Canada. Besides being the Mounties' headquarters, Depot also served as the supply and ordinance center for the Force, thus the name. On and off since its inception, it has also been the primary training academy for all new Mountie recruits.

The first thing Dennis did when he got there was to take a long walk around the grounds. The place was buzzing with activity. Recruits normally trained in troops of thirty-two members and new troops were being brought in every second week. Over six hundred recruits in various phases of their training were on site. New members in khaki fatigues scurried back and forth among the buildings. Troops of more experienced trainees dressed in long blue pants and brown serge jackets marched smartly along the roadways.

The grounds were divided by a number of streets that criss-crossed through a maze of sturdy buildings of various sizes and shapes. These housed administration offices, classrooms, gymnasia, an olympic size swimming pool, dormitories, a huge mess hall, a peaked-roof drill hall and a covered hockey rink that had once been the horse stables on the base. The focal point of Depot was a mammoth parade square with the Maple Leaf flying from the top of a mast. Beside the parade square there was a stone cenotaph bearing the names of all the Mounties who had died violent deaths in the line of duty. Two polished brass cannons preserved from the Riel Rebellion of 1885 stood guard on either side.

The crown jewel of the base is a small, white clapboard chapel with a red steeple that sat off the corner of the parade square. The chapel, which had originally been a canteen, is the oldest building in the City of Regina. In the first days of Depot it stood two buildings away from the guard house where Louis Riel was hanged. Inside the chapel, the walls are lined with a variety of plaques memorializing many of the members who had died in service. An open memorial book is encased just inside the entrance door. It contains the names of all those on the RCMP Honour Roll who have given their lives for their country. Each day a page is turned to honour a different fallen member. With all its echoes of the past, the chapel is an historic RCMP shrine.

When Dennis reported to the Orderly Office he was given his bed roll and kit and was advised that he had been assigned to Troop #27. His troop had the distinction of being the first at Depot to have married men in its complement. When he reported to his dorm in B Block, he saw that it was a long, narrow room with sixteen beds lined against each wall. Between every two beds there was a closet for one man, two desks and a closet for the next man. The first person Dennis met in the dorm was a troop mate from Chatham, Ontario named Derrick Reilly. He too was married. Since Derrick had the bed and desk beside Dennis, this made the two of them, by RCMP jargon, "pit partners."

Gradually the rest of the troop straggled into the dorm and claimed their bunks. The recruit who had the bunk on the other side of Dennis was Alex McLean, another married man from Tsawwassen, British Columbia. From the first day they met in the dorm, Dennis, Derrick and Alex became friends.

Of the thirty-one members in Troop #27, ten were married. While most of them were around twenty-one, the married men tended to be five or six years older. The youngest in the troop was a nineteen year-old baby-faced lad from Ontario. The oldest was Byron Hoover from Vancouver. He was only twenty-nine but he looked older than that and was immediately given the nickname "Gramps."

No matter their age or their looks, from this day forward they would be troop mates, a term that carried a special distinction in the RCMP. As a troop they would share months of hard work and good times that would bond them together in a powerful and long-lasting relationship.

The first night together in the dorm was not a good start for Troop #27. When "lights out" was sounded, Dennis climbed into his strange new bed and tried to sleep. But it was too early and he spent the next hour staring at the ceiling, thinking of home. Every time he began to nod off there was a loud cough or a strange moan that woke him up. Finally, around midnight, he fell asleep only to be awakened by the loudest snoring he had ever heard in his life. It was like a chain saw was being rhythmically revved in the room. One-by-one the whole barracks came awake, except for the snorer.

"Who the hell is that?" one recruit called out into the darkness.

"I think it's Borieau—the guy from Montreal," another voice replied.

"Somebody do something!"

Those closest to Borieau took turns banging their boots on the floor. Then they tried shaking his bed. He'd stop snoring for a minute or two then start up again even louder than before.

Neither Dennis nor anyone else got two hours sleep that night. Without sleep, the next long day was pure torture for all of them—except Borieau.

Dennis and his troop mates soon learned that they had enrolled in something much akin to a marine boot camp. Reveille sounded over the intercom at 6:30 a.m. They had an hour to shower, make their beds and clean the barracks. Then they had to hustle over to breakfast in the Mess Hall and form up in their troops by 8:00 a.m. to march to class. Classes were held all morning, then they marched to the Mess Hall for lunch. After lunch they formed up again in troops and marched to the parade square to the strains of the Depot band, a group of twenty-five struggling musicians drawn from all the different troops on the base. The kindest thing that could be said for them was that they were not very good.

After the troops formed up on the parade square there was a March Past with an Eyes Right to the Cenotaph and then they were off to classes again for the afternoon.

No other country in the world trains their national police force like the Mounties. Some countries have extensive schooling like the United States for their FBI, but none have the rigorous para-military training of the RCMP. From their inception the RCMP trained its members like an army. Over the years that same type of training has been modified and modernized to meet the demands of the evolving Canadian society, but the Mounties have retained their military component.

Like any good battle brigade, the RCMP prides itself on its esprit de corps. At Depot one of the principal goals of the training is to have the recruit sublimate his individual needs and wants for the good of the troop. Over and over the instructors stress that no man stands alone. They insist that when somebody shines, everybody basks in his glow; when somebody screws up, everybody suffers. Above all they teach: "if your troop mate's in trouble, lend a hand." This approach permeates every phase of recruit training.

When somebody's bed is improperly made, everybody gets extra work. When a recruit is slow to form up and makes the troop late for a class, everybody gets a mile run to the firing range and back. When a few recruits score low marks on a test, everybody gets extra assignments. Worse infractions earn them "CB"—

confined to barracks. After a few days of this treatment, two things start to happen. First, the whole troop begins raising hell with the individuals who are messing up. Secondly, each individual does his damndest to make sure he isn't the one who causes a problem. But there are so many demands for accuracy and precision, it is hard to stay on top of everything.

The troop was confined to barracks every Thursday night because every Friday morning there was a regular inspection of the dorm by the Sergeant-Major. Members of Troop #27 would spend the evening making the entire room glisten. To get a high sheen on the linoleum, one member would ride the floor polisher while another steered it through the long room. The washroom had to be spotless, toilets and bathroom fixtures scrubbed to perfection. Every surface in the dorm had to be dusted. The sharp scent of lemon polish filled the air as recruits hand polished all the woodwork. Besides being responsible for the general appearance of the room, everyone had to attend to his own personal area. Desks had to be neat and organized, books properly stored. Their clothes had to be neatly spaced in the closets. Above all, their beds had to be meticulously cleaned and tidied. Even the springs under the mattresses had to be dusted. Metal coat hangers were used to smooth out any wrinkles in the bed sheets. Each man's peaked forage cap had to be centered on his pillow before he left the dorm in the morning.

Nothing was left to chance. After the dorm was spick-and-span on Thursday night, the troop would hold its own inspection to make sure everything was in sparkling condition and in proper order. Otherwise, the next day when they returned to the barracks from breakfast, the Sergeant-Major, to show his supreme displeasure, would have torn the place to shreds, clearing the desks and closets, stripping the beds and overturning them. If that happened, the troop would have to start all over again to meet his lofty standards. It was much wiser for them to get the place correct the first time around and avoid his stinging wrath.

As for the snorer in Troop #27's dorm, they took care of him their first week in the barracks. Feeling they had enough to cope with as it was, they knew they couldn't make it through the day without sleep. When Borieau started snoring again, the whole dorm erupted. Some threw rolled up newspapers at him, one threw a boot, another a pillow. Some cursed at him. Everybody yelled at him.

"Somebody put a clothespin on his nose!"

"Roll his ass over!"

"Dump him out of that damn bed!"

"Wake up Borieau, you buzz saw!"

"Get him the hell out of here!"

When Borieau did wake up, he was surprised at all the furor around him. "Who, me?" was his bewildered response. But much to his credit, when the others explained the invasive nature of his snoring, Borieau picked up his mattress and blankets and dragged them out to the laundry room at the end of the dorm where he slept on a big, steel ironing table. This he did for the entire duration of the troop's stay in the dormitory. Every night just before lights out, he humbly lugged his sleeping equipment from one end of the dorm to the ironing room at the other end. As he trudged along between the row of beds, his troop mates made a big deal of his departure, calling out their appreciation.

"You're a good man, Borieau."

"Sweet dreams, Borieau."

"Thanks man, you're a life saver."

This went on for the first few nights. After that, his departure became commonplace and no one noted his leaving. Many of them were already fast asleep.

Most of the classes were enjoyable but the one class that everyone hated was Foot Drill. They had to march up and down the drill hall at the mercy of a miserable little Drill Instructor who strutted about like a peacock in boots and breeches barking out orders with a swagger stick tucked under his arm.

"BY THE LEFT . . . QUICK . . . MARCH!" he would holler.

The troop would stagger forward totally unsynchronized.

"LEFT RIGHT LEFT RIGHT," came the cadence.

Somebody would be out of step.

"LEFT I SAID . . . LEFT . . . YOUR OTHER LEFT!" he would yell.

Then the swagger stick would come out and he'd whip it against the leather of his long brown boot making cracking sounds that could be heard all over the cavernous building.

"WHAT IN THE HELL IS THE MATTER WITH YOU

PEOPLE!" he would bark. "GET IN STEP . . . STAY IN STEP!"

Some of the troop would hop and shuffle trying to get in step.

"WATCH YOUR SPACING!" he screamed. "SEE HIM OUT OF THE CORNER OF YOUR EYE!"

Someone turned his head too much.

"THE CORNER OF YOUR EYE I SAID! YOUR EYE! DON'T TURN YOUR WHOLE DAMN HEAD!"

For the first two weeks, it was a relief for the troop to get out of the drill hall and go to the academic classes, even though most of these were very demanding. A passing grade was 70% but the instructors expected every recruit to get 80%. The Law course was the toughest of them all. Here they studied the federal statutes such as The Narcotic Control Act, The Migratory Bird Act, The Large Game Act, Customs and Excise, the Criminal Code of Canada. No provincial statutes were studied because the recruits were going to different provinces. Dennis worked at the Law course harder than any subject he had ever taken before. Right from the first he began to get the best marks in the class. Derrick Reilly, who had been with the Ontario Provincial Police for three years before coming to Depot, was familiar with the Criminal Code but his test marks always came second to Dennis. Dennis soon earned a reputation with his troop mates for being really sharp, someone they could go to for answers.

English Composition and Typing were a breeze compared to Law. Ident, which is short for Identification, was difficult but interesting. In this course the troop learned how to function at crime scenes. This included taking notes and photos, doing plan drawings of the scene, protecting the scene from contamination, gathering evidence. Murder scenes and auto accidents were simulated for them to investigate. On one occasion an actor ran into the class and fired off a clip of blanks at the instructor then ran out of the room. The troop was asked to describe his actions and provide a full description of his looks and the clothes he was wearing. When the instructor reviewed the recruits' descriptions to the class, Dennis was amazed at the contradictory profiles they presented.

One course that caught everyone's attention was Law and Security. Here the instructor offered them valuable lessons on how to function safely as a police officer. He taught them to be constantly on guard, always on the alert, totally aware of their surroundings. He showed them how to anticipate problems, how to deal with hazardous situations. He also taught them how not to deal with situations, pointing out the dangers and pitfalls in faulty procedures. Case examples were cited where members had been killed or injured because of their lack of diligence. Actors were brought in to simulate domestic disputes where the policeman can often be caught in the middle of a couple's irrational anger.

All in the troop were exposed to a four hour session where they served in a mock detachment office with the phones ringing, the police radio blaring and the CPIC in use. Everything was happening at once and it all had to be taken care of right away. Dennis quickly realized they had to prioritize the problems that came in and handle them accordingly. Although his time in the office was nerve-wracking, he managed to keep his cool as well as anyone.

Driving classes were fun. Here the corporal kept emphasizing, "I don't want any arguments from you jokers. There's the right way, the wrong way and the RCMP way. I'm going to teach you the RCMP way."

Two recruits rode together in each car. Dennis rode with Alex McLean. On the driving track, he and Alex learned to overtake, to safely pull someone over, and when stopped, to stay sufficiently back of the overtaken car so they could see his rear tires. This was in case they had to speed off to an emergency somewhere else. After completing a stop, they learned how important it was to get up to highway speed as quickly as possible so they were back in the flow of the traffic. Some high speed sessions were conducted out on the highway. Dennis had always loved speed so he was thrilled to open his car up when he got the chance.

If the academic and field classes were difficult, the Physical Training classes were punishing. Stations were established where the recruits did calisthenics, sit ups, rope climbing, and weight lifting. Some of the recruits were bigger and stronger than others but they all had a common standard to meet no matter how flimsy or flabby they were. If a recruit couldn't lift the required weight, he'd have to go back to the weight room after hours to work out. His troop mates would help him improve so eventually he could make the standard. Dennis didn't have any trouble with any of the work in the gym. He was particularly good with the weights so he spent a lot of time at night at the gym with other troop mates like Gramps Hoover who struggled with the weight lifting.

Dennis' biggest problem was with swimming. The standard here was high, each recruit had to earn the equivalent of the Bronze Medallion. Dennis had never liked swimming and he'd never been any good at it. He dreaded the first swimming class because he knew he'd have trouble keeping his head above water. When the time came, he was so anxious, he went into the washroom and threw up. As he stood bent over the toilet, he could hear the swimming instructor calling into the washroom: "ONOFREY GET OUT HERE! WE'RE NOT GOING TO START WITHOUT YOU, ONOFREY!"

Dennis knew there was no way out. When he got out on the pool deck, the NCO lined up the troop and then led them towards the deep end.

"Oh, geez," Dennis mumbled to himself.

Alex McLean, who was in line behind him, said, "What's wrong?"

As the line moved along the edge of the pool the Corporal's booming voice called out, "ALL RIGHT YOU GUYS. ONE AT A TIME I WANT YOU TO JUMP IN SO I CAN SEE WHAT YOU CAN DO."

"Oh, no," Dennis complained.

"What's the matter?" Alex persisted.

"I can't swim," he said as the line nudged forward.

"Not at all?" Alex asked.

"No, not really." There was pain on Dennis' face.

"Well," Alex said, "Maybe you better tell him that."

"Are you crazy? He'll take it out on all of us."

"MOVE ALONG YOU GUYS!" the instructor shouted.

"What are you going to do?" Alex whispered.

"I don't know, you tell me." Dennis replied.

"Do you know how to dog paddle?" Alex asked.

"Yeah . . . I think so."

"Like this." Alex demonstrated by clawing the air in front of his chest. "Can you do that?"

"Maybe." Dennis did not look convincing.

"Let me get in front of you and go first," Alex said.

"And then what?" Dennis said as they quickly changed places.

"I'll be waiting for you in the water."

"LET'S GO! GET IN THERE!" the instructor yelled as a recruit ahead hesitated at the brink.

"So what good is that?" Dennis asked in agony.

"And then I won't let you drown if you start to sink," Alex told him.

"Oh, great . . . that's just great but what if . . . "

Then Alex was gone. Dennis watched him disappear under the greenish blue water.

Dennis was not about to give away his weakness. Without hesitating he took a deep breath and calmly stepped over the side. But as soon as his face went under the water, he began to panic. His mind went blank. He couldn't focus on anything let alone how to dog paddle. All he could do was flail his arms about like a wild man hoping that somehow they'd carry him to the surface. But he was going nowhere and he knew it. As he thrashed about, he let out some air but soon began to regret that. He desperately needed to breathe. It seemed like he'd been under water for ten minutes. Then he felt a pair of hands under his armpits and he could feel himself being lifted upward. When he finally broke the surface, he was spitting and gasping and coughing. But he was glad to be alive. Alex was beside him encouraging him to relax and towing him to the safety of the other side of the pool.

"ONOFREY, YOU BETTER BE BACK TONIGHT FOR EXTRA WORK," the instructor bellowed across the pool.

"Yes, Corporal," Dennis sputtered.

Dennis went back to the pool only because he had to. Night after night Alex and Derrick Reilly worked with him and slowly he learned how to stay afloat. Still every time he appeared for regular swimming class, he felt like throwing up.

Two weeks later everyone in the class was expected to tread water for twenty minutes without touching the bottom or the sides. By then Dennis could dog paddle and keep his head above water but it was still a struggle and very tiring for him. After ten minutes of fighting the water, his arms felt like lead. To relieve his agony, he worked his way over to the side and surreptitiously grabbed the edge of the pool for support. Just as he did, the swimming instructor spotted him.

"ONOFREY," he bellowed, "IF YOU TOUCH THE SIDE OF THIS POOL JUST ONCE MORE, YOU'LL BE OUT OF HERE AND WORKING AT LOBLAWS FOR A DOLLAR-FIFTY AN HOUR."

With that compassionate piece of advice, Dennis never touched the side again except to climb out of the pool. But this only added to his dread of swimming class. From that time on, even changing into his bathing suit gave him a feeling of desperation. It was an emotion that plagued him until late in the course when he eventually learned to swim. Ultimately, by sheer determination, he made the swimming standard. His success in the water was a tribute to his friends and himself. Everybody in the troop was happy for him.

Others weren't so fortunate in dealing with their deficiencies. Half way through the course, one of the troop, an ex-mortician from Manitoba, left of his own volition. No one was surprised. He hadn't seemed very interested in anything and had made little effort to keep up with his work.

Around that same time, Troop #27 was moved out of the barracks into C Block, a senior residence across from the Mess Hall. This was the standard progression for all troops as their seniority increased. Dennis shared a room with five other married troop mates. These included Alex and Derrick and Gramps Hoover. By this time they had become a tight little group. During the week there was so much work to do they seldom went off the base at night, but on Saturday night they liked to go out and unwind. Dennis was a key member of this little clique because he was the only one among them who had a car. They'd all pile in his Barracuda and head for a downtown pub. Over beer and pickled eggs they got to know each other better and to like each other more. Often those evenings off the base were stretched to the limit; lots of nights they made it back to C Block only seconds before the curfew.

Sundays posed a different problem. On Sunday in Regina the only places that sold liquor or beer, were private clubs. The simple solution was that Dennis and his pals chipped in and bought a membership in the German Canadian Club where they could go to have some beer and a bite to eat on Sundays.

All of Dennis' roommates were family men who missed their

wives and children. The rare weekends they got to go home were treasured. When they came back to Depot, they shared their stories about their trips and their special receptions at home. Dennis liked to tell about the long weekend he drove home. It took him ten hours through blowing snow to get to Winnipeg for Christmas with his wife and his mom. He was there for less than two days and then spent another ten hours driving back. He said it was a Christmas he would never forget.

As the term progressed, another class that Dennis learned to like was self-defense. Here they taught a few throws and kicks from karate, jiu-jitsu and tae kwon do. These were combined with some police holds into a crude form of self-defense called ground fighting, sort of the poor man's martial arts. Here almost anything, except biting, was permitted. Recruits were taught to pull hair, gouge eyes, clutch the voice box in the throat and grab the groin. The object was to cause an opponent so much pain he gave up. A recruit was to signal his surrender by tapping the gym mat several times. Once he "tapped out," his partner would release his hold and let him up. It took the instructors a fairly long time to get the paired opponents to fight seriously enough to tap their partner out.

"C'MON USE YOUR THUMBS . . . PUSH HIS EYES BACK IN THEIR SOCKETS," the corporal would yell. "C'MON ONOFREY, TAP HIM OUT, TAP HIM OUT."

At first Dennis found it difficult to do. He was a strong ground fighter but he wasn't mean enough to tap people out. That changed when he was matched with Guy Gagnon, a troop mate who stood 6'3", weighed 230 lbs. and had a black belt in karate. Gagnon was an ex-football player who had once tried out with the Montreal Alouettes. Besides being big he was quick, agile and mean. He could tap most people out in a matter of seconds. When Dennis fought Gagnon, he soon realized that he was in a battle for survival. In their first go at each other, Gagnon tapped him out quickly. He grabbed Dennis by the hair, rammed him into a head lock and thrust him forward so that the first thing that hit the mat was Dennis' face. Dennis almost blacked out right then but he woke up fast when Gagnon yanked his arm behind his back and began forcing his elbow in against its natural flexion. The pain was horrible and Dennis tapped out immediately. They got up and went at it again. This time Gagnon kicked him in the face with his bare foot and Dennis went down like a sack of potatoes. Gagnon was on him like a cat with his knee in his back and began pulling his head backwards by the hair. Dennis tapped out again. His nose was bleeding and his head ached but he wanted to go again. This time he got smart. He didn't get too close to Gagnon and was wary of his feet. When they clutched each other, Dennis reached up and grabbed his hair with one hand and dug the fingers of his other hand into Gagnon's throat. He could hear him let out a grunt of pain. Then Gagnon's superior strength kicked in and he flipped Dennis to the mat. They scrambled around for a few minutes before Dennis was forced to tap out again. From that time on Dennis became more aggressive. He couldn't beat Gagnon or a tough kid from Nova Scotia named Talbot but he punished a lot of his troop mates and became one of the better scrappers in the class.

Another activity Dennis enjoyed was shooting on the firing range. For the first while they fired service revolvers at targets from varying distances. Then they used rifles in the same way. After that they taught him to shoot a revolver with both hands. This was not a frivolous amusement; it was a practical necessity. If he was ever in a gunfight where his right side was restricted, he would be foolish to expose his whole body so that he could shoot with his right hand. Dennis soon proved he was good with a gun. All the hunting he'd done as a youngster came in handy. As long as he was wearing his eyeglasses, Dennis could hit the bulls-eye.

In early April the troop was greeted with a welcome announcement. Due to the heavy volume of recruits going through Depot, their training session would be shortened by three weeks. This meant they would graduate on May 9 rather than May 31. The instructors compressed everything to make sure nothing was omitted in their courses. The workload became even heavier, but all of them knew there were better times ahead.

In the middle of April each man in Troop #27 was given his posting. Derrick Reilly was going back to Chatham, Ontario, the one place he had asked not to be sent. Alex McLean was going to Kamloops, B.C., Gramps Hoover to Summerland B.C. Dennis Onofrey was posted to Virden, Manitoba. He knew where it was; he had driven past it on the way to Winnipeg. When he asked some of the experienced NCOs about Virden, it didn't sound too bad.

They said it was a good, safe, sixteen-member detachment. Dennis was relieved that it was close enough to Winnipeg that his mother could come and visit. He phoned Paula and then his mom to tell them the news.

Three weeks before graduation an unsettling thing happened to the troop. One of their members, a young recruit from Ontario, was asked to leave Depot. Dennis had been concerned about him because he seemed immature. He spent a lot of his time reading comic books and seldom did any studying. The fellow had been warned repeatedly about his low marks and generally poor performance but hadn't taken the admonitions to heart. When he was finally told to leave, he was very resentful because he had already made arrangements for his parents to attend his graduation. The last time the troop saw him was while they were marching in the Drill Hall. He came in to return some gear and as he was leaving, he waited until the troop was facing him and gave them all the finger. Some of the troop laughed, but others were offended. Dennis felt sorry for him because, when he saw him do that to the entire group, he realized he hadn't felt accepted by any of them. He thought how painful that must have been for him.

If that was a low point for the troop, better days lay just ahead. Classes were coming to an end and most of their exams were over. At Depot a combination of academic grades and field scores are used to determine a recruit's rank in his class. The most satisfying moment of Dennis' training came when the Drill Instructor publicly announced to the troop the top three rankings in the class. After naming number three and number two he proclaimed: "The person ranked number one in Troop #27 is . . . Dennis Onofrey." At the sound of his name, all of his troop mates applauded. There was no rancour or envy in any of them. Because of his hard work and dedication, they all knew Dennis was deserving of such commendation.

As the time at Depot wound down, Dennis began looking forward to Paula and his family coming out to his graduation or his "Pass Out" as the RCMP called it. He phoned the Regina Inn and reserved rooms for himself and Paula, his mother and grandmother and his uncle, Stan Kaskiw.

Graduation day was busy. In the morning the invited guests went from building to building watching Troop #27 participate in swimming, physical training and self defense. At 1:30 p.m. the troop donned their dress uniforms—red serge, Stetson, long boots and breeches, Sam Brown belt and holster—and proudly marched to the Drill Hall to perform their Passing Out drill in front of their family and friends. The troop had been working on this for months and it went beautifully. Not a man was out of step. Their boots hit the floor as if one man was marching. Their Drill Instructor beamed with pride. Throughout it all Rose was busy taking pictures with her camera. At the end of the drill, a kilted piper played "Amazing Grace" as each man was awarded his badge. Rose got a picture of Dennis receiving regimental # 32104, another in a long line of consecutive numbers issued since the beginning of the Force.

Then the Drill Corporal turned to the audience in the bleachers and said, "These men are now members of the Royal Canadian Mounted Police. To keep the peace they are ready to die for you." Rose silently sent up a little prayer that such a thing would never happen.

Then the troop was officially dismissed. As they broke ranks, the new Mounties let out a roar of celebration and milled about slapping backs and shaking hands. It was a bittersweet moment for them. Each man had successfully attained his difficult goal; all were on the brink of saying farewell. Many knew they would never see one another again.

That evening there was a formal banquet in the Mess Hall for the troop and their guests. As tradition has it, Troop #28, now the senior troop, served the dinner which included wine, shrimp salad and sirloin steak. Alex McLean was emcee. There were toasts to the Queen, to the parents and to the Force. Throughout the dinner roars of laughter went up as they recounted their experiences at Depot. Dennis laughed as much as anyone and Rose was delighted to see him so happy and so animated.

At 9:00 p.m. the entire party made its way back to the Drill Hall for the graduation dance. Tables were spread over a section of the hall and there was ample room for everyone to walk around and socialize. This was the best opportunity of the day for Dennis and his friends to finally meet and get to know their troop mates' wives and families. Paula was so glad to be with Dennis again she seldom left his side. He introduced her to so many people it was difficult for her to keep them all straight. But she knew Derrick and Alex were Dennis' closest friends and made sure she spent some time chatting with their wives. Rose was content to visit with whomever dropped by their table. She loved watching Dennis and Paula dance together.

Later in the night the band leader announced he was about to play the mother's waltz. Over the microphone he said, "OK now . . . I want all the mothers that are here up on the dance floor . . . dancing with your sons."

Dennis came back to Rose's table and said, "You want to dance, Mom?" He held out his hand to help her up.

Rose didn't hesitate. "I sure do," she said.

As they stepped out on the floor and waited for the waltz to begin, Stan Kaskiw said, "I got to get a picture of this. Where's your camera, Rose?"

"Right there beside my purse," she answered. "But I don't think there's any pictures left . . . and that's the only film I bought."

Stan looked the camera over and said, "Well, we may as well give it a try."

As Rose and Dennis began to waltz, Stan moved into position with the camera to his eye. "Look here," he called. When they turned, he clicked the shutter. "Must be all right," Stan said, "the flash went off."

Rose was glad to hear that; it was a picture she would treasure from a night she would always remember.

The next morning Dennis and all his family had breakfast at the hotel. By noon they were ready to go their separate ways. Rose and Stan drove their mother back to Shoal Lake. Dennis and Paula headed straight for Virden. Both of them were excited about the move; a new adventure was unfolding in their life. They had every reason to believe that many wonderful years lay ahead.

BRUCE AND DOROTHY

As Dennis and Paula Onofrey were driving towards the start of their new adventure in Virden, hundreds of miles away in the bowels of Vancouver, a troubled couple, who supplemented their income by catering to the dark fringe of society, were settling in after a marathon trip across Canada. For the last two years, thirty-nine-year-old Bruce Archer and his twenty-five-year-old girlfriend, Dorothy Malette, had flitted like gypsy moths from city to city engaged in a series of sordid activities that most people would find hard to believe.

Occasionally Dorothy worked as a prostitute. Sometimes she played a crude game of extortion by having her johns photographed during their sessions with her. Then she demanded payment from them by threatening to use the photos to expose them. Bruce was her partner in crime. By day he worked at a variety of jobs; by night he served as Dorothy's protector or acted as her photographer.

By the time they arrived in Vancouver, a substantial portion of their income came from their organization and administration of a club magazine that served as a contact agency among homosexuals, bisexuals and lesbians. People from all over the west coast in Canada and the United States paid a $10 membership fee to join their *Double Gators Club*. This entitled them to receive a monthly catalogue about other people of similar persuasion who advertised their wares, their services or their specific sexual preferences. Each advertisement cost $5 plus another $5 for a photo. Those who wanted to contact an individual advertised in the catalogue sent in $2 and either Bruce or Dorothy forwarded their response to the appropriate party. It was a thriving and lucrative little business. Archer advertised *The Double Gators Club* in papers such as *Tab* and *Hush* as well as in a number of legitimate newspapers in British Columbia, Alberta, California, Oregon, even Alaska. One of the items advertised in the monthly magazine was Archer's Great Dane, Thor, who, it was claimed, was sexually trained.

41

Archer hadn't always lived like this. In truth his life had been rather straight, albeit unstable, until the time he was thirty-five years of age.

What made Archer's low life in Vancouver even more bizarre was the fact that his wife Lucille (not her real name) and two daughters lived only minutes away. Archer had abandoned them two years before in Ontario. Although he no longer had any feelings for Lucille, he loved his daughters and had purposely set his family up in Port Coquitlam so he could be close to his teenage girls. Since Archer didn't give his wife much support of any kind, she had to scrape by, working extra jobs to pay for the rent and the groceries. Even then there was seldom anything left over for frills or special treats. No matter how often Lucille begged him for financial help, Archer rarely sent anything to assist her.

His was a pathetic existence. In three years he had gone from being a relatively decent family man who had had only minor scrapes with the law, to being a pimp and a purveyor of pornography. His preoccupation with satisfying his own wants and needs, his lack of feeling and callous disregard for the welfare of others, including his own flesh and blood, were symptomatic of a personality disorder. In all probability, Bruce Archer was a sociopath.

He was born into poverty as Herbert Bruce Archer in Belleville, Ontario, in 1935. His father, Herbert Sr., in all likelihood suffered from the same personality disorder himself. He had little schooling, few marketable skills and a penchant for quitting jobs to look for something better when there was precious else available. He and his family were always on the move looking for greener pastures. Because of this instability and his limited income, the marriage of Archer's parents was volatile and unhappy. A sister, Lemoyne, was born in 1941 and her arrival made the home situation all the more unstable. Only when Herbert Sr. found steady work in Courtland, Ontario, at a manufacturing shop did family conditions begin to improve.

Bruce's personal problems started to emerge when he first enrolled in school and quickly discovered he didn't like it. His was not the common aversion for school that most children profess. Bruce really and truly hated school. He found it confining and regimented and he had difficulty paying attention. Some subjects were a little better than others, but arithmetic was indecipherable to him. His restlessness often led him into difficulty and he soon was considered a troublemaker by the teachers. Before long he was labelled a "problem child."

Then Herbert Sr. lost his job again and the Archers, in a desperate attempt to generate income, decided to go out to work as migrant farm laborers. In the spring they went from farm to farm to hoe and plant; in the summer they primed tobacco. Like gypsies they moved their little family caravan around from Delhi to Simcoe to Tillsonburg, often living in shacks and barns. Sometimes, when they couldn't find even that accommodation, they all slept in the car. Herbert Sr. and Bruce's mother, Olive, slept sitting up in the front seat; Bruce and his little sister slept in the back.

When summer finally came to an end, they went further west to Leamington and helped with the sugar beet harvest. With this constant moving around there was no more school for Bruce and that suited him fine. While his parents worked in the fields, he stayed home to mind his younger sister and to help prepare the supper. Olive would leave him instructions and he would spend the day washing the vegetables, peeling potatoes or cutting up beans so they could be put on the stove at the time she indicated. There was very seldom any meat for dinner and, when there was, it was always salt pork. Until he was eleven years old, Bruce spent almost every day like this in a variety of tumble-down shacks, preparing meals and minding his sister Lemoyne.

During the winters the family lived where it could find refuge. Usually they squatted in old abandoned shacks where the heat was often supplied by a borrowed wood stove. With money so scarce, winter clothes were always at a premium. Bruce had only rubber farm boots and never any gloves. When he went on an errand, his mother would heat rocks and put them in his coat pockets so he could keep his hands warm.

Olive Archer hated living like this and hounded her husband to get out and find something more permanent and stable. After a long job search, Herbert found work in a factory in the city of Hamilton. When they moved into the tough north end of the city, Olive went looking for a job too. By then Lemoyne was six and old enough to go to school herself. Once Lemoyne enrolled and the family was registered with the school board, the truant officer insisted that Bruce be in school. After a cursory assessment the Hamilton school system placed him in grade four, three grades behind his age group. This was embarrassing for him because he was much bigger than his classmates in Hess Street School and he was taller than some of the teachers. Right from the start, Bruce felt the other kids saw him as a sort of monster in their midst. They were so afraid of him they didn't even tease him. What they did was worse; they shunned him. They stayed away on the playing field and avoided him in the classroom. Added to the embarrassment of that isolation was Bruce's inability to do the school work. He would do anything to avoid his seat work and get out of class. Everyone, including his teacher, was happier when Bruce asked to leave the room. A lot of his time was spent in the boiler room talking with the janitor.

If things were unpleasant at school, they were dramatically improved at home. With both parents working, there was more money coming in than they'd ever had before. Christmas in 1948 was the first time in years that they celebrated the festive season with a permanent roof over their head. And there were gifts under the tree. Herbert splurged and bought Bruce his first expensive present, a .22 repeater rifle. When Bruce unwrapped the gift and discovered what it was, he couldn't believe his eyes. From this gift at age thirteen began a fascination with guns that would last all his life.

In an attempt to find a placement suitable to his needs, Bruce was moved from school to school in quick succession—Cannon Street, King Edward, West Avenue. Wherever he went, nothing much changed for him, except he became more and more a loner. His classmates gave him a wide berth. He seldom attempted to play with them because he was embarrassed by his size and his awkwardness. In the classroom he hated the rules and regulations. He was impetuous, blurting things out in a demanding manner. And he was impatient; when he wanted something, he detested being ignored or being asked to wait. Even at the movies or the malt shop, he could not stand to wait in line. Inevitably his behaviour frequently brought him into conflict both in and out of school.

When Bruce was fourteen, his father bought him another rifle, a .32 Winchester Special. That winter, he and his dad went on their first real hunting trip together up to Algonquin Park. After trudging through the bush for hours, Bruce spotted a deer in the distance and dropped it with one shot. From that time on, hunting was the sport for him. He loved the splendour of the outdoors and the peace and solitude of being on his own in the bush. And, most important of all, he knew he was good with a gun.

But school was another matter. In September 1950 his mother had him transferred to the King George Handicraft School so that he might learn a trade. This was a school for children with learning problems and, by then, there was no doubt that Bruce qualified. He was fifteen years of age but had only completed grade five. He was tested at the new school and his IQ was recorded at 81, well below average. Although this was probably more a reflection of his accumulated ignorance than an accurate assessment of his ability to learn, his enrollment at King George labelled him a slow learner and made him the object of ridicule with the kids on his block. This distress was compounded by the fact that he didn't like this new school any better than the others he had attended. After two months of frustration, Bruce applied for permission to leave school.

If his impetuousness and problems at school were early indicators of a personality disorder, his bizarre employment history was a further symptom . His first full-time job was as a dough boy at Mammy's Bread where he lasted two months. As soon as he became dissatisfied there, he quit and went to work with his dad at the plating company. This hasty movement from one job to another was the beginning of a pattern that he would follow most of his working life.

With all his troubles at school and at work, Bruce had very few problems with the law. The one exception was when he was fifteen he was charged with breaking and entering a dry cleaning store with two other boys and given a suspended sentence. This was his only criminal conviction for the next twenty-five years. One reason he was able to keep his record clean was the control his wife, Lucille exerted over him. They met when they were both seventeen and Bruce spent so much time with her he didn't have a chance to get in trouble with any of his neighbourhood friends. At eighteen, against both their parents' wishes, they married. The parents objected partly because they were too young and mostly because Lucille was a devout Catholic and Bruce was Protestant.

Notwithstanding their parents' complaints, Bruce and Lucille were both glad to be out of their respective homes and happy to be bringing in two decent paychecks that afforded them a comfortable living. Still, right from the beginning of their marriage, Bruce bounced from one job to another. As a general labourer he helped widen the Jolley Cut up the Hamilton mountain. Then he drove a moving van for Wonder Furniture and then for Tippet Richardson. He cleaned buses, drove buses, sold aluminum siding and worked in the plant at Robinson Cone. All of this he did in a span of less than three years.

He told Lucille that he moved from job to job because if he didn't feel he was accomplishing something, he got restless. He wanted to be able to prove to his family and his friends that he was doing well, that he could afford to buy things—a car, furniture, nice clothes. If he didn't feel satisfied with a job, he would quit it and walk away. When another job looked more promising or seemed more rewarding, he took it.

Sometimes he left a job by choice; sometimes he got fired. Usually that was because he was difficult to manage. Bruce was getting bigger and stronger and did some amateur wrestling at a downtown gym. This combined with his trigger temper tended to make him touchy and defiant. He detested being ordered around at work and when that happened he became enraged. On one occasion he was piling sugar bags in a factory when the foreman made the mistake of upbraiding him. "C'mon you damn dumb Irishman," he said. "Get to work." Bruce hit him and knocked him down the stairs. Then he walked into the plant office and quit.

Somehow this didn't seem to bother Lucille because the economy was flourishing and no matter how often he left one job, he always got a new one right away. Besides, she was working in the diet kitchen of the Hamilton General Hospital and together they were making more money than their parents. They went out to dinner and a movie almost every night of the week. When they saw something they liked, they bought it. Life was wonderful for them. Why should they care about some mouthy foreman or another lost job? The present was comfortable and the future was so far away that they gave it little thought.

Bruce was never violent at home but once in a while Lucille

would witness the fury of her husband's temper. At a family picnic in a park beside Lake Ontario a stranger insulted his cousin Orliff's wife. Bruce confronted the man and a terrible fight broke out between them. When it was obvious that Bruce had the fight won, Herbert Sr. and several others tried to pull him off the badly bloodied stranger but Bruce wouldn't stop hitting him. It was as if he had gone berserk and couldn't be brought back to his senses. He stopped beating on his opponent when Lucille, who was pregnant at the time, began screaming at him, "Bruce, I'm going to lose the baby!" That seemed to jar him back to reality. By that time, Bruce had not only beaten his opponent to a pulp but had also hit his own father and his uncles when they tried to subdue him. He didn't lose physical control like that very often but it didn't take much for him to get irate and attack verbally.

A pivotal change in Archer's life occurred when his first daughter, Beth (not her real name) was born in 1955. Although Bruce and Lucille loved her dearly, her arrival required radical adjustments in their lifestyle. First, Lucille had to quit her job and secondly, Bruce had to learn to keep his. Their dining out and going to the movies had to be stringently curtailed. With these new demands crowding in on him, Bruce began to feel trapped. He'd run out of jobs in Hamilton, so he rationalized that if things were no good here, they had to be better somewhere else. He wanted a dramatic change in his life, something totally new, somewhere completely different. He suggested to Lucille that they move out to British Columbia. Lucille not only agreed, she was enthusiastic about the idea. In the spring of 1956 they set out on the first of their family's three transcontinental migrations to the west coast.

At Sault Ste. Marie, their car broke down. With no cash reserves to repair it, Bruce was forced to get a job locally. They stayed in the Sault for the winter and, when the thaw came, started out again. Bruce put his wife and baby on a train and sent them to Calgary where Lucille rented a two room flat. Once she was settled, he hitchhiked across the prairies and caught up with them. He stayed a few days in Calgary doing odd jobs to pay their rent, then went ahead by thumb to Vancouver. Once he was settled there, Lucille and Beth caught up with him by bus. This might seem like a strange way to move a family across the country but, to the impoverished Archers, it seemed the only way. He was proud of his determination and resourcefulness.

All of his ingenuity went for nothing once they got to Vancouver because there was no steady work that appealed to Bruce. Lodging was so expensive that they were forced to live in a cheap motel room. By the fall they'd had enough of the coast and headed back to Hamilton where they moved in with Lucille's family. When that became unbearable for Bruce, he took a job as a breadman in Midland, over 100 miles away. That venture ended abruptly when all three of them contracted jaundice and had to move back to Hamilton to recuperate. Once he recovered, Bruce got a job driving a moving van. After a few weeks, to get away from Lucille's parents, he asked the moving company for a transfer to Barrie. The Archers just got settled there when he was laid off and, to make ends meet, he spent the winter in the bush cutting cordwood. In the spring he sold brass fittings that he retrieved from junkyard cars. Once again he had worked himself into a position where there was barely enough money coming in to pay for the groceries.

In a futile search for something better, the jobs and the moves continued. In Fort Erie he worked as a hospital orderly. Here in 1960 his second daughter Sheila (not her real name) was born. As Bruce's family responsibilities increased, so too did his restlessness and his unhealthy dissatisfaction with his lot in life. He moved his family to Kitchener where he registered in a course for the unemployed that was referred to euphemistically as "Diefenbaker's Army." When the six month course ended and he was discharged from the army, Bruce suggested they try Windsor where he'd heard things were booming.

As usual, Lucille mildly resisted but eventually gave in. She had learned not to oppose him on these matters because, if he didn't get his way, he became surly and made life miserable for all of them. Besides that, she felt reasonably secure knowing that her husband would do almost anything to earn a living and provide for her family. It was difficult to accept but she had learned from experience that her husband would not stay at the same thing in the same place for a very long period of time.

Something new happened when the Archers departed Kitchener. For the first time in their married lives they left behind some unpaid debts. It was a portent of things to come.

In Windsor he went back to his original trade as a metal polisher and he was doing fine until he was joined on the job by his cousin, Orliff, from Belleville. When Orliff started bringing his guitar to work and playing it at the break, the owner of the shop got angry and fired him. Impulsively Bruce quit in sympathy with his cousin. Before he and Orliff left the shop, they vindictively put a bar of soap in each plating tank—one in the copper, one in the chrome, one in the nickel. This caused a chemical reaction that played havoc with the plating process. All the tanks had to be dumped at a cost of thousands of dollars to the owner.

After this the Archers began their second western migration. They drove straight out to Calgary where Bruce landed a solid job as a warehouse supervisor. He truly liked this job because he was more or less the boss and that made him feel like a person of significance. No one was forever giving him orders or treating him like an inferior. He also felt good about the fact that the he was successful dealing with the men under his supervision. They liked him and were happy working for him. Almost miraculously, Bruce Archer had found his niche.

Calgary was a good place for his entire family. Both his girls were in school and, for the first time, they could have friends over to visit. Sometimes they stayed overnight. There was plenty of opportunity for the family to do things together. The four of them went hiking and camping in the mountains or went for long drives and picnics in the foothills. Many times they drove downtown for a movie and dinner out. Lucille loved their family life in Calgary. It was so stable, so normal. They could save their money and plan ahead like everyone else.

Bruce particularly loved living there because it gave him the opportunity of getting away by himself to go hunting. There was nothing he loved better than spending a weekend alone in the bush. He didn't like to go hunting with other people because he didn't trust them with a gun in their hands. He told his wife, "You never know what kind of a stupid move they'll make." Besides he didn't have any close friends who would go with him.

Bruce thought Alberta was fabulous for hunting. He had shot lots of ducks in the swamps of Ontario but the number of wild birds back there was nothing compared to Alberta. The variety was greater too. He could head down to Medicine Hat for pheasant

49

or partridge or go over to Red Deer for grouse. What he really wanted to do was go after the big game in the Highwood Range west of Calgary. The problem was his .32 Winchester Special was too light for that. It didn't have enough stopping power for moose or elk. So, once he had put enough money aside, he went down to a specialty gun shop in mid-town Calgary and bought himself a .308 Savage rifle. Now he owned a powerful weapon that could bring down anything short of an elephant. It was a gun he would keep and use right up until the end.

Problems at work in Calgary began for him late in 1966. The front office didn't give him a promotion that he thought he deserved and after that he rapidly became difficult and defiant. Like a child, he adamantly refused to take any orders from the newly promoted supervisor. When the company gave him an ultimatum to do so, he quit his job. Lucille couldn't believe it when he came home and told her. The happy existence of their family had just gone up in smoke.

Of all the irresponsible behaviour that Bruce Archer had exhibited so far in his life, this was the worst. It was as if some dark force had clouded his mind and forced him to act without any consideration for the consequences to himself or his family. Even though he loved his wife and adored his two daughters, he was prepared to sacrifice their security and happiness in one impulsive act of uncompromising stubbornness.

Yet there also may have been a method to his madness because the Archers had been living beyond their means in Calgary. As a result, they had accrued over two thousand dollars in insurmountable debts. It is possible that Archer precipitated his firing at the warehouse as an excuse to move on and escape the burden of his unpaid accounts. Furthermore, he knew from experience that his family would soon recover from the wrenching process of being relocated. No matter the reason for his quitting or the problems it caused, the Archers were on the road again.

First he got a job metal polishing in Edmonton where they stayed for eighteen months. Then it was on to Lethbridge, Alberta. Archer's work there wasn't much but he liked the area because it was great bird country with lots of partridge and ducks. They stayed around that part of the province long enough for Bruce to learn how to hunt with a bow and arrow. Then the family took to the high road again. Next stop was Quesnel in the caribou country of northern British Columbia. Archer loved this place because, as he said, "I can walk a hundred yards out of town and shoot a bear." Unfortunately, he didn't love his job as a stationary engineer at the hospital quite so much. Within months he walked away from it and once again the travelling Archers were off to Vancouver.

It was now 1968 and several times in the next year Bruce started his own little metal polishing business only to grow dissatisfied and fold it up. As soon as he felt any kind of pressure or boredom, he'd pack it in and start something else. Most of these moves meant a change of address. It was amazing that Lucille tolerated this constant uprooting but it appears she was prepared to suffer almost any hardship to keep her family together. The constant change was toughest on Beth. By now she was thirteen and had left behind school friends in almost every major city in western Canada. She never complained. To Sheila, moving regularly was an occupational family hazard, like being an army brat. When her mom or dad informed her of the next relocation, she would simply shrug her shoulders and say, "Oh well, here we go again."

All this family upheaval didn't prevent Bruce and Lucille giving their children love and understanding. They were good parents. They always knew where their children were and seldom let them stay out after dark. They spent a lot of time talking with them, encouraging them to discuss their personal problems. Together they discussed the dangers of drugs and smoking and stressed the importance of getting a good education. They always took time to help them with their studies and praised their performance at school. They had confidence in their two girls and conveyed that to them. They encouraged them to develop their strengths to become unique individuals. In so many ways they provided a good home for their family. They just didn't stay in one place very long.

In 1969 the Archers moved back to Toronto. Lucille found work at St. Joseph's Hospital; Bruce drew wages at a plating company. He loathed the city from the moment they arrived and hated his job from the day he started. It was too hot, too noisy, there was too much traffic, too many people, he hated standing in line. Nothing was right about Toronto. He told Lucille, "This place is driving me nuts." Then he saw an ad in the Toronto Star for a job at the Ovaltine Company in Peterborough. He guaranteed Lucille that all of them would love it there. He told her that Peterborough was in beautiful cottage country and there were a lots of wonderful things they could do there as a family. When Lucille agreed that he should reply to the advertisement, she had no idea what terrible consequences lay ahead. To her, moving to Peterborough was just another in their endless series of relocations.

Once in Peterborough, they discovered that the city offered everything he promised and more. Bruce was hired as a shipper and receiver. He liked his work for about three months until he convinced himself that the job was leading nowhere. He told his wife, "I'll be slugging my guts out until I'm ninety. I want to be more than that. This job is no good!"

After he quit there, he tried plumbing and heating for a month and a half until he got in an argument with the foreman and left. Even Bruce was becoming discouraged.

"I'm out of work again," he told Lucille.

"What are you going to do now?" she asked.

"I think I'll start my own business."

"You haven't got enough money, to do that."

"I'll get it."

He put an ad in the *Peterborough Examiner* and a retired man in his sixties answered and agreed to loan him $1,000. With that Archer set up a little shop at the corner of London and George streets and was back in the metal finishing business again under the name of Customized Metal Enterprises. This time he was primarily engaged in making magnetic signs for truck doors. He also did some buffing and polishing of metal items from antique shops in the area.

From the start, business was good and the work kept him busy. During the day he travelled about selling orders for signs and picking up antique items for buffing. At night he worked in the shop filling his orders. The next day he would deliver them to his customers and then call on other accounts looking for more work. Things were so good that he repaid his benefactor in three months and had to hire a sales staff of four to help him. As busy as he was, he still made time for his family. Life here was even better than Calgary. The girls were getting older and the four of them could do more together. In the winter they skated or went tobogganing on the hills by Trent University. In the summer they rented canoes and went on weekend camping trips. Often on a Sunday the Archers would drive out along the Otonobee River road until they found a nice spot to have a picnic and a swim. Bruce loved the water and was a very strong swimmer. He taught his two girls how to swim and have fun in the water without fear. The girls would wrestle with him in the river and loved it when he picked them up over his head and threw them through the air with their legs flying. At the end of the day he would take them all for ice cream at the dairy bar in Lakefield or for curds and buttermilk at the cheese factory.

Everywhere they went, they sang to their heart's content. Bruce would lead the singing and encourage the others to join in. As they drove along he taught them the words to every country and western song he knew. He even tried to teach his daughters how to yodel. When the Archers went camping, they harmonized around the campfire. Neighbouring campers, drawn by their singing, were invited to join in.

In many ways he was a typical father. For two summers in Peterborough, Bruce coached his daughters' teams in the local girls' softball league. With all the practices and games, he had to drive a carload of players around town two or three times a week. But he didn't mind because he loved to see his daughters play. Once when Beth wanted to try out for girl's basketball at school, she asked him to teach her how to play. Bruce agreed and when he came home after work, the two of them went out to the park and played together for hours. As much as Bruce loved sports, he loved animals even more. With all their moving around there was never a time that the Archers didn't have a dog or a cat around the house. His daughters could see his love of nature and animals and they learned from his example that pets were to be respected and treated kindly, just like members of the family.

Once his business began to prosper, Bruce fulfilled a life-long dream by renting a house out in the country. Knowing how much his girls loved horses, he went out and bought two of them, an appaloosa for Sheila and a quarter horse for Beth. Without a corral to keep them in, Bruce had to scramble around for materials to erect one before the sun went down. Living in the country was great for all of them. Lucille loved their home life and enjoyed her job at the hospital. For the first time in years she talked about getting involved with the church. Because she married Bruce outside the Catholic church, she could no longer receive the Sacraments. To reverse that restriction, Archer arranged for them to be married again by a priest. As they stood before the altar, with his daughters looking on as witnesses, all the Archers were aware that this was the best time of their lives. None of them, including Bruce, could imagine the calamity that lay ahead.

It began with Bruce desperately needing some help in the shop. In February 1971 he put an advertisement in the newspaper looking for a Girl Friday, someone to keep his books, send out invoices, type correspondence, set up the signs and so forth. There were several applicants but he gave the job to Dorothy Malette, a twenty-two-year-old married woman from the rural area outside Omemee.

Dorothy had a partial high school education, was a very good typist and had some experience as a salesperson in the local Firestone store. She had two young children at home but said she could arrange for their care while she worked. From their first meeting Archer could see that Dorothy was clever and pleasant and very well spoken. Although she had a soft, pretty face and a nice smile, she was a heavy woman of close to 200 lbs. on a 5' frame. Some might have found her bulk and heavy hips unattractive but her size was of little concern to Bruce. He actually preferred it. He was a big man himself at 240 lbs. and he liked buxom women. Lucille herself was heavy and Dorothy was built much the same as Lucille.

Dorothy had a troubled past. Born into poverty on a small backwoods farm outside of Lindsay, she was sexually abused by an older brother. At fifteen she was pregnant and at sixteen she married a local dead stock trucker who was a heavy drinker. By seventeen she was the mother of two daughters. Her relationship with her abusive husband was grossly unhappy but she was too dependent on him to leave. When her beloved mother died, Dorothy was thrown into the grips of a depression that was so severe she tried to commit suicide.

When she came to work for Archer, Dorothy was so poor she had few nice clothes to wear. For the first week she reported to work in the same somber black dress she had worn to her mother's funeral. Bruce lent her some money and took her down to K-Mart so she could buy some new clothes.

Right away Archer could see that Dorothy was a great addition to his business. Being intelligent, she learned things quickly. She was extremely efficient and organized and very good dealing with the customers. Often she came to work early so she could read everything available about metal polishing and the sign business. Bruce was so impressed that, when transportation to work became a problem for her, he bought her a used Pontiac station wagon for $150.

Dorothy, who came from such poverty and unhappiness at home, appreciated his kindness. The two of them soon grew comfortable with each other and had fun working together. They joked and flirted with each other. Flattered that such a pretty young woman would pay attention to him, it wasn't long before Bruce realized that he was physically attracted to her. Within weeks of her arrival he was infatuated. Their pairing was inevitable. Dorothy wanted out of her marriage. Bruce, an immature thirty-six, couldn't resist the allure of this attentive twenty-two year-old woman. His impulsive nature and disregard for consequences sealed their pact. He lunged ahead with no consideration for the pain it would bring to his wife and children.

Bruce had remained sexually loyal to Lucille throughout their marriage but, after one frenzied tryst with Dorothy, he became sexually obsessed with her and their relationship developed into a full-blown affair. Archer was soon suffering from the ultimate mid-life crisis, a choice between the good woman at home and the wild woman outside.

The difference between the two women was dramatic. In many ways they were direct opposites. Although both of them were intelligent and well-read, Lucille's grade five education may have contributed to the fact that she was very shy and retiring. Dorothy was more outgoing. She tended to be personally aggressive. Lucille lacked confidence in social situations and much preferred to stay at home in the private company of her family. Dorothy was much more socially venturesome and quite comfortable meeting new people and engaging them in conversation. Lucille's most outstanding qualities were as a mother and a homemaker. She was also a wonderful cook. One of the reasons Bruce was so heavy was that she fed him like a king. Dorothy took care of her children but she did as little as possible around the house. She disliked cooking and despised housework and spent most her time at home curled up in a comfortable chair with a good book. Although Lucille had many qualities that were vastly superior to Dorothy's, she simply could not compete in the intoxicating realm of sexuality. For Bruce this meant it was no contest. Although Lucille was not aware that her husband was running around with another woman, there was little she could have done about it, even if she had known. The sad truth was that her years of caring and devotion, of moving back and forth across the country at her husband's slightest whim, could not compete with a few brief moments of another woman's passion.

With Dorothy all of Bruce's secret erotic dreams began coming true. She had a ravenous appetite for sex and was imaginative and uninhibited in her lovemaking. Bruce was astounded by her stamina alone. She could go on for hours at a time and seemingly never tire. For years Bruce had been bored with Lucille's dutiful approach to lovemaking and had fantasized about other possibilities. With Dorothy all the wild and wonderful sex that he had only imagined was happening time after glorious time.

For weeks Bruce and Dorothy surreptitiously went about their pleasure in various nooks and crannies around Peterborough. This made it difficult for Bruce to keep his mind on his business. Gradually it began to fail but not only because of his fixation on Dorothy. In recent months competition had moved into the city and they were aggressively undercutting his prices. Archer found himself in an impossible position. If he kept his prices up, customers wouldn't buy; if he lowered his prices, he couldn't pay his bills.

In an attempt to consolidate and save the business, he asked Dorothy to resign. Somewhat reluctantly she obliged. Once Dorothy walked out the door of Archer's sign company, she decided to leave her husband too. She went home and packed her bags, collected her children, piled everything into her station wagon and headed for the welfare office in Belleville. While she was living there, Archer managed to get away and see her about two days a week by telling his wife that he had overnight business trips to eastern Ontario. As time went on it wasn't just her performance in the bedroom that he enjoyed. Bruce saw her as beautiful and was thrilled by the fact that, despite their age difference, she repeatedly professed to love him.

By late spring the business was finished and once more Bruce had to tell his wife they were facing insolvency. "The business is finished, we got to get out of here. Where do you want to live?" It was a question she'd heard many times before.

"The only place where I'll be happy is in Vancouver," she replied.

Her response didn't even faze Bruce. He immediately had her car tuned up and helped her pack for the trip out west. Once Lucille and the girls were on their way, Bruce sold his daughters' horses and got rid of the inventory and equipment in his shop. Then he loaded up his own car and a rented trailer with all the rest of his family's furniture and gear and headed out in pursuit of his wife and children. Before he left Peterborough, he promised Dorothy he'd be back to get her as soon as possible.

Out on the coast Lucille had rented a house in Port Moody. Bruce got there about a week after she and the children had settled in. He unloaded the trailer then immediately headed back to Ontario. He told Lucille he had to go back for a couple of months to clean up some unfinished business. In truth he was going back to live with Dorothy and her two children.

As soon as he got back east, Bruce moved this second family to Toronto. With Dorothy on welfare and Bruce out of work, money was scarce. Bruce started using amphetamines and barbiturates. Then, in July of 1972, Bruce and Dorothy took a fateful step. Bruce decided they should support themselves by using a primitive form of extortion. After taking out an advertisement in a sex tabloid called *Flash*, they made contact with a young single male named Robert who worked for a firm in Downsview. When they got together for sex, photos were taken of him in a degrading and compromising position with Dorothy. Later, on July 28, Dorothy telephoned Robert at work. Not realizing that he had contacted the police and his phone was tapped, Dorothy threatened to show the snapshots to Robert's boss unless he came up with $200. Robert agreed to pay her for them.

They arranged to meet at a local hotel and it was there that Dorothy was arrested by two policemen who were tailing Robert.

The police also found Archer waiting outside the tavern and questioned him about his complicity in the matter. Dorothy was charged with extortion but the authorities didn't feel they had enough evidence on Archer to charge him as a party to the offense. Malette was held on bail and released on an Undertaking to Appear for trial on August 9. At this time she gave her name as Dorothy Lillian Malette, born April 24, 1949 and claimed that she had been moving around Toronto from place to place and, at the present, had no fixed address. Further she admitted she was married to a dead stock butcher working out of R.R.#7, Peterborough. She claimed she was living with a Stephen B. Kellar (Kellar was Archer's mother's maiden name.) She said she was supporting two children and was attending an adult training program at Humber College in Toronto.

With the possibility of Dorothy's prosecution hanging over their heads, they decided to make a run for western Canada. Because Malette didn't want to take her children on such a trip, she arranged to have her father pick them up and take them to his home. When Dorothy failed to appear for her trial, a warrant was issued for her arrest.

Bruce and Dorothy set out through Ontario over the top of Lake Superior. When they got to Winnipeg, their car broke down and they had to look for work. Bruce phoned Lucille to explain the problem. He told her he couldn't get to Port Moody right away because his car needed a new motor and he had to stay where he was in order to earn the money to get it fixed.

Bruce was able to get himself a job in Winnipeg driving a truck for a moving company but decided it wasn't enough income for them to live the good life. He wanted Dorothy to get out and make some big money working the downtown hotels as a full time hooker. They both knew this could be dangerous work so Bruce devised a plan that would protect her. Dorothy would only work at night when Bruce was free. When she picked up a john, Archer would follow them to the hotel they were using and wait outside. Up in the room, Dorothy would put an ashtray on the window sill and, if trouble arose, would knock it to the street below. Archer would stand guard below and come to her aid if he saw the ashtray fall.

This sordid existence went on for over two months. By then Dorothy was pining for her children and asked Bruce to take her back to Ontario so she could retrieve them. Bruce complied and off they went back east where they went into the children's school and plucked them right out of the classroom. Then, with hardly a chance to catch their breath, they turned the car around and drove back to Winnipeg.

As winter arrived, they had enough money coming in but Bruce was troubled. He was missing his daughters in British Columbia yet had to be concerned with the responsibility of caring for Dorothy's children in Manitoba. At Christmas, he flew to Port Moody and had a wonderful time, reunited with his girls. But, as time went on he began to think more and more about Dorothy in Winnipeg; he realized he was trapped in a double life that offered him the worst of both worlds. When he was with Dorothy, he longed for the joy of his children. When he was with Sheila and Beth, he yearned for the physical excitement of Dorothy. As torn as he was, he told Lucille he had to get back to his good-paying job in Winnipeg. He returned to his erotic life with his mistress.

But Bruce didn't stay there long. He and Dorothy had just got her children nicely settled in school in Winnipeg when Lucille phoned to say she and the girls were being evicted from their house and she desperately needed his help relocating. Without hesitation, Bruce got in the car and headed for Port Moody. Once he got there, he found them another place in Port Coquitlam and stayed for a while to help them out.

During the time he was there, he telephoned Dorothy once a week. In one of these calls she told him that the police were on her trail for the extortion charge in Toronto. To evade them she needed to get out of Winnipeg right away. Archer told her he'd meet her half way. He didn't want her travelling in Canada where she could be nabbed by the Mounties so he said he'd meet her at the bus station in Great Falls, Montana.

When Bruce told Lucille that he was leaving again, she knew their marriage was finished. Although Lucille had long suspected that her husband had found another woman, she never once confronted him with her suspicions. Keeping her pain to herself, she'd hoped that he would come to his senses. Now she knew he never would. Still, other than being morose at his departure, she made no attempt to challenge him or prevent his leaving.

Back in Winnipeg, Dorothy, who had left her children with a

local family as baby-sitters, boarded a bus for the States. After a long, tiring ride she found Bruce in Great Falls and they immediately drove due north for Edmonton. Dorothy slept most of the way; Bruce seemed to have tremendous endurance behind the wheel of a vehicle. When they got settled in Edmonton, Archer took a job as a salesman for North American Van Lines and Malette went out and hit the streets again. She now was bringing in big money, working five nights a week from Tuesday to Saturday. Although their life together in many ways was sordid and depraved, it paid for a luxurious standard of living that neither of them had known before. It was the one way that Archer could attain his goal of "having everything that other people have."

As comfortable as life was with Dorothy he still missed his daughters and, once again when Christmas rolled around, he flew home to be with them. Realizing that this might be their last Christmas together, Lucille set aside her distress and tried to make their family celebration as joyous as possible. Bruce did his part by making sure there were plenty of presents under the tree. Even though that Christmas was one of the nicest times they'd ever had as a family, in three days he was back in Edmonton with Dorothy.

Early in the new year, Archer took another major step towards establishing himself as bona fide felon. When Dorothy went with a john named Dunston (not his real name), he refused to pay and an argument ensued. Dunston hit her. Archer, as usual, was not very far away and, hearing the disturbance, charged into the room and laid a beating on Dunston so severe the man needed hospital attention. In the process of assaulting Dunston, Bruce stole his wallet. Besides the cash that was in it, Bruce wanted his credit cards and his personal documents. He figured that if the need ever arose, he could use them to forge himself a new identity that could provide him with an alias. This new combination of violence and theft established a dangerous precedent. It also seemed to indicate he was headed for more criminal activity down the road.

When Dunston reported the beating to the police, it became necessary for Archer and Malette get out of town. They quickly packed and fled by car to Prince George, high in the rugged interior of British Columbia. From there they travelled through the northern wilderness that Archer loved so well—to Prince Rupert, up to Alaska, then back to Prince George. All the while Bruce was complaining that he wanted to move back to Vancouver and be closer to his daughters. At the same time, Dorothy was insisting she stop hooking and get a regular job so that they could live a more normal type of life. In an attempt to force Bruce's hand, she found herself a legitimate position as a secretary at a car dealership in Prince George.

But that didn't last long either. Because Bruce was angry at a bisexual stripper named Rose, who had rejected his suggestion that he manage her as a hooker, Archer decided to teach her a lesson. While she was working, he bought two quarts of muriatic acid, got into her apartment and poured it on almost everything she owned—curtains, clothing, bed sheets, furniture, even the food in the fridge. The extensive damage made this a serious property crime and so, once again, the two of them had to leave town as quickly as possible. A notable aspect of Archer's violent or destructive behaviour was that it was never tied to serious alcohol or drug impairment. He didn't drink much at all and the drugs he took were relatively mild barbiturates. The fact is, he seemed to do stupid things when he needed a reason to move on. That may have been the reason for his destructive binge this time.

In any case, since they had to get out of town, it gave him a chance to convince Dorothy to give Vancouver a try. To further entice her, he offered her a shopping spree in Seattle. They had saved about $6,000 and he was ready to let her splurge if she would consider living in Vancouver. Dorothy consented. She was delighted by the prospect of shopping in a big city where she would have the widest selection of the size twenty-two clothes she required.

After their shopping session, they found an apartment in Vancouver and went looking for work. Slowly they also got acquainted with the swinging community in the Vancouver area and began attending its parties. As an adjunct to this, to bolster their income, Bruce conceived the idea of starting a sexual clearing house catalogue. That set the wheels in motion for the formation of *The Double Gators Club*.

Daily Bruce had to face the disreputable life he was living and measure it against the wholesome existence he wanted for his girls. By now Beth was going on nineteen and Sheila was fifteen. He didn't want to do things that would hurt them or cause them embarrassment but he wasn't prepared to change his way of life and diminish his self-gratification. Although he would never admit it, what he wanted for himself came before consideration of anyone else.

He couldn't seem to stop himself spiraling downward. In the future things would only get worse.

LIKE A FAMILY

When Dennis and Paula Onofrey arrived in Virden they stayed at the Countryside Inn for a few days, while they made arrangements for more permanent lodging. Then they moved to the home of Molly Forrester, a widow who specialized in caring for Mounties new to town. Her son, a member of the RCMP, was stationed in Saskatchewan. While living at Molly's, Dennis and Paula shopped for a house and finally decided to have one built in town.

Dennis soon learned that the detachment was in transition. Three young male members who lived together in a house in town had developed a reputation for partying and the powers that be decided to split them up and have them transferred elsewhere. To replace them, four new members arrived that summer. A new detachment commander, forty-two-year-old Staff Sergeant Fred Westerson was brought in to tighten things up. With twenty-three years on the Force, Fred was from the old school of detachment policing. On a personal level he was kind and generous but on the job he had a distant, autocratic manner that demanded members function on strict rank and file discipline. He believed that Mounties should have little say about most aspects of their job—their placement, their transfers, their assignments. But times were changing and young members expected to be given reasons for what they were being told to do.

Since Fred was so distant, members were thankful that one of the NCOs was approachable. Corporal Syd Barrie had been in Virden for almost three years when Dennis got there. Hard working and unpretentious, Barrie was popular with the members. So was his wife, Vivian, whom Paula liked immediately.

The other corporal in the detachment was a new arrival named Larry Keyes. His problem was that, although he had fifteen years experience with the RCMP, most of it was in Toronto in Customs and Excise. That wasn't sufficient to convince members that he would be an effective detachment cop on the prairies.

Detachment cops have their own form of reverse snobbery.

63

They see themselves as the backbone of the Force, out on the front line dealing with the everyday problems and dangers of the real police officer. They're wary of anyone coming in whose primary experience has been in some cushy office job in one of the big cities, especially in Ontario and Quebec where they only enforce federal law. They wonder if anyone with that kind of sanitized background is willing to dig in day after day on the firing line. To a certain extent their concern is well founded. A detachment cop's job is a tough one; they have to get by on their wits and guile to survive. Normally they work alone in a cruiser patrolling hundreds of square miles of territory with the nearest backup sometimes thirty-five miles away. It isn't a rare occurrence for them to be unable to raise anyone on their radio. Atmospheric conditions, low-lying dead spots, obstructions and distance often prevent them from getting through to help. City police might face more dangerous incidents than detachment police on a regular basis but they have the comfort and advantage of knowing help is close at hand. Sometimes in small detachments there is only one member on duty. If he is attacked on a desolate back road, especially by someone heavily armed, he is, more often than not, on his own for a long time before help will arrive.

Corporal Larry Keyes, coming from his tidy desk job in Toronto, was going to have to prove his mettle in the field. This is not to say that Virden was a rough place. It was one of the safest detachments in all of D Division, which encompassed the entire Province of Manitoba. The province was divided into four huge sub-divisions: Winnipeg, Thompson, Dauphin and Brandon. Virden was part of the Brandon Sub-Division which, because of the industrious, mostly rural population in this part of the province, was thought to be the most law-abiding sector of them all.

Dennis couldn't concern himself with passing judgment on the new command. As a new recruit, he was far too busy trying to prove his own worth. He spent the first few months getting to know all he could about the detachment area and making sure he didn't get involved in office politics. Two of the members he liked were Jake Cullins and Clem MacInnis. Both of them were experienced. Jake, who was from New Brunswick, had been a Mountie for six years and had already served in three small Manitoba detachments. Without being pushy, Jake shared his knowledge with Dennis and did what he could to make him welcome and comfortable. They spent a lot of off-duty time together which worked out well because their wives liked each other. When Paula first came to Virden, she knew no one in the whole town. Joan Cullins was one of the first to invite Paula over for coffee and they became instant friends.

Joan was an operating room nurse who worked at the Virden Hospital. It was a busy place. Besides the usual domestic and hunting accidents there were often major accidents on the Trans-Canada Highway. In the summer, it seemed the road was always under construction and this caused many problems. In the winter, driving conditions were often hazardous. To handle this kind of trauma, the hospital had two operating rooms, a fully functional laboratory, and sophisticated X-ray equipment. The only thing it didn't have was an Intensive Care Unit.

When Dennis arrived in Virden, Clem MacInnis was assigned to be his trainer. Riding together every day, they got to know one another well. MacInnis was a big, raw-boned Cape Breton Islander standing 6'3" and weighing over 200 lbs. He and wife, Irene had come to Virden a year before after two postings in northern Manitoba. Clem was a terrific athlete who had played hockey with the Halifax Junior Canadians as a teenager. He still played Senior "A" for the Virden Oil Kings and was one of the best defensemen in the league. A private individual who tended to go his own way, Clem was one of the few members in Virden who appreciated the way that Fred Westerson ran the detachment. He acknowledged that Westerson was a strict, autocratic commander but he thought he was fair and believed his type of leadership was necessary. Being conservative by nature, Clem wasn't totally happy with all the changes that were taking place in the Force at that time. He was glad to have someone in charge with his feet planted firmly in the past.

The Onofreys, after living at Molly Forrester's for a few months, had a prefabricated house put together and moved to a foundation on a lot on Bennett Crescent in the northwest part of town. One of the first persons to stop by the house was Orville Sheane, a pleasant fifty-year-old retired farmer who lived on the lot directly behind the Onofreys. Orville was a part-time civilian guard for the detachment who was hired to keep an eye on prisoners and make sure there were no incidents in the cells while the police were away from the building. Orville had spoken with Dennis at the detachment office but didn't know him well at all. When he saw that Dennis was moving in behind him, he went over and offered to help in any way he could. From that time forward they became the best of friends. Paula got to know Eileen Sheane and the four of them spent a lot of time together. Orville helped Dennis prepare the soil to plant grass seed in the Onofreys front and back yards. Eileen helped Paula with her first batch of preserves. Over time the four of them were together so much, Dennis came to think of Orville as the dad he had never known.

From time to time, Dennis, Orville and Clem MacInnis would go hunting together but they seldom brought home any game. They weren't interested in that. For them, going hunting was an opportunity to spend some time together walking in the woods on a beautiful fall or winter day.

John and Marion O'Ray were another couple who welcomed Dennis and Paula to town and went out of their way to make them feel at home. John had been in Virden for over four years, which made him the senior man in the detachment. He was a pleasant but outspoken man who had opinions on a wide variety of topics. He also had a lot of interests outside policing. One of these was playing the bass guitar. Three years before, he and three other local musicians had formed a band called "Revival." They practised together long and hard and eventually got hired to play at some of the dances in the Virden Legion.

John was also one of the best hockey players on the RCMP team in the town's industrial league. Having played Junior "C" hockey in his native Ottawa for the Minto Cardinals, John was a good skater and a great stick handler. When he carried the puck, it seemed to dangle on the end of his stick as if it were glued there. He also had a wicked shot that made him one of the highest scorers in the league.

Another big interest of John's was his motorcycle. He owned an XS 1100 Yamaha that he loved taking on the road on his days off. Whenever John got the chance, he and Marion would put on their leathers and go roaring off to Brandon for a movie or dinner at the Suburban restaurant. In the last little while they hadn't been able to do that because Marion, like Paula Onofrey, was expecting in March.

John met Marion at his first posting in Cranberry Portage. They were married prior to coming to Virden in June of 1973. Marion was very outgoing and, when Dennis and Paula Onofrey came to town, she and Paula soon became friends. They had lots in common. Both of them worked as sales clerks at Timms Jewellers in town, both had sons under two years of age and both were expecting in March.

Marion's expected baby would be the O'Rays' second child. Their son Adam had been born in Virden two years before. The new baby was coming at a perfect time. It hadn't interfered with Marion playing on the Virden women's softball team last summer and probably wouldn't prevent her from playing again next summer. That suited her teammates perfectly because she was their star pitcher.

Gregarious, hospitable and attractive, Marion loved a good party. The O'Rays often hosted celebrations for their RCMP colleagues and their wives. At Christmas they would invite everyone in the detachment to drop in for a visit. As soon as they could, the O'Rays had the Onofreys over for dinner and included them in any parties they hosted.

This worked out well for Dennis and Paula because there was seldom a dull moment in the O'Ray household. With Marion playing on the softball team and John playing in the band, they had a lot of friends in town and were very busy socially.

Another of the RCMP transfers to come to Virden in 1975 was a young couple from Windsor, Ontario named Steve and Simone Howell. To make them feel as welcome as she had been made to feel, Paula had them over for a visit as soon as they arrived. They got along very comfortably and went on to develop a warm and long-lasting relationship.

The last of the new arrivals that first summer was a twenty-four-year-old rookie from Depot named Debbie MacLean. Debbie was the first female Mountie to serve in Virden and before she got there, Paula was surprised to hear some of the member's wives express concern about her arrival. Over coffee some admitted they didn't like the idea of their husbands being alone in a cruiser all day with a single woman, driving around the back woods of the detachment. Others weren't convinced that a woman could provide their husbands with the same kind of backup that a man would. All of the wives changed their opinion about the safety factor once they got to meet Debbie MacLean.

Although she was pretty and refined in her manners, she was a big woman at 5'9" and 190 lbs who had a strong, honest way about her that would not tolerate any nonsense from anyone. And that certainly included married policemen. Once the wives got to know her, their concerns abated. It wasn't long before the wives and the members in the detachment came to see that Debbie would be as good a partner as any man in the office. She was tough as nails. Not long after her arrival, she and Dennis had to lock up a drunk in the cells. They didn't have any trouble getting him inside the cage but once he was in there, he became verbally abusive. Debbie had to speak to him several times to get him to settle down. Just as she was about to leave and go upstairs, the prisoner asked her to come to the bars because he wanted to tell her something important. When Debbie went over to hear what he had to say, the man poked his arm through the bars and punched her in the face. Bleeding from the nose, and without saying a word, she opened the cell, went inside and hit the drunk between the eyes. He flew backwards against the wall and slowly slid down into a sitting position on the floor. Then she walked out of the cell and still without comment, walked past Dennis and went upstairs to finish her paperwork.

Like the Onofreys, she stayed with Molly Forrester when she first came to Virden and then got herself a little apartment downtown. This was a temporary move because Debbie liked to entertain and the apartment was too small for the kind of parties she liked to throw. A few months later she found a three bedroom bungalow and rented it with two other women. From that time on, her place became the detachment's informal meeting place. Besides the regular parties she had there, the members used to drop by her place for a drink and a sandwich when they were going off shift. Sometimes that was at five in the afternoon, sometimes that was one in the morning, or later. The wives didn't mind their husbands going there; it was a good place to unwind in private.

Virden was a typical small town where everyone knew everybody's business, so members didn't like to socialize in public. Even though both downtown hotels weren't particularly rough places, it wasn't smart to drink there. If some of the local rednecks got feeling good and were looking for a fight, a cop who might have recently given one of them a speeding ticket could be a perfect target. The only place the members drank in public was at the Legion. To get in, patrons had to have a membership and once they were admitted, the regular members wouldn't tolerate any nonsensical behaviour in such hallowed quarters. Since all the Mounties were automatically entitled to membership, it was a perfect place to go except after night shift, when it was closed. Rather than disturb their wives and children at home, they went to Debbie's place.

Dennis and Paula's Christmas in Virden was their first one away from home. They invited Rose to come out and spend a few days with them and she was delighted to be asked. When she came in from Winnipeg by bus, Dennis picked her up at the station in a police cruiser and put her in the back seat. Arriving at the house, she discovered she couldn't get out because there were no handles to open the back door. For a joke, Dennis got her suitcase out of the trunk and began walking away from the car. Rose pounded on the window and called for him to let her out. When he did, they both had a good laugh, just like they used to have when they walked to work together in Winnipeg. They were still laughing when they went inside.

Rose and Paula hugged and kissed hello and were holding hands when Dennis whispered, "Mom, do you want to hear a secret?"

Rose said, "Is it good news?" She looked at Paula who nodded.

"Sure it's good news," Dennis replied.

"Well, OK tell me then," Rose said.

"We're going to have a baby," he said.

"Oh Dennis," she cried out. "That's wonderful." She pulled Paula towards her and hugged her more tightly than before. With their faces touching Rose said, "Paula, I'm so happy. I'm so happy."

"Me too," Paula whispered.

The next few days were special for the three of them. Dennis introduced his mother to all the visitors who came to the house. The Sheanes dropped over for a long visit and Rose was glad to get to know them because Dennis had told her so much about them. Jake and Joan Cullins, Clem and Irene MacInnis and Steve and Simone Howell came by too. The Howells were quickly becoming favourites of the Onofreys. On Christmas day Dennis, Paula and Rose were invited to drop in at the O'Rays and the Barries. Vivian Barrie was also becoming a close friend of Paula's.

When Dennis introduced Vivian to Rose, Vivian said to her, "You know, Rose, I'm Ukrainian too."

"You are?" Rose exclaimed.

"Yeah, my maiden name was Stasiuk. I'm a Ukie from Wadena, Saskatchewan. Everybody's Ukrainian from out there."

That was all that Rose needed to hear to feel comfortable. From that point on she and Vivian had a long, animated conversation about the places in the old country that their ancestors came from. Before their talk was over, Vivian suggested that all the Onofreys should come back to her place that year to celebrate Ukrainian Christmas on January eighth. Rose was thrilled to be asked but she had to decline.

"I'd love to," she said, "but I'm sorry, I can't stay that long. I've got to get back to work."

"Well," Vivian said, "one year you have to come out here and stay longer. We got to have a traditional dinner with the wheat and honey and everything . . . like they used to do back home."

"I'd love that," Rose said.

Dennis joined in, "Yeah, Mom, we should do that sometime. Instead of regular Christmas, we should celebrate Ukrainian Christmas. We could have a big party and invite everybody over."

They all agreed that would be fun. Rose and Vivian talked about doing it sometime in the future but didn't finalize any plans. When the Onofreys left the Barries, Rose and Vivian promised to keep in touch. Two days later it was time for Rose to go back to Winnipeg. She had enjoyed her stay in Virden so much she was sorry to have to leave. Dennis and Paula made her promise to come back soon.

During the winter Clem MacInnis talked Dennis into playing for the RCMP hockey team in the local industrial league which was comprised of teams sponsored by the teachers, the downtown merchants and one from the Sioux Valley Reserve. It was supposed to be a non-contact league but occasionally tempers flared and the sticks came up. There were seldom any fights.

Dennis wasn't much of a hockey player but he gave it everything he had. The only thing he was worse at than swimming was skating. For some reason he had never learned how to skate properly and, once he got out on the ice, he had a difficult time standing up. Turning and stopping were pretty much out of the question. Even though he was always behind the play, he enjoyed getting out and being part of the team. Sometimes he would be going in one direction while everybody else was coming back the other way, but he never got discouraged. When it was game time, he was always the first one in the dressing room tying on his skates.

In January, Ralph Mahar, a slim, lithe twenty-two-year-old from a three-man detachment in Manitou was transferred into Virden. He was a lively bundle of energy who would eventually become one of Dennis' closest friends. Like many Virden Mounties before him, he moved into Molly Forrester's place and then into a downtown apartment. Coming off two years in a small detachment, Ralph was sensitive to the fact that, as the new member in town, he was going to have to prove himself and earn his spurs. Assessing new members in a detachment is a natural process with the Mounties. Not only do they have to work with them and live with them on a daily basis, they literally have to trust that person with their lives.

The very first week Ralph was put to the test. Riding alone, he was called to a domestic disturbance where a homesteader had badly beaten his wife. The farmer was a huge man who outweighed Ralph by at least sixty lbs. When Ralph tried to arrest him, the fight was on. For ten minutes they wrestled and rolled in the snow with the odd punch thrown in for good measure. Ralph finally got the man subdued but his wrists were so big he had trouble getting the cuffs on him. By the time he put him in the cruiser his uniform was a mess and he was totally exhausted. The assailant was well known to the Virden detachment so when the word got around that Ralph had brought him in alone and locked him up, his colleagues were impressed.

That week, when Dennis and Ralph were riding together, they talked about the wife-beater Ralph had arrested. "You know," Dennis said, "I had trouble with that same guy when I first came here."

"Really?" Ralph replied.

"Yeah. I had to fight him too. He's a real handful."

"You're telling me."

"But I'll tell you something," Dennis confided, "it's a good thing you took him on. He's a constant problem around here but once he knows you won't back down, he's a lot easier to handle."

Ralph nodded that he understood.

"He won't cause you any more trouble," Dennis said.

"Good," Ralph replied.

"And he won't fight with you any more either."

"That's even better."

They both chuckled. It was the first of many laughs they would share together.

All the Virden members warmed to Ralph as, day by day, he demonstrated he was capable and dependable. Like the others in the detachment, Ralph had his share of traumatic experiences. One night he had to disarm a violent prisoner in the detachment office. Another time he had to wrestle a pair of scissors from a woman bent on suicide. Several times he was called to fatal automobile accidents where broken bodies were strewn along the highway. The most wrenching of all his duties were the times he had to notify parents of the death of a young son or daughter.

Besides being a solid member of the detachment, Ralph endeared himself to everybody, especially the detachment wives, when he performed his comedy routines at their parties. Ralph didn't have to drink very much before he became a happy and talented entertainer. With very little coaxing, he could become Monkey Man, grunting his way around the room with his lower lip protruding and his long arms swinging below his waist. Or he could squawk and strut around doing his Chicken Dance to whatever tune was playing on the tape deck. His most requested routine was Being Born where with a contorted face he conveyed the agony of his painful trip through the birth canal into the bright light and joyous freedom of the outside world.

Some nights, when Ralph and Dennis were on the same shift, they would contravene detachment policy and double up together after midnight. Patrolling the highways and rural hamlets at that time of night could be boring and lonely. Riding together made the time pass a lot more quickly and pleasantly. Ralph found Dennis mature beyond his years and valued his point of view. When things were quiet, they had a chance to discuss their families and their future. Ralph talked about his fiancee, Sonja Matthys, and their wedding which was set for the following spring. Dennis spoke of his plans to someday move into undercover narcotics work in one of the big western cities.

They discovered that late at night on the open prairie, they could bring in AM radio stations on the car's standard radio from hundreds of miles away. On Friday nights they liked to listen to a series of ghost stories that came from Chicago at midnight. As Dennis drove, Ralph would fiddle with the dial until they heard a snippet of the announcer's familiar voice.

"That's it!" Dennis would say, "you just went past it."

Ralph would turn the dial delicately until the announcer's voice came back in. "That's him, I got it!"

"Yeah, that's it. Turn it up."

Then they both settled in to listen. There was little talk between them as they cruised along in the darkness lost in the world of imagination. Occasionally they would look at each other and make a face to convey their enjoyment. At the commercial, one would say, "Geez, what do you think's going to happen now?"

"I don't know," the other would reply, "but it sounds like that guy's in for a big surprise." Then they'd go on to speculate about the direction of the plot until the drama began anew. Their only concern was that the show might be interrupted by the dispatcher sending them out on a call. On the rare occasions that happened, Dennis would grumble, wheel the car around and head for the trouble spot. But when they got there, it had to be something pretty serious before both of them would get out of the car and abandon the story in progress.

One or the other would say, "You stay here and tell me what happens." Seldom did one of the ghost stories finish without their knowing the ending.

In the summer, Ralph's fiancee Sonja came to town to work as a sales clerk at Timms Jewellers. She met Marion O'Ray and Paula Onofrey who worked there too. Although Sonja was eighteen years old and fresh out of high school, she was an independent woman who looked to the two older women for companionship and a chance to share her concerns about being married to a policeman. Over coffee and Coke, Sonja and Paula became acquainted and, as the summer wore on, they bonded like Dennis and Ralph.

Paula was busy that summer. She and Vivian Barrie planted

vegetable gardens in the dark rich soil of their back yards. Paula had never done this before but Vivian was an old hand at it. They travelled back and forth between their homes preparing the soil and planting rows of tomatoes, cucumbers, beans, peas, almost every vegetable imaginable. For Paula it wasn't just a novel idea. With the baby coming, she liked the idea of saving money and she loved the access to fresh produce all through the summer. Sometimes Dennis helped her hoe or weed but he really preferred working inside at little maintenance jobs. Orville Sheane was invaluable in teaching him how to do electrical and plumbing repairs.

Dennis felt he was really blessed because not only were all these good things happening in his life but, besides, he truly enjoyed his work as a police officer. Occasionally he would go into the office on his day off just to see what was happening. When he was on duty, he was very serious about his work. He spent a lot of time poring over the criminal code and provincial statutes and soon developed a reputation for being one of the more knowledgeable members in the detachment. Out on the road, there were occasions when his intensity made him seem officious. He would stop someone who was speeding recklessly on the highway and not only give them a ticket but also a gratuitous lecture about being more sensible and responsible.

Dennis and Paula were finding that they liked the people in the community. Most of them were friendly but not too pushy or nosy. They appreciated the presence of the police and, unless they had reason to think otherwise, held them in high regard. Within months most people in town knew Dennis by name and a lot of them knew that Paula was his wife. Paula was always surprised when a stranger in the supermarket said hello and called her Mrs. Onofrey.

Although Virden was just a small place, there always seemed to be something interesting to do. There was a movie theatre and a drive-in movie just outside of town. Every month there was a dance sponsored by one organization or another either at the Legion or the Elks Club. If they wanted a special night out, a trip to Brandon was easily arranged. Otherwise most people in town did their entertaining at home. They played cards or had pot luck house parties or barbecues. The RCMP couples tended to stick together and the Onofreys went to every party they could manage when Dennis was off-duty.

At the end of June, Paula went into the Virden Hospital and delivered a healthy, handsome boy they called Corey. Dennis was so thrilled that after he phoned his mother and Paula's, he made a regular tour around town to tell the Sheanes and their other friends. Then he dropped by the office to pass out cigars. Because Dennis was usually so serious looking, everyone was surprised to see him with such a beaming smile on his face. He told anyone who would listen that this was definitely the happiest day of his life. And although he wasn't known for his extravagance, he even brought flowers to Paula in the hospital. They both felt a happy, new chapter in their lives had just begun.

Paula was only home from the hospital a week when Joe and Elaine MacDougall were transferred to the detachment in Virden. Their arrival sparked a special, new friendship between the two couples. From the first day Joe arrived in Virden, Dennis liked him and he quickly became another of Dennis' close friends.

Joe and his wife Elaine became a popular couple. A tall, attractive woman, Elaine was a university graduate who had been raised on a 540-acre farm in the Assiniboine Valley near Brandon. She met Joe when she went up to The Pas, 300 miles north of Winnipeg, to teach high school. Both she and Joe were happy when they were transferred to Virden. He liked what he'd heard about the detachment and she was glad to be so much closer to her parents.

As soon as they arrived in town the MacDougalls got a pleasant taste of the Virden Detachment hospitality. Syd and Vivian Barrie offered to let them live in their house for the first three weeks while they went away on holidays. Elaine couldn't believe a family that they didn't even know could be so trusting and so gracious. Joe was surprised too; he wasn't about to turn down such a generous offer from his corporal. It would give them a chance to live comfortably while they looked around for a permanent place to live. Paula made a point of inviting Elaine over for coffee the first week they arrived. So did Marion O'Ray and Simone Howell. The next week two other detachment wives had her over. That was the Virden way. Elaine and Joe were very pleased.

Joe was a good addition to the detachment. A chunky fellow at 5'9" and 200 lbs., he had a rare combination of personal qualities that made him an exemplary policeman. He was very outgoing and personable, always ready to have a good laugh, even at his own expense. He was kind and fair with everyone, always trying to help them solve their problems. In the most turbulent circumstances he could remain calm and patient and understanding. But he was firm and when his patience ran out, he could be as tough as nails. True to his Scots heritage, Joe could fight if he had to. He came to Virden from three years of hard RCMP duty at The Pas, one of the toughest detachments in the province. To his credit he was the first recruit from Depot to be sent directly there. Every member sent to The Pas had to be prepared, at one time or another, to stand up and take care of himself. Once they proved they could do that, they were usually left alone. Typical of a good fighter, Joe didn't go around showing off his toughness but kept it quietly in reserve for when it was needed. He much preferred to talk his way through a problem in an attempt to get it resolved.

In Virden too he was forced to prove he could fight. Not long after he arrived, he was challenged by a young rowdy with a tough reputation who egged him on and eventually tried to hit him. Joe swung back and the fight was on. It was a good battle with a lot of hard punches exchanged until Joe landed a heavy one to the young fellow's nose that sent him down for the count. The lesson was not lost on the crew of gawkers who had gathered round to taunt the Mountie hoping to see him humiliated. From that time on, when he was called to a public disturbance at one of the hotels or to a heated domestic dispute, people paid attention to what Joe had to say.

"Stop your nonsense or you're going to jail," he would warn them. Usually they stopped but if he had to say it again, Joe would snap the cuffs on them and ram them into a cruiser so fast they didn't know where they were.

Joe quickly established himself in the detachment as being dependable, the one quality that all policemen prize in a fellow officer. Every police officer keeps a mental list of whom they would call if trouble breaks out. Dennis had Joe MacDougall high on his list. The members who were low on everybody's lists were usually the ones who did a lot of whining and complaining. They were the ones who didn't like working shifts, didn't like working nights, who kicked up a fuss when they were sent out to investigate a disturbance on their own. Dennis suspected these were the members who would be afraid to go into a dangerous situation, reluctant to help a fellow officer in a bad spot. The others Dennis didn't trust were the big talkers who didn't seem to know anything. They didn't read the manuals or the literature on the changes in the law or the new policies and procedures that were regularly circulated around the office. They always seemed to bluff their way through things. What good would they be in a tight spot where action was required? It was comforting for Dennis to know that there were very few in the detachment who were like that.

As strong and trustworthy as MacDougall was, Dennis soon learned Joe was human. Both of them were opinionated and disagreed on a wide variety of subjects. Both were stubborn as mules and wouldn't give an inch on their beliefs. Some of their discussions on abstract topics like justice or morality were refined and dignified. Others, like those on politics, were heated. Dennis loved the NDP; Joe was a true-blue Conservative. Some of their discussions were mundane, like Dennis' refusal to eat pork.

"It's a dirty, filthy animal," he said. "I will never serve it in my house and I don't intend to eat it in anyone else's house."

"Oh don't be so crazy, Dennis," Joe argued. "There's nothing wrong with pork. It may get a little dirty on the outside . . . from the slop in the barnyard but it's fine once it's been butchered and cured and all that."

"Well you eat it if you want to but I'm not going to. I want no part of it."

"Aw, geez, there's no sense talking to you," Joe complained.

But that never stopped the two of them from debating again the next time they got together.

The one thing they strongly agreed on was their Roman Catholic faith. Both of them attended church every Sunday without fail, often at the same mass at Sacred Heart Church. Strangely enough both their wives were Protestant and that soon became the topic of little jokes among the four of them.

As time went on Joe became one of the most active members of the Virden community. He served on the parish council, sat on the Co-op board, belonged to the Optimist Club, coached the town hockey midgets, coached swimming at the outdoor swimming pool, volunteered to collect for the Red Cross, played on the police hockey team. He did all this so quietly and effortlessly most people never noticed how busy he was. But Dennis noticed and he admired him for it.

In August 1976, Russ and Kim Hornseth were transferred in from Flin Flon. If the social life of the detachment was good before they came it became appreciably better after they arrived. Although Russ was quiet and dependable at work, off the job he could be a hellion. He and his wife, Kim quickly became the zany live-wires of the detachment. Wherever they went, people had more fun. Any kind of social outing became a real party once the Hornseths arrived on the scene with their crazy antics.

Russ had come a long way to become a Mountie. A true westerner, he was a country boy born in Humboldt, Saskatchewan and raised in the tiny village of Kandahar, 100 miles north of Regina. He and his older brother, Bob, learned to hunt and fish with their dad. They spent days together in the bush looking for caribou and moose and hours at the nearby lakes pulling out strings of jackfish and pike. He was able to handle a horse before he could ride a bike and had his own buckskin mare by the time he was twelve-years-old. Since he was the only kid for miles around who owned his own horse, he loved to ride around town showing it off.

After graduating from high school, he got a job on a "green chain," cutting logs in the bush. It was tough work because the work gang went into the bush camp in the fall and didn't come out again until the spring. In between times they had to enjoy each other's company and entertain themselves to survive. Although Russ liked the isolation of the bush, he could see the work offered him a very limited future. So, like his brother Bob before him, Russ joined the RCMP. After graduating from Depot Division in 1967, he was assigned his first posting in Burnaby, B.C. It didn't take him long to decide he didn't like it there. The city was too big and crowded. There were too many buildings and cars, too much noise and not enough wilderness to suit him. Feeling very much out of place, he began asking for a transfer. It took three long years to end his misery in Burnaby.

In 1970 his superior horsemanship got him a spot with the RCMP Musical Ride. The move transformed his life. From the minute he joined the Ride in Ottawa, he was in heaven. He loved riding; he loved practicing the maneuvers; he loved grooming and caring for the horses. When the troop went on an extended show tour for six months, things got even better. The Ride performed all across Canada and the United States and everywhere they went the single girls flocked around the men in red serge on the black horses.

It was while he was stationed with the Ride at Rockcliffe in Ottawa that he met Kim Proulx, a Quebecoise from across the Ottawa River in Hull. Above everything else, Kim was an original who went her own way. Dark and attractive, she was fluent in French and spoke English with only the slightest hint of an accent. Blunt and outspoken, she could swear fluently in both languages. When Russ and Kim got married, it was a melding of kindred spirits.

When Russ' tour on the Ride was ended in 1972, he and Kim were posted to Flin Flon in the wilds of northwestern Manitoba. They spent four happy years there, both of them heavily involved in the life of the community, both of them loving the outdoor life.

Russ liked the police work in Flin Flon with one exception. Almost every pay day at the zinc or copper mines, the hardrock miners would collect their money and head for the bars to get drunk. When they got drunk, they liked to fight. When the Mounties were called to break up the fights, the combatants often turned on them. They still tell the story in Flin Flon about a local family of brothers who interrupted their fighting just long enough to pick up a peacekeeping Mountie by the ankles, turn him upside down and thump his head on the barroom floor. Although Hornseth never suffered such a humiliation, he did have his two front teeth knocked out when he went after a thief in a dark alley. The guy was trying to break into a store and as Russ snuck up on him, another crook attacked him from the shadows hitting him in the face with a two-by-four. He didn't wake up until one of his fellow officers found him lying in the alley and shook him into consciousness.

Although Hornseth wasn't much of a boxer, he was wiry enough and strong enough to take care of himself in a fight. In Flin Flon he learned to get by on his ingenuity and his positive attitude. When he was forced to fight, he usually took some punishment but was always able to subdue his assailant and get the cuffs on him. Then, cussing a blue streak, Russ would jam him into the back seat of his cruiser and haul him off to the cells. In those Flin Flon years there were many occasions when Russ

Hornseth was bruised and battered; nevertheless he managed to survive.

When Russ was transferred to Virden in August 1976, he felt the move was an acceptable compromise. Although Virden was a town detachment, it was one with a substantial rural component. Here Russ could still enjoy the benefits of the open country that would let him fish and hunt on his days off. Things worked out well for him in Virden; he was promoted to corporal in October 1977.

Kim enjoyed Virden too. She could fit in anywhere and was immediately popular with the detachment wives. They loved her not only because she was kind and considerate but because she was brash and venturesome. She dressed outrageously in leopard skin vests, huge floppy hats and bright coloured boots. She carried herself flamboyantly with loads of gold coloured necklaces and earrings that sparkled in the light and jangled when she walked. She was the first person they'd seen who hung a huge macramé chair from the ceiling in her living room. She dared to mock the Musical Ride with a small figurine of a black horse she kept in her curio cabinet. Seated on the horse was a miniature red-coated Mountie and behind the Mountie rode a bare-breasted woman dressed in a wedding veil and a half length bridal gown.

When she learned that Syd Barrie was from Richmond, Quebec, they struck up a special relationship and spoke French every time they got together. That tended to be often because the Hornseths loved to party. As soon as they moved into their house, which was only a short walk from Dennis and Paula, they began inviting people in the detachment over for get-togethers. There was lots of drinking, dancing, singing, sometimes crazy games and always good food.

They weren't the only ones to throw a good party. It seemed as if everybody did, the O'Rays, the Onofreys, Debbie MacLean and others. The unofficial motto for the Virden detachment seemed to be: "we work hard; we play hard." Some of the best parties were held at Ray and Lynn Needham's farm. The Needhams were an older couple who lived in a house in Virden but also owned a fifty-acre farm five miles out of town near Oak Lake. They had one son in the Mounties and another son, Dave, who was interested in becoming one. Their farm had been used for several detachment parties before but once the Hornseths became good friends, the place was always open for action. These parties weren't exclusive to the detachment. Many civilians like the Needhams, the Sheanes and Hart and Ardelle Devonish, who owned the Shell station on the highway, were invited too.

The farm house was just an old frame shack with no running water or sewer but it offered the Virden Mounties and their wives a private place to kick up their heels. The men would dig a barbecue pit and cover it with a grate to cook their meat. Everyone brought salads and breads and lots to drink. After dinner they sat around the fire drinking and telling stories. When the alcohol began to take hold, they would start singing. Invariably it began with the old favourites and, as more and more joined in, the group would start to make requests of individuals to sing their special songs. They would pester Joe MacDougall mercilessly until he sang his song from the Maritimes.

Standing erect with his chin held high and a beer in his hand, Joe would sing the verse loud and clear:

> The sun was setting in the west
> The birds were singing on every tree
> All nature seemed inclined for a rest
> But still there was no rest for me

Then he would make them all join in and sing the chorus:

> FAREWELL NOVA SCOTIA, the sea-bound coast
> Let your mountains dark and dreary be
> For when I am far away on the briny ocean tossed
> Will you ever heave a sigh and a wish for me

When the song was over, a great cheer would go up. But before Joe could sit down, they'd insist he do a jig. This normally didn't take much persuasion. Humming another east coast tune, with his arms down by his sides and his back ram-rod straight, Joe's feet would start flying. When he was done, he'd get a bigger cheer for his dancing than for his singing. As he'd sit down to the applause, a big Cape Breton smile would break upon his face.

As soon as the group tired of singing, a tape deck would be rigged up and the modern dancing would start. To the pulsing music of the Eagles and the BeeGees they danced on the prairie grass under the light of the moon. Paula and Vivian Barrie and Steve Howell were always the last to quit. More than anyone Paula loved the music and the dancing and never wanted to say good night.

Throughout the evening, things could get loud and boisterous but never completely out of hand. Kim and Russ Hornseth, or Horny as he was called, were the hardest drinkers of the bunch. When they got wound up, the two of them and crazy Ralph Mahar were the life of the party. Eventually Mahar and the Hornseths would fall asleep and somebody would drive them all home. That was an understood rule. Nobody drove home under the influence. When the party was at one of the houses in town, everybody lived so close they could walk home.

The parties weren't always big, planned affairs. Sometimes there was a spontaneous fish fry. Throughout the summer different couples would go fishing on the banks of the Assiniboine River. Even though the river was only ten feet wide in some places, there were times when it was filled with pickerel. It was not unusual for the Onofreys and the Howells to catch a bucket full of good-sized fish. They'd head back to the Howell's big, old house in Virden and invite as many friends as they could feed to come over for a fish fry. In twenty minutes the Howell's kitchen would be bustling with six or seven couples eagerly preparing for a fresh fish dinner.

One special event took place every summer. Teams of fire fighters came in from Manitoba, Alberta, Saskatchewan and North and South Dakota to compete in a series of events. These included hose rolling, ladder climbing and shooting water. Teams were timed as they rushed into smoke-filled rooms to rescue dummies. The Virden RCMP detachment was always invited to enter a team and although they never finished high in the standings, they put up a good fight and had lots of fun. At the end of it all, the detachment threw a huge barbecue out at Needham's place and this gave the competing teams a true taste of Virden hospitality.

In October Russ Hornseth was promoted to corporal and assigned to be the shift commander for the rural section. Syd Barrie was in charge of the town and Larry Keyes was responsible for the highway. Although Russ had only been in Virden a short time, he was so honest and self-effacing his former equals had no difficulty accepting him as their boss. One of the things they liked about Russ was the fact he didn't always go by the book. If there were a fast solution to a problem that involved an unorthodox approach with a little risk involved, Russ would usually take a chance.

This immediately got him in some hot water with an Inspector in Brandon. One night Morris Cameron, an aboriginal Special RCMP constable, called Russ from the Sioux Valley Reserve.

"Russ," he said, "I got a problem out here."

"What's the matter?" Russ replied.

"I arrested a guy for being drunk and put the cuffs on him but I didn't get him in the cruiser."

"What happened?"

"He got loose and ran away on me."

"Can't you find him?"

"No, he's hiding some place and it's too dark out here to see anything."

"Well the hell with him. Come on back in."

"Just leave him out there with the handcuffs on?"

"Sure. Let him wander around for a while. When he gets tired of wearing those bracelets, he'll call us. C'mon back in."

"OK, whatever you say." Morris wondered at Russ' solution but he knew if any trouble arose, his corporal would back him. So he left. Within two hours, the escapee called the detachment to get out of the cuffs and Morris went back to the reserve to pick him up.

The problem was that Russ and Morris' conversation was picked up over the radio and heard by an Inspector in Brandon. The next day he called Russ on the carpet and told him he didn't like the way Russ operated as a policeman. He also assured Russ he would not be receiving any further promotions. Russ was unconcerned with what he had to say. He'd always been a little bit of a renegade.

One time he contravened the Force's regulations on hand guns. On this issue, he was not alone. Many members felt that the Smith and Wesson .38 Specials they were issued were virtually useless. They were inaccurate beyond fifty yards and didn't hit hard enough to knock a criminal down and put him out of commission. For his own safety Russ, like other members in the Force, began carrying a .357 Magnum in his holster.

He explained what he was doing to Kim: "There's a lot more whump to her. If I ever get into a situation where I'm in real trouble, I can defend myself. Afterwards the brass will be all over me but I'll still be alive to answer their stupid questions."

Russ carried the Magnum for about two months but it bothered him. He knew somebody would eventually spot it and he'd be in deep trouble with the administration. Reluctantly he decided to put it away and slipped his old .38 Special back in his holster. He felt he wouldn't need the Magnum in Virden anyway.

Still, as tranquil as the detachment could be, it had its dangerous moments. One afternoon Debbie MacLean was just about to go off shift when a distraught woman called. She identified herself and Debbie knew her to be an old widow who lived out by the highway.

"Please help me," the woman implored. "There's a crazy man in my house and he's taken it over."

"Who is he?" Debbie asked.

"I don't know. He's a stranger off the highway."

"What do you mean, he's taken it over?"

"He just barged in my house and started yelling and acting crazy. I ran away."

"Where are you now?"

"I'm at my neighbour's next door but I'm afraid he's coming in here next."

Debbie went out in the office and told a member who was still on duty the nature of the call.

He didn't seem too interested. "I'll get out there in a few minutes," he said.

Debbie couldn't believe his nonchalance in the face of such an emergency.

"Don't you think you better get out there?" she insisted.

"Don't worry about it," he replied. "I'll take care of it."

Debbie wouldn't accept that. "I'm going out right now," she announced hoping to shame the other member into going with her. But he didn't respond to her challenge and continued dawdling with his paper work. Debbie put on her gun and left the office by herself.

When she arrived at the house that had been invaded, she went up on the porch and opened the front door. Inside she could see a young, long-haired man moving around in the kitchen.

"Hey, you," she said. "What are you doing in there?"

He stared at her with fierce eyes.

"Come out of there, I want to talk to you."

Paula and Dennis Onofrey on their wedding day

Paula, Dennis and Corey Onofrey fifteen months before the Virden incident

Graduation photo of Troop 9. Candy Smith back row second from left, Katie Wiegert third row third from left, Candy Palmer back row third from right, Jane Greenwood third row third from right Courtesy of Corporal Brenda MacFarlane, Stn. Johns, Newfoundland (third row, second from right)

Russ and Kim Hornseth after the Virden incident

Dennis Onofrey 1950 - 1978

*John
and Marion
O'Ray*

*Russ Hornseth,
John O'Ray and
Candy Smith
at a house party
after work, 1977*

The Countryside Inn showing the Trans-Canada Highway, the frontage road and the houses on Nelson Street

The RCMP model used at the trial showing the parking lot at the time of the gunfight as well as the houses on Nelson Street
Photo by Robert Knuckle

Room 20 of the Countryside Inn showing the jut-out where Onofrey stood and the iron support for the roof overhang that O'Ray hit
Photo by Robert Knuckle

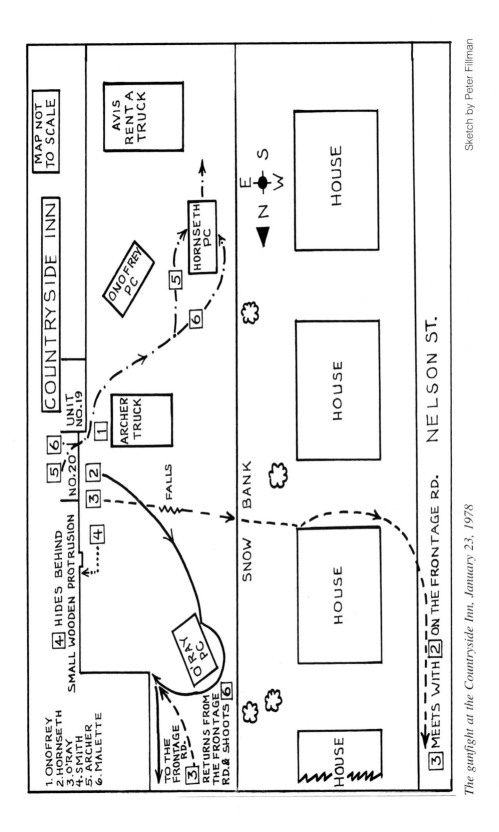

The gunfight at the Countryside Inn, January 23, 1978

Sketch by Peter Fillman

23 JAN 78

Corbett : Bullock + 1 :

Bed Messed up :

Bullet hole in door⁻

Two holes in wall :

151 Shell casings 20 GA :

→ 10 Empty Shells.

x 2 Knife   Knife

Rifle Casing. Bed

TV

Dresser

Garbage

Night STAND

Chair

Lead Fragments

20'

15'

W   S   N   E

Box Remington X Press
20 gauge⁻ 3" Magnum
on Bed : Empty

A page from Cpl. Gerry Coulter's notebook showing his sketch of the interior of room 20 at the Countryside Inn

The invader continued staring at her.

"Did you hear what I said, come on out of there. RIGHT NOW!"

The invader picked up a kitchen chair and walked towards the door. When he got outside, he raised it over his shoulder. Then, as he began advancing toward Debbie on the porch, she started backing down the stairs. The look in his eyes told her he was high on something. When they were both standing on ground level, he kept on advancing. Debbie drew her gun.

"Put that chair down or I'll shoot you," she said.

He hesitated momentarily then put the chair down and stepped away from it. But he refused any attempt on her part to handcuff him. As he stood there breathing heavily and glaring at her, Debbie cautiously slid into her cruiser and radioed Brandon for backup. They relayed her emergency call to Virden and, within minutes, the detachment commander, Fred Westerson arrived. There was no sign of the member she had left behind in the office. After they subdued the house invader and took him away to the cells, Debbie never said a word about her reluctant colleague to Westerson or anyone else in the detachment, but she never forgot what the man did in the face of danger.

As it turned out the house invader was another transient who had gone strange on some acid or LSD. These people are dangerous because they are so unpredictable. The next day when Russ heard that Debbie had gone out on her own and handled the situation, he said to Dennis, "You know she's as good as any man. If I ever get in trouble, I'd have no hesitation to call her for help."

Dennis, who had seen her in action in the cells, was quick to agree.

Another nasty situation occurred when a member stopped three drifters who had been speeding in an old car on the highway. Suspicious because of their appearance, he called for backup. Once it arrived, he and his partner discovered a machete under the front seat and found there was a warrant outstanding for their arrest under the caution "armed and dangerous." They were taken into custody and returned to Ontario where they were wanted.

Not long after that, Syd Barrie and Dennis pulled over two men on a routine spot check. Their plates were legitimate but a further check with the Crime Index Section indicated they were both wanted in the States for their involvement in a contract killing. Although they were arrested without incident, Dennis couldn't help but comment to Syd, "Thank goodness there was two of us. I wouldn't want to take those guys on by myself."

"I know . . . and it's always out on this damn highway. The town's fine but you never know who's coming down this highway."

There were so many break-ins at the service stations and restaurants along the highway that, when it got late, the police picked up any transients who were hanging around and put them up for the night in one of the local hotels. The next morning they gave them a voucher for breakfast and told them to get out of the area or they were going to end up sleeping in jail. If they came across a transient close to the Saskatchewan border, they'd drive him across the line so the next detachment at Moosemin would have to deal with him. Moosemin would drive him right back and dump him off outside Virden.

Hornseth picked up a young fellow one night and was driving him toward the border when he said, "Where are you taking me?"

"I'm going to let you off in Saskatchewan so the boys in Moosemin can take care of you."

"Aw c'mon," the youth complained, "I've been back and forth to Moosemin three times already tonight. I'm just trying to get to British Columbia."

In town things could be fun. One time they got a call at the detachment that there was a pig loose at the hotel downtown. One of the members responded and spent an hour chasing it around trying to catch it. While he scurried back and forth behind the fifty lb. chunk, the patrons in the hotel were splitting their sides laughing. When he finally caught it by the tail, it wiggled so fiercely he had a terrible time loading it into the trunk of his cruiser. By the time he arrived back at the detachment, the pig had made a horrible mess in the trunk. They couldn't get the smell out of it for months.

When the winter came, a lot of the detachment couples got involved in curling at the arena. The hockey team started up again and people began getting ready for Christmas. Dennis wasn't scheduled to work over Christmas so he and Paula and Corey drove to Winnipeg to spend a few days with Rose, his brother, Jerry, and

Paula's family. Corey wasn't old enough to really enjoy his presents but Dennis knew it wouldn't be long before he would be. He and Paula looked forward to that.

On New Year's Eve, Dennis and Paula went to the party at the Legion with the MacDougalls. Almost everybody from the detachment was there except the members on duty. There was such a nice feeling among the group that it was like a big family celebrating together. Paula and Dennis enjoyed themselves so much, they were surprised when the time came for everyone to put on their silly hats and start counting down to midnight. When the count came to zero, Dennis held Paula close and gave her a long, rich kiss.

"Happy New Year, honey," he whispered.

"Happy new Year, Dennis," she said. They kissed again, this time even longer.

Then they went from friend to friend, kissing and hugging and exchanging best wishes. It seemed like only minutes later that the band was playing the last dance and everybody was heading out of the hall. It would have been a perfect evening except when Dennis went to start his car, big plumes of smoke came billowing out from under the hood. As Dennis and Paula scrambled out of the car, Joe MacDougall and the others gathered around and stared incredulously.

"What the hell is it?" Dennis asked.

"Your car's on fire," MacDougall answered.

"I CAN SEE THAT!" Dennis said in exasperation. "But WHY is it on fire?"

As they were speculating, flames started to flick out from under the hood. A crowd began to gather around.

"Holy geez," Dennis exclaimed. He reached in the car door and released the hood latch. As he did, a local mechanic, who had more than his share to drink, rushed over and opened the hood. When he saw what was happening he heaped handfuls of snow onto the carburetor until the flames were extinguished. Dennis, who was shaken, could only stand and stare.

"What happened?" he asked the mechanic.

"Looks like you started off the New Year with a bang," he chuckled.

Dennis was not amused. As the Onofreys and MacDougalls

rode home with another couple, Dennis didn't say a word. Joe thought the whole thing was hilarious and wanted to say something to alleviate the tension but Paula put her finger to her lips to indicate that he should be quiet. Joe didn't mind holding it in because he knew he would get good mileage out of the story later.

The following May, Ralph and Sonja were married in the St. Leon Church near Manitou. Dennis was one of the ushers in the wedding party and was asked to pick Sonja up at her parents' farm and drive her to the church. The wedding was spectacular. Not only were Sonja and her bridesmaids beautiful but all the men in the ceremony were RCMP and wore the Mountie red serge tunics, dark blue pants with wide yellow stripes, black Wellington boots with silver spurs, and their traditional, brown Stetson hats. The ceremony was followed by a huge reception in the Somerset Community Hall. Almost all the members of the detachment and their wives were on hand. They sat together through dinner, laughed and called out comments during the speeches and danced with one another until the party ended. The Virden group had been a close unit over the last two years but that night, more than any other, they seemed like a family.

When Sonja moved into Virden, she became a buddy of Kim Hornseth. In the summer when she and Kim and Elaine MacDougall went riding around in Kim's red convertible with the top down, the townspeople dubbed them "Charlie's Angels," after the three women in a popular television series of the time.

After softball season ended for Marion O'Ray, Sonja was invited to join Marion's Stitch and Bitch Club where the detachment wives met once a week to do crafts and enjoy each other's company. They were all surprised to find that Kim Hornseth was the most skilled craftsperson of the bunch. She was so good at macramé, they asked her to teach it at the night school.

The biggest detachment bash of the year was the 1977 Grey Cup party, held at the Hornseths. Everyone gathered in the basement recreation room to watch the game but by half-time Montreal had such a commanding lead over Edmonton that only the die-hards continued to pay much attention. When the women went upstairs to visit, the men began singing in the basement. Mahar and Hornseth were feeling no pain and started singing into a microphone connected to a sound system that carried their duet into the living room on the main floor. They were trying hard, but unsuccessfully, to imitate a novelty singer of the time named Nestor Pister who had a small time hit called "Wine Stoned Ploughboy," a take-off on Glen Campbell's latest hit Rhinestone Cowboy. Their off-key singing drove everyone in the house to search for the electrical cord that fed the sound system. Once they found it, they pulled it and hid it.

When hockey season rolled around again, the one consolation that Dennis could now enjoy was the fact that he was no longer the worst player on the detachment team. That honour was reserved for his pal, Ralph Mahar. On the way home after one of their games, Dennis shared a bit of news. "I hear we're getting a new recruit from Depot."

"Oh yeah, that's great. Now I won't be the youngest guy in the office," Ralph replied.

"Oh, yes you will," Dennis responded.

"Why, is he an old guy?"

"It isn't a guy . . . it's a woman."

"Really! Do you know anything about her?"

"I hear her name is Smith. She's due in here early in December."

"So she's still on course now?"

"As far as I know."

"I got to go up to Depot in a couple of days . . . to pick something up at the forensic lab. Maybe I'll look her up."

"Yeah, that would be nice. You could do a Chicken Dance for her. Show her how we do things out here in Virden." Dennis smiled.

Ralph chose to ignore his little joke. "What are you doing for Christmas," he asked, "going to Winnipeg?"

"No, we're staying here this year. My mother's coming out. Nothing is completely firmed up yet but I got some big plans this year."

"Yeah?"

"Yeah," Dennis said, "and some of them include you . . . and Sonja."

"Yeah, like what?"

"We're thinking of having a Ukrainian Christmas celebration at my place . . . on January 6. Paula and me and Vivian Barrie are going to put it together."

"What's it all about?"

"Ah, it's kind of a special meal . . . lots of good Ukrainian food . . . traditional stuff."

"Sounds good."

"We're inviting everybody in the detachment."

"Great. Sonja and I will look forward to it."

"Yeah, should be lots of fun. My mother's going to love it."

After Dennis let Ralph off he had a pleasant ride home thinking about the future. Like most of us, he enjoyed looking forward to things. First there would be regular Christmas, then New Year's, then Ukrainian Christmas. Then, best of all, his new baby would arrive. Wonderful times were ahead.

VANCOUVER

Throughout his relationship with Dorothy, Bruce Archer had been magnetized by her youth and her sexual prowess. His obsession with her made him constantly fearful that these very qualities might cause her to grow tired of him and walk away with someone younger and more attractive. In an attempt to alleviate his fears, Bruce agreed to join the swinging clubs. He knew their regulations required that, after two participating members spent the night together, they were not to make any attempt to contact each other again. To Bruce this made them more impersonal and less threatening.

Still, once he and Dorothy got caught up in these clubs, their life of debauchery approached its zenith. One of the most elaborate of the sex clubs that they belonged to was the *C-Y Club* in New Westminster, B.C. It was the largest swingers' club in the country with over 600 couples enrolled. The members came from all walks of life and included a good number of professional people such as doctors, lawyers, accountants and teachers. Every month hordes of these people came from as far away as Oregon and California to attend the parties and dances in various cities that were often referred to as "meat markets." The dances were lavish affairs held in major hotel ballrooms with live bands and open bars. Men and women members were allowed to attend either as couples or as singles to go shopping for new and different sexual adventures. Almost everybody had their own business card, which they exchanged with other people who showed an interest in them. Sometimes their liaison would take place right after the dance; sometimes it wouldn't materialize until several weeks later. Even though it was against the rules, there were rare occasions when longer-lasting relationships developed. Through the C-Y Club, Bruce and Dorothy met Margaret Rose, an attractive bisexual woman of twenty-one. She was a sad soul who was very confused about her sexual identity. Dorothy established a relationship with her first and Bruce got to know her later. For a while they lived together as a threesome. Eventually there was too much tension among them and she moved out.

91

Although Bruce and Dorothy's private lives were strange, their whole existence wasn't consumed by sex. Bruce loved country and western music and when the big country stars came to town, he often got tickets to see them. After one concert at the Pacific Coliseum, Bruce waited for an hour outside the stage door to get Roy Clark's autograph. When the singer finally came out, Bruce had his picture taken with him and eventually had the photo framed as one of his prized possessions.

From time to time Bruce and Dorothy did things that regular couples might envy. When Dorothy got a job as a secretary in New Westminster, Bruce would drive her into work in the morning. About twice a week, he'd go home and pack a picnic lunch with bread and cheese and cold cuts. At noon he'd go back and take her to a nearby park where they spread out a table cloth and shared a bottle of wine with their sandwiches.

They often ate out but when they stayed home, Bruce, who did most of the cooking, made sure they ate well. His lack of concern about the richness of his diet, combined with his sedentary life, caused him to balloon to 270 lbs. Uncomfortable with his size and awkwardness, he sought out a doctor's help to get his weight down. The physician recommended Ionomin. He gave Archer a prescription that would last a month at the strongest dosage he could prescribe. This was most unwise of him because Ionomin is an anorectic, a diet suppressant that has a strong stimulating effect on the central nervous system. It is also an amphetamine. Amphetamines are known to produce imitative psychotic behaviour. This means that when a physician is first diagnosing a patient presenting psychotic behaviour, he will normally begin by determining whether or not the client has taken amphetamines. Ionomin is a particularly dangerous amphetamine and was later taken off the commercial market.

The Ionomin did reduce Archer's appetite so that he didn't want to eat, but it also chemically supercharged his body and hyper-energized his nervous system. Bruce could no longer sit still. He couldn't relax, couldn't stay in one place long enough to watch TV. Worst of all, he couldn't sleep. His mind and body were on a constant search for something to do. He lost twenty-five lbs. in a month but felt as if his nerves were shattered.

While he was losing this weight, Bruce got a well-paying job working for British Columbia Housing as the superintendent/ manager of two high rise apartments in Surrey. These were subsidized housing units for people over fifty-five with limited incomes. It was a substantial position for Archer but to get it he had to use false identification. His wife Lucille was already working for the Province of British Columbia and, at that time, a husband and wife could not both be employed by the government. Archer solved that problem by writing to his relatives in Ontario and asking them to send out the identification of a cousin who had recently passed away. Without asking any questions, they obliged. As soon as Bruce received the credentials in the mail, he began identifying himself as Donald Alfred Archer. With this identification in hand, he got the job.

Once he was comfortable in his new position, Bruce began visiting his family in Port Coquitlam more often. He stayed with Dorothy most of the week but went to see Lucille and the children on his days off. He often stayed overnight on the couch. Because he was so frequently on the scene, many of Lucille's neighbours believed the Archers were a normal little family. A couple of days a week they saw him cutting the grass or going out with the children in the car so they assumed he was some sort of travelling salesman.

On the days and nights that Bruce was with Dorothy, they continued their hedonistic lifestyle. Because Dorothy was still wanted for extortion in Ontario as Malette, Bruce suggested she begin using his sister Lemoyne's identification. From that time on, Dorothy identified herself as Violet Lemoyne Archer. Everyone called them Don and Violet.

With his superintendent's responsibilities, his wild night life and the demands of maintaining his double life, Archer began to unravel. The daily doses of Ionomin only added to his anxiety. On the job he became overbearing and began to show signs of paranoia. Trusting no one, tenants or tradesmen alike, he went so far as to take Polaroid pictures of substandard repair work done by the maintenance men in his building.

"Look at this," he said to Harry, his boss, showing him the photo. "Have you ever seen such a mess?"

"I can't really tell," Harry replied. "The picture's too dark."

"Well, I can tell. It's awful sloppy workmanship for what these guys are getting paid," Archer protested.

"That may be, but there's a bigger concern here than their workmanship."

"Yeah, " Bruce countered, "and what is that?"

"I don't like what you're doing with that camera."

"What do you mean?"

"Look," Harry said, "if you have a problem with someone's work, just come and tell me."

"That's what I'm doing."

"No, you're not," the boss insisted. "You're bringing me pictures . . . like some kind of detective or something."

"What's wrong with that?"

"I'll tell you what's wrong. These guys know what you're doing and they don't like it. They told me they don't like working in your buildings because you hassle the shit out of them."

"Well, they're getting paid good money and they have to . . . "

"Jesus, boy, don't you get it? These guys stick together. You keep messing with them and they won't do a damn thing for you. We'll be lucky to get them to come out here at all."

"Yeah but . . . "

"No 'yeah buts.' Get off their back and leave them alone. You'll get a hell of a lot more work out of them. Now I don't want to hear anymore about it. I'm telling you, stop taking those damn pictures."

Archer refused to accept Harry's admonition. His solution was to go over his head and submit a lengthy complaint to the chief supervisor about the way he was treated by his immediate superior. Nothing came of it.

Then Bruce went too far. When he smelled liquor on Harry's breath, he reported him again to the chief supervisor and tried to get him fired for being drunk on the job. He didn't realize Harry and the supervisor were friends. They were both from Newfoundland, as were most of the maintenance men he had complained about. The next thing Archer knew, he was transferred to a much less desirable job in one of the roughest parts of the city near Hastings and Main. To make things worse, he was now responsible for three buildings instead of two. All three buildings were filled with a lawless and unmanageable clientele. They littered the hallways and the grounds, destroyed or damaged the apartments and partied till all hours of the night. Their behaviour drove Archer crazy; he felt as if his nerves were going to jump right through his skin.

As he became more anxious, he became more childlike. At the least provocation, he would lose his temper and explode. One evening while driving to Lucille's place, he inadvertently cut off another car. When he stopped at the next red light, the other driver came running out of his car with a flashlight in his hand. When Bruce put down the window, the man began screaming at him.

"You cut me off," he screamed with the flashlight trembling in his hand. "What the hell's the matter with you?" he yelled.

"I signalled," Bruce yelled back. "Why don't you watch what's going on?"

"Where'd you learn to drive?" He shook the flashlight in Bruce's face. "You almost sent me over the curb, you idiot."

"You're the idiot . . . and get that damn flashlight out of my face." Bruce went to push it away.

As the other driver swung it away from his grasp, he hit Bruce smartly on the forehead, drawing a little blood. Bruce went wild. He threw open the door and came flying out of the front seat. When the other driver saw Bruce's size and the fury on his face, he began running towards his car. Bruce reached down on the floor of his back seat and pulled out a two foot length of heavy chain. As he ran towards the other car, the driver, in panic, tried to get his vehicle started. When Bruce got there, he went crazy with the chain. Like a madman, he lashed at the hood over and over. He broke one headlight, shattered a huge section of the windshield and completely mangled the hood. Finally, the frantic driver got his vehicle started and raced away. Archer was left standing in the street like a giant ogre, bent over and gasping for breath with the piece of chain dangling from his hand.

Considering the damage he'd done to the car, he was lucky the other driver took off without taking his licence number and reporting him to the police. He would not be so fortunate the next time.

Archer's only hope for a respite from all the anger and anxiety in his life came when, as usual, he spent Christmas at home with his kids. But even while he was there he was jumpy and fretful, preoccupied with his inner confusion.

In the new year he and Dorothy continued with their work on *The Double Gators Club*. There was lots to do. Memberships continued to come in and had to be processed. The magazine had to be laid out, photos had to be arranged, files and correspondence had to be maintained. Many nights Bruce stayed up into the wee hours trying to stay ahead of things. Before long they had 300 members and the money kept rolling in. Letters came from all across Canada and the U.S. Bruce was astounded at one club member who sent in over two 200 requests at $2 a piece to contact other members.

As a natural adjunct to their club Archer had compiled an extensive library of pornographic photos as well as a considerable collection of hard core pornographic movies, which they sold or rented out. One young man paid Bruce $75 to have him arrange a voyeur session where he got to watch another couple having sex. And, of course, there was Thor, who Bruce advertised as the Harlequin Great Dane who was sexually trained to please. The more Archer dealt with the strange inclinations of club members, the more baffled he became at their preferences. Through the club, Archer learned of three couples in Vancouver who not only swapped their wives — their wives swapped their dogs.

This was not something that appealed to him and Dorothy or any of their friends. They preferred the ordinary swinging orgies that were so readily available in the area. At these parties it was not uncommon for twenty couples to be engaged in sex at the same time in the same room. As wild as these orgies could be there were also some tacit rules that had to be adhered to. There was to be no individual contact between party-goers other than that mutually agreed on by both couples. While participating in swinging, married partners were expected to control any inclination they might have toward jealousy. Female homosexuality was allowed; male homosexuality was forbidden.

While all this was taking place, Bruce continued to play the role of the devoted father and family man. He visited his daughters about two days a week. He never missed a family celebration or one of his girls' birthdays and always brought beautiful presents. At least four times over the course of the summer, Bruce took the whole family out canoeing and picnicking. They loved it.

He also took Sheila and three of her girlfriends to Seattle to see Paul McCartney in concert. Bruce made all the hotel arrangements, stayed in a separate room beside them and paid for all their meals. On many nights throughout the summer he would pick up Beth from her part-time job, take her out for a sundae or a snack and then drive her home. Archer loved his time with his daughters but the duplicity and depravity of his hidden life weighed heavily on him. When he compared the sordid way he was living with the sparkling purity of their belief in him and their love for him, it drove him into depression. He wanted to give up his double life but wasn't strong enough to do it. His feebleness made him feel lost and useless.

Then on January 16, 1976 Bruce was involved in an automobile accident. While waiting at an intersection, he suffered a severe whiplash injury to his neck and shoulders when a big truck rolled back and violently struck his car. As a result he was treated several times by a Vancouver doctor who, while tending to his injuries, began to detect the warning signs of psychological trauma. The doctor could see that Archer's physical pain was overshadowed by his acute anxiety state. To alleviate his back pain, this doctor prescribed Darvon for Archer. Darvon is a potent pain killer containing codeine. Like Ionomin it is somewhat addictive. So now, every day Archer was ingesting a potent elixir—Ionomin that kept him wired and Darvon that dulled his pain. Pharmacologists will attest that anytime a person mixes drugs that influence or alter the mind, the effects can be unpredictable. In Archer's case, he was becoming a walking time bomb.

By now Dorothy was doing everything for him. She did the shopping and chose the daily menu. She cooked for him. She cut and styled his hair. Almost every day she shaved him. She back-combed and sprayed his hair before they went out anywhere. She picked out the clothes she wanted him to wear.

With each medical examination, it was obvious that Bruce was becoming more depressed and withdrawn. His doctor also noted that Archer "was becoming more and more dependent on his wife (Dorothy) whom he was now regarding as a mother figure rather than a spouse."

In February 1976, Lucille made her one and only approach to Bruce, asking that he come home to her and the children. Her request made things all the more confusing for him. He still loved Lucille and at times even thought about ending it with Dorothy but he couldn't bring himself to do it. He was so infatuated with

Dorothy that the thought of losing her was too much to face. He couldn't decide anything. He couldn't admit to Lucille how badly mixed up he was.

As hopeless as things seemed, Bruce did manage to make a symbolic choice between the two women. In early spring he and Dorothy took a trip to Reno, Nevada and on March 10, 1976 they were married in the Court House Wedding Chapel in the presence of Bea and Lawrence Tuttle. Using their false identification and assumed names, they registered as Don and Violet Archer. The fact that both of them were legally married to other partners made their marriage unlawful and bigamous but that didn't seem to matter to either of them. From that day forward, Archer referred to Dorothy as his wife.

Shortly after they returned to Vancouver, Bruce drove his daughter Sheila down to Seattle to help her buy her grade ten graduation dress. Days later she was delighted when her dad attended her graduation ceremony. He seemed so proud of her, scurrying around taking pictures of her and her classmates. All the other girls thought Sheila was lucky to have a dad who was so vitally interested in her and one who was so nice to all her friends.

In the early summer Bruce took both his daughters on a long and joyous holiday driving tour. They travelled down to Mexico and, like the old days in Peterborough, sang songs as they went. It was the trip of a lifetime for the two girls. They visited Reno and Virginia City in Nevada as well as Los Angeles, San Francisco and Disneyland in California. All along the way, Bruce was pleasant and generous and the three of them enjoyed themselves immensely.

It was when they got back home from that trip and Bruce returned to his job in the housing units, that he really began to sink. He started the day with Ionomin for his weight and by 10:00 a.m. he needed a Valium for his nerves. His paranoia was steadily deepening to the point where he began setting up traps to catch the young vandals that roamed around his buildings. He went to management and asked for a night watchman and when they refused his request, he went out and bought a pair of binoculars and a set of walkie-talkies so that he could spy on the hoodlums from the roof. He would watch for illegal or destructive behaviour and call his reports back to Dorothy. She, in turn, would report his sightings to the police. They informed on drunks, dope sniffers, thieves and menacing bikers who rode their choppers in the hallways of the buildings. Dorothy even got a commendation from the Vancouver Police Department for assisting in the arrest of an escaped convict.

Then on July 24, 1976 Archer took a major step towards his ultimate fate.

He was working at his desk one evening when he heard a knock at the apartment door. When he opened it, he was confronted by one of the scruffy low lifes who lived in the building, a well-built man with liquor on his breath.

"Are you the superintendent?" he slurred.

"Yes, I am," Bruce replied. "What can I do for you?"

"You can get the goddamn halls cleaned up in this place . . . that's what you can do."

Seeing the man was going to be trouble, Archer began to close his door.

"No, no, no," said the man, forcefully holding the door open. "I'm still talking to you."

Archer waited for him to say more.

"Are you the superintendent or not?" he insisted.

"I already told you I am. Now what do you . . . "

"And I already told you this place is a mess. There's a whole bunch of pails and shit in the entrance way. I tripped on the stuff and almost broke my neck."

"The janitor must have left them there. I'll get him to move it."

"When?"

"As soon as I can."

"Why don't you do it now?"

Archer glared at him.

"Why don't you get off your fat ass and move it yourself?" the man insisted.

"Why don't you get the hell out of here?" Bruce started to close the door again. As he did he caught the man's hand between the door and the jam.

"Hey!" he yelped in pain. Then with all his might he pushed the door back open with both hands. When Bruce stepped towards him, the man hit him in the face with his fist.

Bruce came charging through the doorway like a rhinoceros. As he did, the man kicked at him so hard his boot flew off. Before

Bruce could get a hold of him, the man hit him several times in the face. Bruce wasn't much of a boxer but he was big and strong and knew some wrestling holds. After a couple of failed grappling attempts, Bruce got him in a headlock. Once he had him like that, he started to slam his face against the wall. The last smash was so hard the man almost lost consciousness. Sensing the man's weakness, Bruce changed grips and got him in a full Nelson. Then he drove him headfirst into the door jam. By now Dorothy was out of the apartment and a crowd had gathered in the hall. Bruce was beating him with his fists, pummelling him like a defenseless rag doll. Dorothy tried to get him off the man but she couldn't. Finally a couple of bikers who lived down the hall helped her to subdue him. When he came back to his senses, he stood in the hallway trembling and hyperventilating.

The police arrived and called for an ambulance. As the injured tenant was carted off on a stretcher, Bruce gave them his statement as to what had happened. They said they were going to finish their investigation and would get back to him as soon as they could. Two days later, the officers came back.

"We're going to have to charge you, Mr. Archer," one of them said.

"Charge me? With what?"

"Assault causing bodily harm."

"What!" Bruce was stunned. He knew this was a serious offense. "I was only defending myself."

"You went too far, Mr. Archer," the other policeman said.

"He hit me first. I had to defend myself."

"Mr. Archer, you broke this guy's collarbone. You punctured his eardrum and you broke two of his ribs. He's still in the hospital."

Bruce tried to argue with them but it was to no avail. They arrested him on the spot and took him down to the police station. Much to his surprise they put him in a cell and left him there for the night. It was the first time he had ever been locked up like that and it really got to him. Claustrophobic and panic-stricken, he didn't sleep one minute through the night. The next day, after he was released from jail, things got worse. His employer, the B.C. Housing Corporation, suspended him indefinitely without pay, pending the outcome of his trial.

Archer began to come apart at the seams. He went to a psychiatrist who examined him and declared that Bruce was suffering from an acute anxiety reaction directly attributable to his assault charge. He further noted that he was suffering from headaches, chest and stomach pains and an inability to eat or sleep properly. In conclusion the doctor stated in his report: "I had seriously considered having him hospitalized because of the intensity of his anxiety and depressive symptoms, but he is suffering from claustrophobia and refused to enter the hospital."

Valium was prescribed to ease his anxiety. Archer never told the doctor he was also on Ionomin and Darvon.

Bruce no longer cared about anything. During the day he sat around the apartment immobilized, relying on Dorothy for almost everything. Dutifully she waited on him hand and foot and catered to his childlike regression. At night he couldn't sleep and was sexually impotent.

Two months after his session with the first psychiatrist, Archer visited a second by the name of Dr. Schwarz who wrote in his report: "since Archer has been suspended from his job, he sees no prospect of employment and has begun to suspect that the police, and even his lawyer and his physician, are in some kind of collaboration with B.C. Housing to keep him unemployed."

Dr. Schwarz also stated that Dorothy appeared to be generally very smothering and, in so doing, was encouraging Bruce's somewhat paranoid stance. The psychiatrist did not get the impression that Bruce was overtly psychotic, but felt he was essentially an angry man, no longer able to lead a productive life. Aware that Dorothy was forever waiting on him, the doctor encouraged both of them to get Bruce to show more initiative in his life.

Archer's trial on the assault charge was held over until June 1978. This was done on the advice to the court from his family doctor that: "at this time he (Bruce) is not mentally able to advise his lawyer."

Bruce's paranoia continued to deepen to the point that he felt all the people in his building were against him. He didn't trust anybody and he believed he had no friends. It's hard to imagine how things could get worse for him but they did, because now he found himself in a situation where he didn't have enough money to pay the rent or buy the groceries.

He couldn't hold a job. Dorothy was willing to look for work but things were really tough. Nobody was hiring. They had heated arguments about her going back hooking but Dorothy didn't want any part of that. Their solution to their problem was foolhardy. Bruce convinced her they could get through the down-turn by writing bad cheques.

Once they started, they did it with a vengeance. They wrote cheques for their groceries. They wrote bad cheques to buy expensive equipment that they sold for cash. When the money wasn't coming in fast enough, they spread out and wrote bad cheques in West Vancouver, in North Vancouver and many of the small suburban towns surrounding the city. At no time did they consider the consequences of their actions. Getting caught was the furthest thing from their minds.

On June 10, 1977, RCMP Constable William Hiney arrested Dorothy on two charges of false pretenses in connection with the purchase of a tape recorder and some groceries, both valued at less than $200. She was taken into custody and released on a promise to appear for trial on June 27. Five days later a Constable Gorley arrested her for three more counts of false pretenses and once again she was released on a promise to appear.

On June 27 she failed to appear for trial and a warrant was issued for her arrest. Now a fugitive from justice, she managed to evade arrest by constantly and cleverly moving from one address to another with Bruce.

Early in September the psychiatrist felt that Bruce was improving. In his records he wrote: "He now relates with me more freely and is less dependent on his wife." The doctor had him medicated on Triavil, 292's and 10mgs of Librium to be taken as required.

On September 20 it was discovered that Archer had used false identification and received illicit student loans to a value of $1,220 from Simon Fraser University. Three days after this, Dorothy fraudulently applied for a student loan of $1,050 from the Surrey Campus of Douglas College. Investigation revealed both of them seldom attended classes and their academic grades were non-existent.

November 3, Bruce was charged with one count of false pretenses on the purchase of a movie projector and screen worth $197. November 15, he was arrested for trying to pass a worthless cheque in Bellingham, Washington. When the police there contacted the Canadian authorities, a search of Archer's residence was undertaken. During the inspection the police found six different sets of identification that belonged to neither Bruce nor Dorothy. Some of them belonged to relatives, both alive and dead and some belonged to various people that they had ripped off along the way. Besides this, the police also retrieved a .380 Browning semi-automatic pistol that had been stolen from a senior citizens' home where Archer had been employed as a maintenance man.

Elsewhere in the apartment several hundred letters were found that were addressed to *The Double Gators Club* in care of Box 69327, Station K, Vancouver. The correspondence indicated that the Archers acted as a clearing house for getting people together. There were references to Thor, their infamous Great Dane, as well as clear indications that both Bruce and Dorothy chronically made false representations about the numbers subscribing to their magazine. In an effort to enhance the prospects of their sex club, they lied and misrepresented their own appearances to readers and correspondents.

Three days after this search, Archer was given a suspended sentence in Bellingham, Washington and placed on two years probation. He was then deported from the U.S. under escort and was immediately arrested at the border by the Canadian police. Taken into custody, he was charged with four counts of false pretenses and one count of possession of an unregistered firearm.

Bruce was held over in the Surrey cells for three days where he got his first real taste of imprisonment. Typical of people suffering from sociopathic personality disorder, he hated being confined. It was physically painful for him. He couldn't sleep and lay curled up in the corner of his bunk for hours trembling. After his first night in jail, he broke out in hives and his whole body was covered with lumps.

Beth came to visit him and brought him some personal things that he needed. Lucille even came to visit him once.

"I don't belong in here," he told them. "I am not one of these people. They're lowlife scum. I don't want to deal with them . . . any of them."

Lucille tried to calm him down and soothe him but nothing seemed to work.

103

"Lucille," he whined. "These are bad people in here. I keep asking myself what am I doing in here? I gotta get out or I'm going to go crazy."

Bruce appeared before Justice of the Peace J. Henneghan on November 21 as Donald Alfred Archer and an agreement was reached that he would be released on $1,000 bail. After raising the required amount for the surety through one of their relatives, Bruce was given an undertaking to appear in court for trial on two conditions:

1) that he be under the supervision of a bail officer

2) that he notify the court of any change of his address

The bail supervisor, Shawn Christie, met with Archer in the Surrey cells for about twenty minutes while he completed the appropriate paper work and issued the bail document that outlined Bruce's agreement of his promise to appear. Bruce was to report to him once a week.

In the meanwhile, Dorothy had been arrested and remained in custody until November 30 when she had a show-cause hearing before Judge Holmes to decide if there were enough evidence to proceed to trial. Once that was decided against her, she was released on her own recognizance under a strict bail supervision order that would also be administered by Shawn Christie, the same man who was dealing with Bruce. Dorothy was ordered to report to Mr. Christie in person every day of the week. On Saturdays and Sundays she was to report to the NCO in charge of the Surrey RCMP detachment.

On Tuesday, December 6, Archer reported to his bail supervisor and agreed he would be back to see him again on December 13 at 1:30 p.m. Even while Archer was checking in with Christie, another summons from another court was being sent out to him. Archer was never served with it because it was addressed to a vacant lot.

Both of them could see that their universe was crumbling. Bruce painfully told Dorothy, "In a matter of days the whole world is going to start coming down on us. It's only going to get worse."

Dorothy's trial was set for the following Wednesday. She and Bruce feared she would be sentenced to jail for about a year. Furthermore, they were both worried that the extortion charge from Ontario would catch up with her and cause her added problems. As for his own situation, Bruce wasn't too concerned about the fraud charges against him. It was the assault causing bodily harm that plagued him. For some reason he had convinced himself he would get the maximum sentence for that. He was sure he was going to jail for a good long stretch, possibly as much as five years. This petrified him. They both decided that their only chance was to get out of Vancouver and make a run for Ontario.

The following Sunday Bruce and Dorothy drove over to Lucille's place. Archer parked about a block away. Leaving Dorothy in the car, he walked over to the house. Once he got there, he had little to say to Lucille but he asked his two daughters to come with him for a few minutes. They had no idea what he had in mind but were more than willing to accompany him down the street. When he brought them over to the car and introduced the girls to Dorothy, they recognized she was the "other woman" in their father's life and were not all that pleased to meet her. They thought their father's idea of introducing them to her was strange. Their awkward and brief encounter amounted to little more than a strained silence.

After Bruce walked the girls back to the house he privately told Lucille he was leaving for Ontario. All she said to that was, "I want a divorce."

With typical twisted logic Bruce answered, "No, I'm not giving you a divorce. You are my wife." Then he turned his back on his wife and his children and walked out of their lives.

The next day, December 12, he and Dorothy went to a rental agency in Surrey to lease a truck.

CANDY

Candy Smith was raised with four other children by her foster parents, Orlean and Leo Strom in Sault Ste. Marie, Ontario. Always quiet and reserved, she was a bright young girl and a voracious reader who wanted to become a police officer ever since watching a movie about police work in grade four at the Anna McCrae Elementary School. At Sir James Dunn Collegiate she was an active member of the student body and was particularly good in music and athletics. Candy was not only a member of the school choir but an avid participant in the singing group at St. Giles Presbyterian Church. At Sir James Dunn, she was one of the few girls in the school to seriously take up karate. Lithe and quick, she liked the physical challenge of the sport and wasn't afraid to fight the boys in the class. There were lots of nights she went home with a swollen lip or a bloody nose but she never complained and always went back for more. She was equally intense and serious in her school work. As active as she was, Candy kept her marks at a very high level.

After graduating in 1973, she began studying for her B.A. in English at Algoma College in the Sault. While she was there, she applied for a position with the Ontario Provincial Police. When the RCMP started accepting women in 1974, she applied to them as well. After finishing her degree, she worked at a few minor jobs in the Sault including six months as a security guard in a department store. She stayed there until the Mounties contacted her in the spring of 1977 and advised that she had been accepted as a recruit. It was like a dream come true. In June, after a farewell party at home, she set off in her car for the long drive to Regina. Although she was travelling alone on unfamiliar highways, she was thrilled at the prospect of what lay ahead.

When she arrived at Depot, she reported to the Orderly Office, received her initial kit and was assigned to Troop #9. Unlike the men on the base, the women were not housed in an open dormitory. From the beginning of their training they were quartered two women to a room on the second floor of C Block, across from the Mess Hall. The rooms were Spartan containing only beds, closets and desks. They ran down one long hall with a lounge at one end and a large common washroom near the middle. The entire floor was known as the women's dorm.

No men were housed on the other floors in the building and none were allowed on the women's floor at any time for any reason. Since there were no female NCOs in the RCMP at that time, whenever a corporal wanted to inspect something on the floor, he had to call to one of the women to come out and escort him into their sanctuary. As time went on, this would be to the women's advantage.

The first day and night on the base were interesting for Candy. Women from all across Canada were in her troop. At first the maritimers tended to stick together but it wasn't long before they were mixing in with the rest. They were easy to distinguish because of the beautiful lilt in their speech and their habit of saying things like "Lord t'underin' Jesus!"

Most of the women were between twenty-one and twenty-three. The youngest was nineteen, the oldest twenty-eight. Candy's roommate was Terry Buchanan from Regina. Blond and bespectacled, she was a tiny dynamo of a woman who had barely made the height restriction of 5' 4". Because of her assertive nature and her husky voice that sounded like a man's, Buchanan was appointed to be the right marker of the troop. She marched on the right side at the head of the troop's column and called out all the marching orders when they were on parade.

At their first troop meeting, their counsellor Corporal Desaulniers gave them some important information and some sound advice. He reminded them that women were still a new phenomenon at Depot; only thirty-two of the 300 recruits on the base were women. He told them that Troop #9 was just the sixth female troop to train at Depot and less than 200 female members were working in the field. In some quarters, he said, there was still resistance to the idea that women could make effective police officers. He told them that right from the start, Troop #9 had to prove themselves superior at Depot. They certainly could not afford to indulge in any form of inappropriate behaviour.

"This is not a college campus for fun and games," he said. "This is a workplace where you are being trained to become a professional police officer."

He pointed out that rumours can start at the least provocation and all of them needed to avoid any hint of scandal, at the risk of dismissal.

That night in their lounge the women discussed the implications of what the Corporal had said. The first female troop had come to Depot late in 1974. Its entry into the RCMP was impelled by political pressure on the Force. There was a great deal of resistance in many quarters of the RCMP against women breaking into what had been an all-male bastion for over 100 years. Inevitably unfair rumours abounded. The word spread from detachment to detachment in the field that the first couple of female troops at Depot resembled the Green Bay Packers. Other rumours suggested there was hanky panky between some of the women recruits and the NCO instructors. Female recruit troops were accused of having sex with their male counterparts in the residences, in police cruisers, even in the graveyard. Since no one was ever dismissed for such infractions, they remained in the realm of rumour.

Candy's troop got an inkling of the rough road that lay ahead from their Drill Instructor, Corporal Roux.

"There's nothing worse than a fat woman in uniform," he scolded. "If I see or hear of any pizza being delivered to your floor, I'll parade you." This meant he'd take away their privileges or give them extra duties.

Roux was a slight, trim man who obviously took great care with his own physical condition.

"And don't let me catch you at that Sticky Bun or you'll be in worse trouble yet." The Sticky Bun was a room in C Block with a number of dispensing machines that sold chocolate bars, candy, peanuts and soft drinks. One of the machines offered glazed donuts from which the room got its name.

He told them that starting from the first day, they would be learning a marching routine that would culminate at its presentation to their guests at their graduation. To be good at their drill and sharp as a unit, they had to be in shape.

"Follow your schedule. Go to bed at night. Get the hell out of bed in the morning and move smartly all day. Get a good run in every day and you'll be all right."

Troop #9 appreciated their corporals' cautions and took them very seriously. They were bright, industrious and very serious about their work. Each member wanted to excel and make their troop a unit to be admired. Right from the start, everyone helped each other towards attaining that goal.

They wanted no allusions comparing Troop #9 to a fat and ugly professional football team. They intended to be high achievers and the most attractive, well-groomed group of female cadets ever assembled in one class at Depot.

Like all other troops before them, their physical pain began from their first day. To determine their conditioning, their Physical Training instructor had them repeatedly run up and down the stairs of C Block until they almost dropped. Then he ran them over to the grass beside the chapel and made them do kick-outs and push-ups until they writhed in pain or collapsed in fatigue. That night most of them were in bed long before lights out at 10:45 p.m.

For the first two weeks they ran as a unit everywhere they went. By the time they arrived at their destination, most of them were exhausted. Their P.T. instructor insisted they do some extra running in their spare time. He told them about the 500 Mile Running Club where, on their honour, they were to keep a record of the distance they ran each day towards accumulating 500 miles. Some took to this extra running better than others but in a matter of weeks almost all the women were logging some running miles on their own time. One of their instructor's goals was to have them run down to Wascana Park by the Saskatchewan Legislature and back, a total distance of ten miles. By the time their course was finished, over half the class accomplished this objective.

Their daily duties were punishing. Up at 6:00 a.m.; make your bed; clean and dust your room; store your clothes a certain way, in a specific place; fold your towel and face cloth a certain way; clean your boots; press your uniform; get ready for classes. All of that was before breakfast. Then they were to "stand to" for inspection by the senior class on the base.

These men were usually reasonable and considerate with them because they had been through the same demanding routine themselves. However, they were not about to overlook any glaring abuses or obvious neglect of responsibility. Each day as Troop #9 trudged off to breakfast, their common unspoken prayer was,

"Please God, let me get through this day without falling asleep in the middle of a class or an exercise."

The women soon learned it would be impossible to keep their hair long and wear makeup every day. Regulations called for their hair to be above the collar or swept up on their head. Everyone opted for a short hair cut because they had no time to fuss with it first thing in the morning or after their swimming or physical training classes when they had five minutes to get to the next class.

The academic courses were a salvation for the women because they gave them a chance to rest their weary bones. But every night it seemed there was a major assignment to complete. To get everything done and ready for the next day, the women started to congregate in the communal washroom after lights out. They knew they couldn't keep the light on in their room because it would be seen from outside and they would be called on the carpet. They also knew that the lights in the washrooms had to be left on all night and that no NCO could come on their floor without an escort. When one came calling they always had lots of warning. Katie Weigert from Ottawa lived in the first room beside the stairs leading to the floor of their dorm. On the rare occasion an NCO came for bed check, he would stand outside the double doors and yell, "WEIGERT" to get her to come out and escort him onto the floor. As soon as the women heard that call, everybody crept back to their rooms and quietly tucked themselves into bed until the NCO was gone. Then they headed right back to the washroom.

It was not unusual at two or three in the morning to find fifteen or twenty members of Troop #9 in there. They would be sitting on the floor or in the cubicles, reading, writing, studying or polishing boots and leather. The odd one had a cigarette dangling from her lips.

Some of the classes were fun. They went to the firing range once a week and all the women enjoyed that. Their male instructor told them that he thought women were generally speaking, better shots than men. He said men seemed to deal with guns as some kind of hereditary extension of the male personality. Handling guns and aiming them was taken for granted. On the other hand, since women found guns foreign to them, they seemed to have more respect for them. Once they had them in their hands, they concentrated more and took them very seriously. Women also have a musculature that offers less tension to resist the gun's recoil. Consequently they seem to shoot more accurately.

He claimed the women's only problem on the firing range was that they had smaller hands and weaker wrists. When they were asked to shoot 150 rounds per session, their shots tended to get poorer towards the end of the shooting session.

Although the instructor on the firing range was a gentle person, he said the most callous things when he was teaching them shooting. "To stop someone," he'd yell, "you have to aim for the center of mass. Shoot for the solar plexus, right in the middle of his thorax. If that doesn't stop him, then go to the head or the pelvic area, so he can't stand up anymore."

Although Candy was a very good shot, she wasn't quite as good as Jackie Olsen from Sherwood Park, Alberta. Olsen had lots of experience with guns, having hunted with her father and brothers since she was a little girl. It didn't take her long to establish herself as the sharpshooter in Troop #9.

Candy Smith was close to the top of her class in most activities and skills. She was very strong in the academic subjects. At one point the Law Instructor was handing back the results from a major test in his subject when he said, "You'll never guess who got the highest mark on the test."

No one ventured an opinion out loud.

"Well," the instructor said, "the person with the best law mark is Candy Smith."

None of her classmates was surprised at the announcement because Candy was one of the best-read members of the class and was always on top of her subjects. They gave her a round of applause when she went up to receive her test paper.

Besides being good in academics, Candy excelled in self-defense classes. The toughest woman in the class was Judy Best from Prince Edward Island. She had been a Phys. Ed. teacher before joining the Mounties and was in excellent condition. Judy ran every night before dinner and was well on her way to the 500 Mile Club. As a ground fighter she was strong and agile and, above all, fearless. Judy was the only troop mate that Candy Smith could not tap out. Yet every chance Candy got she went looking for Judy Best to fight.

It was interesting how the various women took to ground

fighting. Katie Weigert was an energetic, bubbly cadet who was very congenial and well liked. At 5'7" and 150 lbs. she was also very strong and tremendously intense. When she fought, she got herself so psyched up against her opponents that, in the heat of battle, she often bit them. Weigert and her opponent would go into a tangle and the next thing the class would hear was a high-pitched yelp. Then they'd see Katie apologizing profusely to the girl who'd have a mean-looking bite mark on her arm or her leg. Katie bit different people about six times, enough for the women in the troop to begin calling her Chomper. When the others chastised her for it, she tried to explain that she didn't mean it to happen, something just came over her in the heat of battle.

"You mean you're like Dr. Jekyll and Mr. Hyde?"

"No, no, not like that," she replied. "I just kind of go blank. I get so wound up, I don't realize what I'm doing."

Opponents became very wary of fighting Katie but, when she was assigned as their opponent, they couldn't avoid her.

Candy Palmer, a tall, dark, ladylike recruit from London, Ontario, who seldom ever had a hair out of place, did not enjoy self-defense classes at all. It was something totally foreign to her. She had only sisters at home and had never been involved in any rough and tumble, even as a child. For her, ground fighting was something she had to endure and she was always relieved when it was over. Even though she found the fighting distasteful, she gave it her best effort every class.

When it came her turn to fight Chomper Weigert, Candy Palmer was very apprehensive. As they stood facing each other before the signal to fight was given, Candy could see that Katie was getting herself ready to fight like a demon. She was breathing deeply, with her fists clenched and her teeth clamped closed. Candy Palmer pointed her finger directly in Katie's face and stared her down. Then she said, "Katie, don't you dare. Don't you even dare think of biting me. Do you hear me?" Somehow that brought Weigert to her senses and they went on to have a reasonably sane fight.

Candy Palmer employed the same strategy the first time a troop of men were brought in to fight against Troop #9. Days ahead, the instructor told them when the men would be coming in. "Don't worry about it," he said. "When you fight them, you can do

113

anything but run."

The women enjoyed his little joke but stewed about fighting the men for a couple of days. When the day arrived, Palmer took the direct approach. Standing beside her first male opponent as the opening instructions were being given, she leaned over and whispered to him. "I won't embarrass you, if you don't embarrass me." The male recruit, a blond, clean-cut young man, nodded that he understood and he agreed.

Candy had been taught enough to know that in a fight between a woman and a man, the man is usually stronger but he has one distinct anatomical disadvantage. She knew that five pounds pressure on his testicles would put him into shock. What's more, her male opponent was aware she had been taught this fact. He was more anxious about fighting a woman than she was about wrestling with a man. She just wanted to get the awkward situation over with and figured there was no reason for either of them to fight dirty with a colleague.

Joyce Graham from Montague, PEI was a fairly tough fighter and she too, like Katie Weigert, was very intense. Joyce had extra long arms and didn't seem to realize how far they reached. When she feinted a punch at someone, she would flash out a fist and invariably end up hitting her opponent flush on the nose with full force. More than one woman in the troop had to be taken to First Aid for a bloody nose after an encounter with Joyce. Due to her zealous intensity, it wasn't long before the women began calling her Billy Graham. She'd been called this before and didn't mind. To go along with the gag, she wandered up and down the hall of the residence at night with a Bible in her hand, calling to the others to come out of their rooms and be saved.

Another tough fighter was tiny Terry Buchanan, or Bucky as she came to be called. Bucky was only 90 lbs. but she was well muscled and liked to fight. And she was as quick as a cat. One minute her opponent would think she had her pinned to the mat; the next thing she knew, Buchanan had wiggled out and was on top of her. Once Bucky got a painful hold on someone, the girl was finished because Bucky would keep applying the pressure until her opponent gave in and tapped out.

The oldest recruit in Troop #9, Carol Rose from Nova Scotia, was another good scrapper. She was a married woman, twenty-eight-years-old who was a graduate psychologist. Nothing about her—her size, her strength or her personality—predicted she would be as good a fighter as she was. Her greatest attribute was that she didn't like to lose and refused to tap out until someone put her in such pain that she couldn't bear it any longer. Most women in the troop didn't like to do that to an opponent but with Carol, they learned they had to or she'd come back and whip them. Fights with her were always long, drawn-out and exhausting. This seemed ironic to the troop, since Carol was a kindly woman whom they all affectionately called Mom.

Unobtrusive, gentle and hard working, the one thing Carol Rose looked forward to was seeing her husband on the few occasions he was able to fly out from Nova Scotia. Since he wasn't allowed to stay on the base, they would take a hotel room in downtown Regina and hibernate for the weekend.

In many ways Candy Smith was like Carol. On the outside she was quiet and reserved, gentle and kind. On the inside she was extremely intense and competitive. She hated losing at anything. As quiet as they were, both Candy and Carol were appreciated by the class and fit in comfortably. Candy didn't like to miss a trick and made sure she was always around when the fun started. She was usually there with the others in the john until after midnight getting ready for the next day. Although she didn't drink alcohol, when the others went out to a pub on the weekend, Candy always went along and enjoyed herself. She didn't talk a lot but when she did, she spoke so excitedly and quickly that the others had to strain to follow what she was saying. Candy seldom told jokes but was a great audience. She loved to laugh and when she did, her whole upper body would shake uncontrollably.

Some of the women in the class dated civilians or other recruits on the base. Two from Troop #9 became engaged during the course of their training. Candy never dated. Although she was attractive and pleasant, she seemed shy and inexperienced. It was no big thing. There were always lots of women in C Block to hang out with and there was always something doing on the weekends that was fun and interesting.

About half way through the course, the troop was badly shaken when one of the thirty-two women in the class quit and went home. A week after her departure, the troop was hit with another shock.

One of their troop mates, Lorraine Rochon from Hull, Quebec, lost her mother. It came as no surprise to Lorraine because her mother had been battling a terminal illness for a long time. Empathizing with Lorraine's loss, the troop rallied around her to give what support they could. Her closest friends spent hours commiserating with her in her room. Lorraine carefully weighed all her options and decided that she would not go home for her mother's funeral. She was afraid if she went home she would be consumed by grief and wouldn't come back to Depot to finish her course. Since she was determined to complete her studies and become a police officer she decided to stay. It was a difficult decision for such a young woman so far from home, but once she made it, the troop supported her like a band of sisters.

Early in October there was great excitement among the women because, one by one, they were given appointments to see the tailor on the base so he could fit them for their red serge tunics. Each took her appointment as the first clear sign she was going to graduate from Depot.

When Thanksgiving weekend rolled around in October, many of the women in C block went home for the holiday. Only a skeleton crew was left in the residence. One of them was Candy Smith, the other was a crazy character from Wolfe Island, Ontario, by the name of Jane Greenwood. Like most of the troop Jane Greenwood was hard working and conscientious. But she was also a devil who loved to pull pranks on her troop mates. She would hide in closets or behind doors and jump out at people, taking their breath away. At night she would hide under beds and reach out and grab an ankle, sending her victim running off screaming in terror. Every time she did this, the frantic response was always the same: "DAMN YOU GREENWOOD, GET OUT OF HERE!"

They wouldn't stay mad at Greenwood for long because she was so much fun and so full of beans. She was talented too, serving as the artist for the troop's yearbook, which was well on the way to being finished. Jane had already designed the cover. It showed a cat with its tail curled into a figure nine. Beside it was the motto, "Tiger by the Tail."

Carol Rose also remained on the floor over Thanksgiving. When the three of them got together, they devised a stunt for the benefit of their missing sisters. On the night before the troop's return, they made a dummy. Using a pair of blue coveralls that had once been worn as fatigues, they stuffed newspapers into garbage bags until the coveralls took on the shape of a human body. They topped the coveralls with a stuffed Halloween mask wearing a fisherman's hat. Then they tied a pair of recruit boots to the bottom of the pants. When they were finished, they had a very realistic looking dummy that they took down to the communal washroom and sat on the toilet in one of the cubicles. They locked all of the other cubicles.

The next day the three of them waited across the hall in Greenwood's room for the fireworks to begin. As the women straggled one by one into the dorm, the first place they visited was the washroom. Each reacted the same. Seconds after entering, a scream would go up and the woman would fly out of the washroom and run wildly down the hall until one of the girls in the know caught up to her and told her what they had done. Then the woman who had been tricked joined the others in Greenwood's room to enjoy the reaction from the next unsuspecting victim.

Greenwood and Smith wanted to throw the dummy off the roof of C Block that night to see how the night patrol at Depot would react. They were talked out of it by their troop mates who feared they might get kicked out of the course if they were caught.

Jane Greenwood was also the recruit who defied Corporal Roux and got the women to use ingenious methods to smuggle pizza and Chinese food onto the floor for late night snacks. Most of her methods of conveyance involved hiding small packages above the waist inside their blouses and sweaters. When the food was eaten, they had to sneak the empty food cartons out to the huge dumpster by the kitchen. Greenwood knew if they were left in the garbage pails on the floor, Corporal Roux would find them out.

Generally speaking Roux was quite happy with the troop's progress in the drill hall. However, they did have one relapse in late October when he was trying to teach them the proper way to perform crowd control. Standing shoulder to shoulder with their batons held in both hands in front of them, the women were to advance slowly but purposefully, one firm step at a time. With each step they were to yell in unison the command, "MOVE!" Their footwork was all right but Roux could not get them to yell with any kind of authority.

"What the hell is the matter here?" he roared at them. "You sound like a bunch of little mice. You got to yell MOVE . . . all together . . . and mean it. Now start again and let me hear you yell MOVE . . . MOVE . . . MOVE!" After his tirade, the women improved somewhat but their performance was not their finest moment in the drill hall.

Thankfully, by the start of November, their marching had become impeccable. The troop was parading so well, Corporal Roux was bragging about them. He even went so far as to predict they would make a good showing at their Passing Out which was scheduled for Friday, December 5.

When drilling other troops, Roux sometimes referred to Troop #9 as a good example of how a marching unit should perform. Consequently, at Depot, Troop #9 became known as Roux's Angels.

The women had come to appreciate Roux and all their instructors for their knowledge and sincerity in preparing them for the world beyond Depot. Corporal Desaulniers had become their special friend and adviser. Several times he and his wife invited the whole troop to his home in Regina for a barbecue and beer. He was always available to listen and help the women with their problems or concerns.

The greatest character of all their teachers was Corporal Parent who taught Law and Security. He was originally from Quebec and still retained a slight French accent. Many years before he had been stationed in Banff, Alberta. He liked to give harrowing examples of his experiences from then to make a point when he was teaching. A trim, balding man in his mid-forties he would dramatically proclaim, "When I was in Banff, Jesus Christ . . . " and then he'd go on with his parable. This expression became such a popular phrase among the women, they used it as the heading for the section of their yearbook that dealt with their experiences in the classroom.

One of the most dramatic days in their training came in early November when, out of the blue in the Drill Hall, they were told the Division to which each recruit had been assigned:

Bucky Buchanan to Manitoba
Billy Graham to British Columbia
Jane Greenwood to British Columbia

Candy Palmer to Nova Scotia
Carol Rose back to Nova Scotia to be with her husband
Katie Weigert to Prince Edward Island
Candy Smith to Manitoba

A week after that they were told the actual detachment to which they were posted. When they told Candy Smith she was going to Virden, she had to look it up on the map. Once she spotted it, she did remember driving past it on her trip west from Sault Ste. Marie. The posting to Virden suited her fine.

Two days later, Candy was sitting in her room talking with her roommate when Katie Weigert came to the door and told Candy there was a male Mountie waiting outside the double doors of the dorm to see her.

"Who is it?" she asked Weigert.

"I don't know. I've never seen him before."

Candy was puzzled but went down to the end of the hall to meet her visitor. When she got there, she found a slightly built man wearing a Mountie storm coat and field uniform.

"Hi," Candy said, "are you looking for me?"

"Are you Candace Smith?"

"Yes, that's me." She cleared her throat. "I'm actually called Candy."

"Hi, my name's Ralph Mahar. I'm with the Virden Detachment in Manitoba."

"Oh, hi! It's nice to meet you."

"Same here," Ralph replied. "We heard you were coming to Virden so I thought I'd drive over and welcome you on board."

"You drove all that way just to do that?"

"No, I'm just kidding," Ralph said. "I had to bring something in to the forensic lab over by the museum . . . so I thought I'd drop by and say hello."

"That's nice of you. I appreciate that."

"Well, it wasn't very long ago that I was coming out of Depot myself. I know how it feels to be assigned to your first detachment . . . kind of scary and exciting all at the same time."

"Yeah, it is kind of like that, isn't it?"

"Well don't worry about coming to Virden, you're going to love it there. There's sixteen of us and it's just like working in one big happy family. Oh . . . sometimes we have our differences but most of the time, we really pull together."

"I've heard good things about Virden. It sounds like a neat place to work. I'm looking forward to going there."

"And we're looking forward to seeing you. Here's my card and if there's anything I can do to help get you settled, give me a call."

Candy looked at his card. "OK, Ralph, thanks a lot. I appreciate this."

"No problem," Ralph said. "See you later in Virden." He turned and began walking down the stairs. "Bye, Candy," he called as he started down the next flight.

Candy waved good-bye and went back to her room with a nice, warm feeling. She opened her Depot yearbook to the page with her photo. Part of the caption under her picture read: *Will Virden ever be the same?* Now more than ever she liked the idea she was going there.

Candy's graduation was one of the special days in her life. Her family came and watched Troop #9 go through its paces in the gym and on the mats. It was so blistering cold outside, the women's hair froze when they left the swimming pool after their aquatic exhibition. In the Drill Hall, the troop, as Roux predicted, was letter perfect.

Katie Weigert was the class valedictorian. She reviewed how Depot had become the women's home in such a very short time. She thanked the instructors, especially Corporal Desaulniers. She thanked the parents for their kindness and support. Then she touched a nerve with everyone by saying: "Though we have worked hard during the past six months, the most difficult part is yet to come. Tomorrow we will say good-bye to each other."

Many of the women were crying. When the ceremony ended, there were hugs and kisses for everyone. One emotional rite followed another. First the formal dinner and its speeches, then the formal dance with all the women looking gorgeous in their red serge tunics and long dress skirts.

The next day was emotionally wrenching for all of them as they went from one to another saying farewell. They hugged and kissed and exchanged addresses of their new detachment offices. They made each other promise to write. Many of them had tears in their eyes as they parted and headed off in different directions for their new destinations in life.

Candy went home to the Sault for a ten day furlough. For the first while she was glad to be among her family and her home town friends. One of the places she visited was the department store where she had worked as a security guard. The associate manager, Larry Gaylord, could see she was proud of graduating as a Mountie and told her he was impressed with her accomplishment. Her time at home was very satisfying but Candy couldn't keep her mind off Virden. She wanted to get started on her career as a policewoman. When the time came to leave, Candy was more than ready to go.

After a difficult two day trip on snow-bound winter roads, she reported for duty at the Virden Detachment on December 15, 1977. On Fred Westerson's advice, she made arrangements to board with Molly Forrester. From the moment they met, Candy and Molly got along well. Candy looked so young and innocent with her big eyes and short brown hair that Molly treated her like a daughter.

Westerson immediately assigned John O'Ray as her trainer and from then on she spent most of her working hours with him. John was a good choice because he was affable and patient. In one of their first discussions while riding in a cruiser, John posed what he thought was a crucial issue.

"Do you know what the police officer's worst dilemma is?"

Candy turned to look at him but waited for his answer.

"The policeman's biggest dilemma is this. What do you do if you come around a corner at night and there's a fifteen year old kid standing there high on dope or booze and he's got a gun?"

Candy pondered the question.

John continued, "Your problem is this. If you shoot him and the gun turns out to be plastic, then you're a murderer. If you don't shoot him and he shoots you, then you're dead. That's the police officer's biggest dilemma."

She knew he was right.

"Do you know what I'd do in that situation? My instinct is to get the hell out of there. Move. Get under cover. I'll soon find out if his gun is real or not. Once I find that out, I'll know what to do."

Candy could see the merit in his thinking. This was the first in many exchanges of valuable ideas between Candy and her mentor.

If John was good to Candy, his wife was even kinder. Marion invited Candy to dinner the first week. When Christmas came, she had both Candy and Debbie MacLean over to open their gifts on Christmas morning. Candy was working the day shift with John but they all came back at 6:00 for Christmas dinner. In time, Marion became one of the few people in Virden that Candy would confide in.

As a newcomer Candy was under the scrutiny of all the members in the detachment. Because she was so quiet and reserved, some of them felt uncomfortable with her. It seemed difficult to have a conversation with her. As the only other woman member in Virden, Debbie MacLean was concerned about Candy's shyness. She wondered how such a quiet, timid person could function effectively as a police officer. How would she draw information out of people in an investigation? Debbie tried to befriend her. She lived with two other women who were always on the go and invited Candy to go out with them. But Candy, more often than not, declined. She preferred to go her own way and was more than comfortable spending her evenings quietly at Molly Forrester's.

Eventually Candy did attend one of the after-shift informal detachment parties at MacLean's and went to the New Year's party at the Legion. This was a bit of a breakthrough for her. Although she didn't drink or smoke, she enjoyed being with the members and their wives. John and Marion were her favourites. She had liked Ralph Mahar when he visited her at Depot and came to enjoy him even more when she saw how crazy he could be at a party. Joe and Elaine MacDougall were another couple she felt comfortable with. They were easy to talk to and had a sense of humour. Candy really enjoyed it when Joe started to sing on New Year's and got her to join in. Russ Hornseth could be a bit gruff in the office but Candy could see he loved having a good time at a party. She appreciated him on New Year's because he made no demands on her. If she wanted to talk that was fine; if she didn't want to talk, that was fine too.

Dennis Onofrey she wasn't sure of. He was always pleasant with her on the job but he seemed to keep his distance. She was impressed when Paula told her that he had taken time before the New Year's dance to call Joan Cullins and ask about her baby.

Joan was two weeks overdue and there was some concern among the detachment wives about the baby coming late. Since Jake Cullins was working New Year's Eve, Joan was at home alone, so Dennis called to ask her how she was feeling and assure her that everything would be all right.

"Do you think it might come tonight?" Dennis asked.

"I don't think so, Dennis," she replied.

"No chance of you having the New Year baby?"

"I don't think so . . . but it's nice of you to call and ask."

Over the blare of the band at the Legion, Candy and Paula struggled at small talk.

"Our basement's a mess right now," Paula said. "Dennis is building a rec room down there with Orville Sheane."

Candy had already met Orville in the detachment office.

"How's it coming?"

"Not bad," Paula said. "They're just doing the electrical now. Dennis says it should be ready in another month or so." Paula looked away for a moment then came back with a different topic. "Will you be able to come to our place for Ukrainian Christmas Eve?"

"I've heard about that but I didn't know if I was invited."

"Oh, sure you are. Will you be able to come?"

"When is it again?"

"On Friday, January 6. Ukrainian Christmas is on the seventh but the big dinner celebration is on the sixth."

"Sure," Candy responded, "that sounds great, I'd love to come."

"Good. Dennis and his mother and Viv Barrie are planning it all. There's a big bunch coming from the detachment."

"Do you do this every year?"

"No," Paula replied. "It's the first time we've ever done it. Dennis never even did this when he lived at home. I don't know what's got into him, he just decided that he wanted to do it . . . well, him and Vivian Barrie."

"Sounds neat."

"Yeah, it should be fun."

Then one of the members asked Candy to dance. When the tune was finished, another member asked her to dance. It was the best night she'd had in Virden since she arrived.

The Ukrainian Christmas celebration at Onofreys' was even better than that. The traditional menu for this celebration is to serve thirteen dishes, one each for Jesus and his twelve apostles. Normally these are meatless dishes but Dennis and Vivian weren't going to stand on ceremony. They wanted to serve little Ukrainian meat balls and city chicken which is veal on a stick. The veal was supposed to be mixed with pork but Dennis wouldn't hear of it. They also wanted to have meat in their cabbage rolls. Dennis made arrangements to drive to his grandmother's place in Shoal Lake the day before the feast to pick up a whopping supply of her cabbage rolls and perogies.

Because fish was such an important part of the Christmas menu, Dennis and Orville Sheane went fishing at Oak Lake. As soon as they got there, Orville snagged a huge jackfish and began to haul it in. But when he went to take it off his hook, the fish bit his hand with its vicious teeth. Orville let out a yell and his hand started to bleed heavily. Dennis didn't hesitate. He pulled out the tail of his undershirt and cut it off with his knife then wrapped it around Orville's bleeding hand. Then they hauled the fish home to the freezer.

Rose Onofrey had come into Virden for an extended stay on regular Christmas. She, Paula and Vivian Barrie spent Wednesday and Thursday making the meatballs and city chicken. Friday morning they started stewing the borsch. By supper time, everything was ready. Except for those on duty, all the members and their wives came to the dinner. By tradition, the first dish served was a spoonful of *kutia*, a mixture of boiled wheat, honey, poppyseeds and chopped walnuts. Normally the host makes a welcoming speech, tries the *kutia* and then hurls what remains on his spoon against the ceiling for good luck. Dennis was happy to welcome everyone but he was reluctant to make a mess of his kitchen ceiling. He took a bite and passed the rest to Paula.

Then he gave Vivian Barrie the traditional greeting: "*Christos narodevsha* (Christ is born!)"

Following custom, Vivian replied: "*Slavita yohaw* (Praise him!)"

Then they all started on the red borsch, baked fish, rolled herring, sauerkraut and peas, mushroom gravy and all the other dishes the women had prepared. There was red wine, white wine, beer and cola for toasts by anyone who felt so inclined. Over the sound of clinking glasses, the unfamiliar strains of Ukrainian music drifted from the sound system. The house was so crowded that people were eating anywhere they could find a place. Some ate in the kitchen or at the dining room table. Others ate off their laps in chairs that circled the living room. All the talking and yelling made it difficult to hear anyone, even if they were sitting close by.

Rose Onofrey loved what she was seeing and hearing. She leaned over to Paula and spoke in her ear. "They're like brothers," she said.

Paula couldn't hear her. "I'm sorry, Mom, what did you say?"

Rose leaned over and spoke more loudly. "I said they're like brothers . . . closer than brothers."

Paula nodded that she agreed. "I know," she said. "They are."

The celebration went on for hours and everyone raved about the Ukrainian food. Dennis and Vivian were delighted at the party's success and vowed to have the same thing next year. They stayed up late into the night talking about it with Rose.

The following day brought an entirely different mood to the members of the detachment. A story was breaking out of Hoyt, New Brunswick that two Mounties, Corporal Barry Lidstone and Constable Perry Brophy had been murdered while investigating a domestic dispute near Fredericton. The incident had occurred the night before when a despondent man named Leslie Crombie used a high-powered rifle to kill both officers in the kitchen of his mobile home. Crombie, appearing calm and sane, had excused himself from the kitchen to get something from his bedroom. When he came out, he shot Lidstone in the back of the head while the policeman stood waiting with his back to him. Brophy he killed while the officer was trying to pull his revolver from his holster. After slaying both policemen, Crombie murdered his wife and then shot himself dead.

The members of the Virden detachment became more and more morose as the gruesome details of the killings filtered into the detachment. The worst part was that the killer had never met these two policemen before. They had never been to his house or spoken to him on the phone. They had never given him so much as a speeding ticket or harassed him in any way. He had no reason whatsoever to end their lives and destroy their families.

The night after the Mounties' deaths in New Brunswick, Joan Cullins went into labour. When John O'Ray heard she needed to go to the hospital, he and Candy provided her with a police escort from the house. She went in at 1:30 in the morning. As soon as Dennis heard what was happening, he dropped by the hospital to see his buddy Jake and find out how Joan was doing. Although there was some concern about the baby being overdue, it arrived safely at 6:20 a.m. after a normal delivery.

That night many members gathered at Jake's house to celebrate the birth of his first child. Mostly they sat around his recreation room and drank. Dennis and Ralph Mahar sat on the rug on the floor, sending up clouds of blue smoke as they puffed on the cheap cigars Jake had handed out. They spoke about Joan and the baby and how good it was that there were no complications.

When Jake left to tend to other business, Dennis switched to a darker topic.

"What about those two guys in New Brunswick?" he said. "That was an out and out execution."

"They shouldn't have let him go into the bedroom without watching him," Ralph replied. "Once he got that gun, they never had a chance."

Dennis was pensive. "I don't know. If a crazy guy wants to kill you, he'll find a way."

"I suppose that's right," Ralph sighed. "I guess you never know when it could be you."

"All you can do is stay alert," Dennis said. "But if a crazy guy is out to get you . . . well . . . ," Dennis' voice trailed off. He shook his head. "I don't know what you can do."

Ralph nodded. Both of them sipped their beer and sat quietly absorbed in their own thoughts. Then Jake came back and they reverted to more joyous topics.

Two weeks later at a hockey game at the arena, Joe MacDougall told Dennis he and Elaine were going to have their first baby. Dennis was delighted. After the game, he went and found Elaine sitting in the stands.

"Joe told me the good news and I just wanted to tell you how happy I am for the both of you," he said.

"Thanks Dennis," Elaine said. "That's nice of you. They'll be quite a crew of kids in town in another year or so."

"Yeah, it should be great. There's lots of stuff we can do together with them. I look forward to that. Anyway I just thought I'd let you know how excited I am for you. Puts a whole new perspective in your life."

"It does, doesn't it?"

"I think Joe's going to be great father."

"So do I."

"See you later," Dennis said.

"Yeah . . . and thanks again."

On Sunday, January15, Dennis and Paula and the two Howells decided to do some ice fishing in the Assiniboine River. They drove out in the Howell's vehicle but, because of the snow, couldn't get very close to the river and they had to walk. Paula was so big she struggled as they followed a snowmobile path that led up hill. But then the path gradually disappeared into a drift and the four of them slogged along in snow that slowly rose to their waists. The deeper it got, the more Paula laughed; the more she laughed, the weaker she became, until she couldn't move. By then she and Simone Howell were in hysterics. Dennis and Steve had to haul Paula out of the drift and help her back to the car. She was still giggling when they poured her into the back seat.

On the way home, Steve said, "So, Dennis, you think you can come over next weekend and give me a hand with that electrical work?"

"Yeah, I don't see why not. I'm tied up Saturday but I could make it over Sunday morning for a couple of hours. I'll be working nights . . . going in at five."

"Well, that should work, " Steve said. "There's not that much to do."

"You come over too, Paula," Simone said. "Bring Corey and we can have brunch before Dennis goes on duty."

"Are we talking about next Sunday?" Paula asked.

"Yeah, the twenty-second," Simone replied. "Is that OK for you?"

"Sure, that would be nice," Paula said. "We'll see you on the twenty-second."

CALGARY

On Monday, December 12, Dorothy appeared before Shawn Christie in the morning and asked if she could make her bail visit with him the next day at 1:30 p.m. She explained that Bruce was to appear in a Vancouver court then and she wanted to be there with him. Christie agreed and Dorothy went downstairs and climbed into Archer's rented car. From there they went directly to Bow Mac Truck Rentals on King George Highway in the Vancouver suburb of Surrey. They told the young service clerk, Nevil Marples, that they wanted to rent a three-quarter ton truck for a couple of days. Marples said that would be no problem but they would have to put down a $200 deposit. Bruce was surprised at the amount required but he told the clerk he would go home and get the money and be right back.

Bruce and Dorothy went home and scrounged up as much cash as they could find. Within an hour they were back at the rental office filling out a lease agreement. They asked Marples if he would accept a deposit of $150 and he reluctantly agreed to do so. The truck, a white, square-backed GMC Magnavan, was due to be returned on Wednesday, December 14. Archer signed the lease with the alias he had been using, Donald Alfred Archer.

Archer told Marples they had to move some Amway products from a garage in Kamloops and because of the snow, they might be a day or two late returning the truck. If that happened, he said they would call the rental agency and let them know. Marples said that would be all right and handed them the keys to the Magnavan, license # 7879AK.

Then they went home and began loading the truck with their clothes and furniture and their pornography collection. Trip after trip they carried out speakers, lamps, curtains, planters, wine racks, everything they owned. They cleaned out their fridge and their cupboards and stowed that on board too. Archer himself took care of loading his personal arsenal. This included two .22 rifles, a .38 Winchester rifle, and a .12-gauge goose gun, a 40 lb. test hunting bow, a 30 lb. test target bow, 2 hunting knives, a sixteen-foot bull

129

whip and over 2,000 rounds of ammunition. His prized possessions, a .308 Savage deer rifle and a .20-gauge shotgun, he stored in the truck cab behind the seats. Within a few hours, they were packed.

Their plan was vague but they knew they had to get out of British Columbia. Neither of them could face the prospect of being jailed for any length of time and Bruce felt sure he was going to be put away for the assault charge. They just wanted to run and hoped they would be able to work their way back to Ontario. This is how Bruce had always operated. When he got in trouble in one place, he just left and went somewhere else. It had worked in the past, why wouldn't it work again?

Archer loved being on the move. It gave him a carefree sense of starting over, starting fresh. He felt he was leaving his troubles behind. Driving long distances was no problem. It seemed to stimulate him. He'd been back and forth across the country a number of times and never tired of the trip. He particularly loved the drive through the British Columbia mountains into Alberta. This time he planned to make it a trip to remember. Once they got past Hope, Bruce headed for Kamloops where they took a motel room. They left early the next morning without paying the bill and leisurely worked their way through the Monashee Mountains into Revelstoke. What little cash they had went for groceries. There was nothing for any frills or meals in a restaurant. The next day they crossed through the Selkirks and spent the night in Golden. The scenery in every direction was spectacular. From Golden they wound their way through the splendour of Kicking Horse Pass into Alberta, then turned down Highway #93, along the spine of the Rockies. Like a couple of vacationing tourists, they stopped to see Lake Louise and then spent the night in Banff at a small motel. By December 16, they had gone down the grade through the foothills and were in Calgary.

Since the van was now four days overdue, Nevil Marples at the Bow Mac rentals reported it missing to the RCMP detachment in Surrey. Bruce figured that would happen. He had counted on having a few days grace but suspected the police would be looking for the truck by now, so he was glad to be in the anonymity of a big city. Calgary wasn't quite as big and complex as Vancouver but it was large enough for their truck to meld into the busy traffic.

130

They stayed at a small motel for a couple of days while Archer looked for work. Although he tried his best, every shop and office in the city was slowing down for Christmas. By now Bruce and Dorothy were almost broke. They could barely afford to eat, let alone pay for a room, so they left the motel without paying the bill and found a fairly nice basement apartment at 2911-16th Street S.W. The rental agent, Nancy Rokana, was a real estate agent who lived above the apartment. She let them move in on the promise they would get the rent to her within a couple of weeks.

On December 19, Archer called the Bow Mac Truck Rental Agency in Surrey and told Nevil Marples they were going to need the van for another couple of weeks. Marples wasn't thrilled by Archer's news but there was little he could do but go along with it. After talking to Archer, Marples advised the police the van had been located. The police altered their CPIC records accordingly.

Once Bruce and Dorothy had the heat of the missing truck off their back, all they had to do was raise a little money to pay for their room and board. One week after settling into the place on 16th Street, Dorothy went down to the office of one of Calgary's major newspapers, *The Albertan*, and put a classified ad in the personal column. It ran in the paper on Thursday, December 29 through Saturday, December 31 and read as follows:

> *Very broad minded couple new in Calgary, wish to meet other couples and singles to establish intimate friendship. Reply Box #A13349 The Albertan (29-12-31-148)*

For those in the game, the language expressed a very clear message: two new swingers were on the scene looking for some sexual action with other swinging couples or with singles who were hoping to be served in a particular way.

The ad drew several replies. One was from the owner of a used car agency. Another was from an unemployed construction worker. The third was from a man named Maurice who said he was in real estate.

To meet the first respondent, Bruce and Dorothy went out to his car lot in the suburbs. As it turned out, Bruce didn't like his looks and they left without anything happening. The second respondent, the construction worker, owned his own house trailer.

131

He wanted to engage in some sexual activity and look at some of their pornographic movies. They stayed about three hours with him while he had sex with Dorothy and got drunk. Bruce stole his wallet and they left him sleeping peacefully.

The third and last respondent was a man named Maurice Crystal. He was a sixty-four-year-old gentleman who was into sadomasochistic sex. When he saw Dorothy's advertisement, he replied to the mail box address at the newspaper, outlining the type of sexual service he was looking for. Strangely enough his letter of reply, which normally would have been treated as private and confidential by the paper, was accidentally put in with the senior editor's morning mail. While the editor sat chatting with a colleague, he opened the letter and started to read it before he realized it wasn't intended for him. When he began to comprehend what the letter was about, he was astonished at its contents and sent it on to the mail box to which it was addressed. He couldn't believe that people did such bizarre things.

Very few people who knew Maurice Crystal would have believed it either. A married man who lived in a beautiful home in the suburbs of Okotoks, south of the city, Crystal was a prominent realtor and a reputable businessman among the merchants of Calgary. He was known not only as an extremely successful entrepreneur but as a man who led an active and productive life. Although small and paunchy with only a fringe of gray hair that circled his head, he was gregarious, enthusiastic and still the little bundle of energy that had made him something special all his life.

Crystal was born in Montreal, the son of a clothing manufacturer. From his earliest days he had developed a broad base of interests and was highly successful in most of them. As a young man of twenty-three, he rose to become the Canadian Dominion Fencing Champion and was slated to represent his country at the 1936 Olympics. Unfortunately those games were held in Hitler's Berlin and, as a Jew, Crystal wasn't welcome to participate.

Once World War II began, Crystal found a way to strike back at the Nazis. He enlisted in the RAF and became a navigator and a paratroop trainer. Throughout the war he served with distinction in the Middle East and in North Africa. For his valour he was awarded the Africa Star, an honour reserved for a very select number of allied airmen. There were more honours to come. In 1948, at thirty-five years of age, Maurice Crystal enjoyed the rare distinction of being chosen as a Canadian witness to the documents establishing the new state of Israel.

Crystal moved to Calgary in 1956 and established his own real estate business in 1961. As his business grew and flourished, he became an active member of the local Real Estate Association. Still a man with many interests, he was an amateur hypnotist and the founding president of the Calgary Hypnotic Society. One of his most impressive achievements was his venturesome spirit in the realm of education. At his late age, he was about to complete his studies towards obtaining a B.A. from the University of Calgary.

Unfortunately Crystal had a dark side to his personal life and enjoyed being bound and dominated while in the act of having sex. Once he established contact with Dorothy through the mail, he made arrangements to meet her in order to satisfy these fantastic desires.

At 6:45 a.m. on Saturday, January 21, Maurice Crystal dropped off his sixteen-year-old son, Sam, at the bus station in downtown Calgary. The boy was taking a commuter bus to the nearby ski slopes at Banff. He was going to ski all day then take the return trip to the bus station to arrive by 5:00 p.m. Maurice told Sam he would be working all day Saturday at his office in the Mayfair Plaza and that he would be back to pick him up when he returned from the mountains. They said their good-byes and each went his own way.

When young Sam Crystal arrived back in the city at 5:00 p.m., his father wasn't there to pick him up. He waited for about a half an hour and then decided that his dad must have been held up and probably wouldn't be coming. Maurice's failure to show up didn't alarm Sam because he knew his father was a busy salesman and often had unexpected demands put on his time. This type of thing had happened before on a few occasions. Sam simply went to the phone and made other arrangements to get to get home.

Sam and his mother finished their supper without any real concern about Maurice's absence. Even when he hadn't shown up by bedtime, they didn't worry. Both were convinced that he was once again working late and was out somewhere closing a deal or finalizing an important listing.

But when Maurice was still not home by 9:00 a.m. on Sunday

morning, his wife became concerned. She phoned his office several times but there was no answer. They knew Maurice had a couch in his inner office and could have slept there overnight but why wasn't he answering his phone? It was a puzzling situation so, after discussing it with her son, she asked him to drive down to his father's Calgary office and see if he could find him.

In the quiet traffic of an early Sunday morning, Sam set out for Mayfair Plaza on Elbow Drive S.W. When he pulled into the parking area, he was mildly surprised not to see his father's orange Datsun in its customary parking place. He quickly walked to the storefront of Crystal Realty and pulled out the key his mother had given him at home. Once inside the general office area, as far as he could tell, everything looked normal. Some of the desks were slightly cluttered, but nothing looked extraordinary. Sam walked directly towards his father's private office located at the rear of the general office.

Just outside the door to the inner office, Sam was taken aback by a curious sight. There neatly folded on a straight back chair were some clothes that he was sure belonged to his father. His pants lay on the seat of the chair and his shirt, tie and suit coat were draped over the back of the chair. His father's shoes were neatly tucked underneath the chair.

Sam was puzzled. Nevertheless, he went ahead and opened the inner office door with only a hint of trepidation. Once he stepped inside and turned on the light, his mind had great difficulty comprehending what he was seeing. There on the couch lay his father with his arms and feet bound together behind his back with a length of blue nylon cord running up to his neck where it had left a deep, dark blue bruise on his throat. He was clothed in his undershorts and socks but part of his head and all of his face was covered with some kind of strange paraphernalia composed of bandages and what looked like pantyhose. His father was utterly still and it was quite clear that he was dead. The sheer shock of it all somehow helped Sam to function. Although terribly upset, he managed to call the police who responded immediately.

Once the police got there, they sealed off the area and began their investigation. Sam gave a detective his statement while other officers, Ident photographers and the coroner went back and forth about their business. The preliminary cause of death was established as asphyxiation by strangulation. Sam was shattered by the experience. He didn't understand what had happened but suspected his father had been murdered in the course of a robbery. Although Crystal's wallet was missing and he had no cash left in any of his pockets, the police knew that more than a robbery had taken place.

From their experience in these matters, it was reasonably clear to them that Crystal's death was some type of sadomasochistic killing, possibly accidental. The office had not been broken into and there were no signs of a struggle. Crystal's clothes appeared to have been removed voluntarily and the ropes and paraphernalia on his head indicated he had been participating in a type of sexual bondage that the police had seen before. Crystal was lying on his left side facing the back of the couch in a semi-fetal position with his hands tied around his back. There was a wide brown tensor bandage wrapped around his eyes and mouth and a pair of pantyhose pulled over the bandage to cover his eyes. The police knew that this had been done to restrict his vision and thereby enhance his sense of helplessness and heighten his dread, thus making his experience all the more dangerous and exciting.

A blue nylon cord was tied around his hands and ran down to his ankles which were also bound and drawn up towards the back of his knees. The same rope then continued up his back and was looped around his neck so that if his legs extended the rope would apply pressure on his throat. It was significant to the police that when they teased the ropes, they found them tied in such a way that Crystal could easily have freed himself from the bondage had he so chosen.

To the untrained eye, it would appear that he had been out-and-out strangled but the police knew that his death could have been caused by something more complex than that. Since his wallet was missing and there was no cash left in any of the pockets in his clothes, the police suspected Crystal probably died in one of three ways.

One possible way was that he died in the heated throes of a S/M ritual that the police termed a "bondage sex act." In this ritual female undergarments are commonly employed. In Crystal's case, the legs of the pantyhose were knotted and used as a ligature to apply pressure to the carotid artery in his neck. This would cut off the blood supply to his brain and take him to the brink of unconsciousness. When a person is sexually stimulated and climax is reached in this state of semi-stupor, it apparently provides an extremely heightened sexual experience. If Crystal's sexual partners assisted him in this way, it is possible they went too far and kept the pressure on too long. Because he was older and out of shape, he could have choked to death in the process.

The general public is not aware of the frequency of this type of death. More often than not, it happens to young people who use this procedure to heighten their own sexual experience during an act of masturbation. Because they are usually alone, they have to anchor their ligature on a door knob or a bathroom tap and in the rush of their climax, they sometimes lose control and keep the pressure on too long. When this happens, such a person can end up dying from strangulation. This cause of death is not widely known because, to avoid scandal and family embarrassment, most deaths of this type are listed by the police as suicide.

In Crystal's case the second possibility was that whoever was doing this to him was choking him to find out where he kept his money. When he wouldn't tell them, they choked him with the rope too hard and too long and he died.

A third possibility is that Crystal was alive when his sexual servers left the office and he choked himself to death due to the way he was tied. This doesn't make a lot of sense because the police felt that if Crystal wanted to, he could have got out of his bonds.

No one knows exactly what caused Crystal's death. What is known is that Dorothy participated in sexual activity with him in that office at some point prior to the time of his death. Several Polaroid photos later discovered in Archer and Malette's possession show her engaged in such activity on the couch in Crystal's office. The photos appear to have been taken by a third party rather than an automatic timing device. In all probability that third party was Archer.

Whether Crystal was dead when Archer and Malette left Crystal's office remains unknown. However, by Archer's own admission, it was he who took Crystal's Datsun that day and drove it to a large parkade in downtown Calgary. After wiping it clean of fingerprints, he left it on the main floor.

Staff Sergeant Bob Hay was assigned to head up the Crystal investigation. In an effort to build up a profile of his social associations, the police started talking to people who knew Maurice Crystal. As the investigation progressed, they began to uncover the dark side of Maurice Crystal's life. It had developed relatively late in his life and he had kept it well hidden from his family and friends. Ironically it was his need for anonymity and propriety that caused him to take the risk of answering such a newspaper advertisement.

The investigation determined he belonged to an informal group of older, physically unattractive people who enjoyed aberrant sex. To this small group Crystal had confided that he'd recently met a new couple in town and he had a new woman he could call on. The police believed that this information made it sound as if he might have had more than one meeting with this new woman.

Over and above the sexual implications of the murder, there were also clear indications that a robbery had taken place. Sam Crystal explained to Bob Hay that when his father was travelling about, he usually kept his wallet in the glove compartment of his car. However, Mr. Crystal's car keys were neither in his clothes nor anywhere to be found in the office. After an exhaustive police search of the immediate area, they were unable to locate Crystal's Datsun, which he usually parked nearby the office.

In Sam's statement to the Staff Sergeant, he revealed his father's intention to pick him up at the bus terminal on Saturday at 5:00 p.m. This information combined with the coroner's comments on the condition of the body led the police to conclude that Crystal's death probably occurred early in the afternoon of Saturday, January 21. This caused the police some concern because over twenty hours had already elapsed since Crystal's death which afforded the killer or killers a great opportunity to distance themselves from the scene.

While the office was being dusted for fingerprints, an all-points bulletin was put out in an attempt to locate Crystal's missing Datsun. Then Hay ordered a search in the immediate area of Mayfair Plaza to ascertain where the nylon cord and tensor bandage might have been purchased.

During the initial stages of the investigation the Calgary Police Department decided to keep quiet about the specific details of Crystal's murder. They had to balance the public's right to know with the attendant scandal that would result from this type of death occurring to such a prominent Calgarian as Maurice Crystal. Detective Superintendent Ernie Reimer issued a very terse statement about the murder saying, "Sex could be something that could have been used to accomplish the motive of robbery."

As the Crystals suffered and struggled with their confusion and grief at home, the police went about their business with a great intensity. Homicide of any kind was a serious matter but this case presented the additional nasty overtones of deviance. They were determined to handle the case delicately and to resolve it immediately. Although they didn't have a specific name or face in mind, they thought they had a general idea of the type of person or persons who were involved. They felt confident that this type of sadomasochistic death had not been the work of a local prostitute or sexual deviant. They believed that no one of that particular persuasion in Calgary would be foolish enough to foul their own nest with such a serious crime. Their suspicion was that it had been done by transients or outsiders who were new to the city. Their concern was that people such as this would flee the city as quickly as possible and, as each hour lapsed, they were getting further and further away.

This is exactly what Archer and Malette were doing. The same Saturday evening that Crystal died, Bruce and Dorothy went back to their suite, loaded all their gear back into the van and left town. They did this even though there was black ice on the highway and their apartment rent was paid up for another two days. At this point, the only risk they faced in running from Calgary was the fact that their truck had, once again, been reported overdue. The previous Friday, Nevil Marples at the Bow Mac agency, having heard nothing from Archer for over two weeks, once again reported the vehicle to the RCMP. Archer and Malette had now kept the truck five weeks beyond its due date.

That evening they drove as far as Lethbridge where they holed up for the night in the Holiday Inn, using Crystal's MasterCard to pay for their room and to draw $50 in cash. The next morning they got up around 5:00 a.m. Before anything else, Archer took his pills to get him through the day. When they left the Holiday Inn, the streets were empty but Bruce was careful not to break the speed limit nor commit any other driving violations. He didn't know if their truck had been reported missing in B.C. but he didn't want to take any chances. Once they got past Coaldale on Highway #3, he felt a lot better. There was a smattering of morning traffic but no police cars in sight.

In two hours they connected with the Trans-Canada Highway at Medicine Hat and began their trek east across Saskatchewan. It was slow going because the roads were slippery and covered with snow. Around 10:00 a.m. they went into Swift Current for something to eat. While they were there, Bruce went into a drugstore and bought a heavy bandage wrap for his right hand. They were going to be using Crystal's credit cards and he needed a good excuse for not being able to replicate his signature. Since he had everything from Crystal's wallet at his disposal, he figured, with any luck, they would have a fairly easy time getting to Ontario. Not only did Archer have his MasterCard but the entire contents of his wallet including his Shell and Texaco cards, his driver's license and his birth certificate.

As soon as Bruce was done in the drug store, they were back on the road again. All the way along the route he held to the speed limit, seldom passed anyone and constantly checked in every direction for the appearance of police. It was warm and comfortable in the cab, there was good music on the radio and every mile they went was a mile further away from the troubles they had left behind. From then on, the only time they stopped was to buy gas and snack food.

From Swift Current to Moose Jaw was a long, boring trip. The only thing that broke the monotony was the little prairie towns that appeared about every five miles along the highway. As soon as they passed one, they started looking forward to the next one. In the quiet of the cab Bruce got thinking about the predicament he was in. He knew he had the use of the credit cards for only another few days until they were reported stolen. Before that he had to stock up on food and gas and draw as much cash from them as possible. He figured he could get to Ontario by Wednesday or Thursday at the latest. Then he would ditch the truck, find some work and start over. For him, the key was to get the van into an area of higher traffic density where it had less chance of being spotted.

By the time they got to Regina it was getting dark. They had covered over 450 miles and Archer had driven the entire distance. When they reached the Manitoba border, he was getting weary so he started looking for a place to spend the night. In another twenty minutes, they were approaching the stretch of the highway adjacent to the business section of Virden. Late on a Sunday night there was very little activity on the roads near town. Everything was pretty well closed up. It was obvious that most of the town folks were either in bed or snug in their living rooms watching their Sunday night programs on television.

When Bruce looked at his watch, it was just past 10:30 p.m. They had been on the road for more than seventeen hours and had put over 600 miles behind them. When he saw the sign indicating the entrance to the frontage road, he pulled off the highway. Then, up ahead on the right, he spotted the big sign for the Countryside Inn. As he got closer, he saw there was a vacancy.

"This looks like all right to me," he said. "Let's pull in here."

He swung the Magnavan hard to the right and drove down the driveway leading to the motel office. Leaving the motor running, Archer went inside to register for a room. At the desk, the motel owner, June Bohonis, was busy registering Dave Melia and Tom Schmidt, two agricultural chemical salesmen for Ely Lilly Pharmaceuticals. The two men nodded to Archer and were amused when they saw him bend down, gently stroke the Bohonis' dog and engage it in a kindly one-way conversation. Schmidt was struck by the incongruity of the little dog enjoying the attention of this burly man who, in many ways, resembled Angelo Mosca, the professional wrestler and one-time football player.

Mrs. Bohonis assigned the two men to room 17 and they left the office.

To Archer June Bohonis said, "Can I help you?"

"Yes," he replied. "I'd like a room with a king size bed for me and my wife."

"I'm sorry we don't have any king size beds. We have a regular double bed that's extra long."

"That'll be fine. I'll take it."

As he proceeded to register, June noticed his right hand was bandaged and he was shaking. It looked as if he was in some pain. He was signing his name very slowly.

"What happened to your hand?" she said.

"I was helping my sister move to Calgary and slipped on some ice," he replied.

"Oh, that's too bad." She waited until he finished filling out the form. "You'll be in room 20. That's right down the west side about half way. That'll be $22 plus tax."

He handed her a MasterCard. "There you go."

She imprinted it and Archer signed it with difficulty. The card and the shaky signature were in the name of Maurice Crystal.

When he was finished in the motel office, Archer wheeled the van around the side of the motel and parked slightly beyond the doorway to room 20. There was only one other truck in the parking lot and it was parked about four spaces to the south. Together he and Dorothy took in their gear from the back of the truck. This included a couple of suitcases and a cardboard box containing the remnants from their refrigerator. Among other things in the box were sherry wine and peanut butter. It also held some ammunition, about twenty-five shotgun shells and twenty bullets for a .308 deer rifle.

Then Bruce alone went back to the truck for one last trip. From behind the front seats, he removed his two expensive guns, the .20-gauge shotgun and the .308 Savage hunting rifle. Both were in their cases. Then he locked all the truck doors, surveyed the stillness of the almost empty parking lot and carefully carried his rifles into the motel.

Inside room 20, it was warm and cozy. Both of them were very tired from the long drive. What he wanted more than anything was a nice warm bath but the first thing he did was turn on the television and look for the news. Seeing nothing that concerned him, he ran the water in the tub, washed his socks in the sink and hung them on the dresser to dry. While Malette got ready for bed and he was waiting for the tub to fill, Archer fixed himself a little snack. The television nattered on quietly in the background.

Their room at the Countryside Inn was typical, modern accommodation. On the outside, to the right of the door, the wall jutted out about three feet and then continued along the face of the motel to the south. The entrance was on the right with a large, partially screened window on the front wall beside it. The room itself was about fourteen feet wide by twenty feet long. There was a double bed and dresser with two incidental chairs and a night table. The bathroom ran along the back wall with a sink and vanity mirror located just outside the bathroom door. A three-foot wooden divider ran up the side wall separating the vanity from the bed/sitting area. The divider was directly opposite the entrance door.

When Archer got out of the tub, he admired himself in the vanity mirror. Even though he was overweight and a bit paunchy, he liked the idea that he looked like a wrestler—240 lbs., big shoulders, big arms, big hands. But then he grimaced in the mirror when he felt the nagging ache in his back. It was frustrating that he couldn't get rid of it. He'd been in constant pain ever since his car accident in Vancouver, almost two years ago. That look on his face reminded him that he needed to take his pills.

Bruce waited until Dorothy came out of the bathroom and let her dole out his medication and serve it to him with a glass of water. First three Valium capsules for his nerves, then four Darvon Compound tablets for his pain. Like always, she took care of him. He liked that.

Once all the pills were down, Bruce walked over to the motel door and rammed the tip of his hunting knife under the inside of the door molding so that the handle rested against the motel door and prevented it from opening. It was a precaution he had learned as a transport driver years ago, to prevent unwanted guests from entering during the night. Then he climbed under the covers.

He wasn't in bed very long before Dorothy climbed in beside him. Once she was comfortable, he turned out the light and they settled in for a good night's sleep.

THE COUNTRYSIDE INN

A rcher and Malette lay sleeping in the Countryside Inn, unaware of the police activity that was beginning to develop outside their room. Dennis Onofrey had gone back into the registration office of the motel and asked Bill Bohonis for a key to room 20. Just as Bill was handing it over, Hornseth arrived in his police cruiser. Dennis went outside to meet him.

"What's up?" Hornseth asked Dennis.

"They're in room 20," Dennis replied. "I got the key from Bill."

"We know anything about them?" Hornseth asked.

"Same as before," Dennis said. "The guy's name is Maurice Crystal and he's with a woman . . . either she's his wife or his girlfriend."

O'Ray and Smith waited for Hornseth to give them instructions.

"Let's take our cars around the side and see if we can wake them up . . . and find out what's going on with the truck," Hornseth said.

They drove their cruisers to the back of the motel. Dennis parked his on the right side of Archer's white cube van with its front facing the motel. Hornseth parked his in the parking lot parallel to the motel just behind Archer's van. He left his motor running. As he and Dennis were walking towards the door to room 20, John O'Ray and Candy Smith pulled into the parking lot in their cruiser. O'Ray kept his cruiser north of room 20 and angled it so his headlights shone on the door of the room. Even though the parking lot was fairly well lit, he put the headlights on high beam. They shone directly on Hornseth and Onofrey who were now standing in front of the motel door. O'Ray left his motor running too.

Then he and Smith got out of the car and started towards Russ and Dennis. As they walked, John noticed that Onofrey had his gun out. This puzzled him and he thought to himself, "What's going on here? Does Dennis know something more about this than I do?" Warily O'Ray undid his holster flap, took out his own revolver and put it in the deep side pocket of his storm coat. He

143

and Candy took up a position on the sidewalk to the left of Hornseth; Onofrey was on Hornseth's right.

When John noticed that Candy was standing in front of the window of room 20, he motioned for her to move away from it. Smith nodded that she understood and retreated to a position on the sidewalk further to the north. Her holster was open. Her hand was on her gun. All of them could feel the adrenaline flowing. Onofrey positioned himself behind the three foot jut-out in the wall immediately adjacent to the door to room 20. He had his back against the motel and held his gun pointed up in the air beside his head. Hornseth was directly in front of the door with his gun in his holster. He rapped three times on the door with his flashlight.

Inside the room, Archer had heard scuffling outside. Then he heard the tapping on the door. He sat up and strained to look out through the window. Unable to see anything, he got up and peered out through the narrow slit in the drapes. The only thing he could see was the silhouette of someone holding what appeared to be a revolver pointed up in the air. Archer went to the bed and shook Dorothy awake.

"There's somebody out there," he said. "You better get dressed."

Fretfully Dorothy climbed out of bed and scurried behind the wood-slatted half wall to put on her clothes.

Hornseth tapped on the door again, this time more forcefully.

Archer turned on the lights in the room, pulled on his pants and then reached for his shotgun, which was on the floor by the television set. He loaded it and placed it on the end of the bed. Then he turned the lights out.

Outside the room Russ asked Onofrey for the key to the door and then tried it in the lock. It didn't work. Onofrey said to Russ, "Tell them it's the RCMP."

Hornseth rapped on the door again with the flashlight. "Open up, it's the RCMP," he said. It was loud enough so that everyone could hear what he said, including Archer. Onofrey, on Hornseth's right, now rotated and faced the motel. Assuming the combat firing position, he pointed his revolver at the door. When Hornseth saw him do this out of the corner of his right eye, he thought to himself, "That's not a bad idea."

Hornseth could hear a bustling noise as if someone was

moving around inside the room. Shortly after that, the lock on the door was released and the door opened a crack.

Although Hornseth couldn't see Archer because he was concealed, standing with his back against the motel wall beside the door, he did hear him say, "The door is open, come on in."

"No, we're not coming in," Hornseth replied. "You come out."

There was a pause and then the door opened a little bit more. Archer who was still concealed, said again, "It's open. Come in."

Hornseth pushed the door open further but didn't step inside. He still couldn't see anyone because Archer remained concealed with his back against the wall beside the door. What Hornseth did see in the shadows was the top of Dorothy's head moving around behind the half wall. She appeared to be putting on some clothes.

Hornseth yelled to her, "Hey you . . . come out from behind that wall."

"Just a minute," Dorothy called back, "I'm getting dressed."

Frantically, Dorothy continued to dress, but she did not come out.

Now Dennis shouted to her, "Come out from behind there." He pointed his gun at her.

As Dorothy struggled with her clothing, Archer stepped into the doorway directly in front of Hornseth. Only the left half of his body was visible. His right arm was completely concealed by the motel wall next to the door. Archer's attention was focused on Onofrey, who was pointing his service revolver at Dorothy.

Hornseth said to him, "Is this your truck?"

Archer replied, "Yes, it is."

"We'd like to talk to you about it," Russ said.

Very firmly Archer responded, "I'll talk to you all right!" Then he took another half step to his left into the doorway and began to raise a shotgun with his right hand.

As soon as Hornseth saw the shotgun, he shouted a warning to everyone. "HE'S GOT A GUN!" he yelled at the top of his voice. Then he turned and started to run for the cover of O'Ray's cruiser.

When O'Ray and Smith heard Russ yell his warning, they began moving for cover as well. Only Onofrey remained in his original position, partially hidden by the jut-out of the motel wall. As Archer raised the shotgun, Onofrey maintained his combat position with his revolver pointed at Dorothy. He and Archer were eight feet apart. There was a pause while both men stared at each other. It was a split second in time that held the future in the balance for many people.

Then Archer pulled the trigger. The shotgun blast hit Onofrey high on the chest near his left shoulder and blew him back into the snow in front of the white truck. He died instantly.

Hornseth heard that first blast as he was running past Archer's truck heading for cover behind O'Ray's cruiser. With his back turned to the action, he had no idea that Dennis was hit.

Candy Smith heard the shotgun go off as she scurried along the face of the motel. She pinned herself flat against the building behind a wooden decorative abutment that ran down the motel wall. It jutted out only four inches from the wall and provided very limited protection. With her back against the wall, she drew her gun. Fixing her stare on the door of room 20, she could see Onofrey's feet and the bottom of his legs lying on the ground, sticking out behind Archer's truck. Candy did not know that he was dead.

When O'Ray heard Hornseth yell his warning, he turned to run and immediately smashed into a wrought iron support that ran from the roof overhang to the sidewalk. He lost his footing and fell face first into the packed snow of the parking lot. His hands had just hit the ground when he heard the first shotgun blast go off. He lost his glasses in the fall but continued to scramble on his hands and knees in an attempt to regain his feet. He too had no idea that Dennis had been shot.

After the first shot, Archer fired again. This time, from his position in the doorway, he got off a volley at the fleeing Hornseth and O'Ray. The second shot didn't hit anyone but Archer's third shot caught Hornseth on the side of the face. As Russ was running, he heard O'Ray stumble and fall so he turned his head to the left to see how he was doing. As he did, Archer's third shot hit him on the left side of the face, doing severe damage to his left eye and forehead. To Russ it felt as if he'd been kicked in the head. He could see nothing out of his left eye and blood was streaming down his face. Still he kept moving until he was safely behind O'Ray's cruiser. It was only when he saw how much blood he was losing that he realized how seriously he was wounded. But he didn't let that prevent him from drawing his gun and returning Archer's fire.

As he was shooting, he kept yelling, "YOU BASTARD! COME OUT OF THERE YOU SON OF A BITCH!"

When he saw that Archer was going to fight to the finish, Hornseth yelled, "SHOOT THAT BASTARD! KILL THAT SON OF A BITCH! SHOOT HIM! SHOOT HIM!"

By then John O'Ray had made it to his feet and dove over a small snowbank at the west side of the parking lot. From there he crawled on his belly through eighteen inches of snow into the back yard of a house on adjacent Nelson Street. As he was crawling Archer and Hornseth continued to blaze away at each other. Through it all John could hear the shotgun pellets rattling off the metal eavestrough of the house immediately ahead of him.

The gun battle between Archer and Hornseth was no contest. Hornseth only had his .38 Smith and Wesson Special and Archer was too far away for his handgun to do any damage. Archer's shotgun was much more powerful. Rapidly loading and reloading, he fired blast after blast at Hornseth who was hiding behind the cruiser. Fierce and desperate, Archer blew out the car's headlights, one of its roof lights, its grill and radiator and flattened one tire.

After his long crawl in the snow, O'Ray positioned himself by the corner of the house and attempted to survey the scene. He could hear the pop, pop, pop of Hornseth's revolver and the cannonlike boom of Archer's shotgun. He could see everything that was happening. The parking lot was well lit and he didn't need his glasses for distance. He could see Hornseth behind the cruiser firing towards room 20 with Archer firing back. Although he couldn't spot Dennis anywhere, he saw Candy pinned against the motel wall with her revolver out.

Inside the motel room, Archer could hear the telltale "ping-g-g-g-g" of the incoming bullets as they ricochetted wildly around the room. Dorothy was still behind the room divider, yelling "They're going to kill us! They're going to kill us both!"

"No they won't," he yelled back. "I won't let them kill you."

Crazed with fear, Dorothy inexplicably began to crawl around the room on her hands and knees picking up items of clothing and throwing them into her open suitcase beside the dresser. One of the few times she glanced up at Bruce, she could see that he had been grazed by a bullet that had torn across his forehead.

In the middle of the gunfight, Tom Schmidt, the chemical salesman in room 17, thought the noise outside meant someone was trying to break into his truck. When he stepped outside the motel in his pajamas and slippers, Hornseth screamed at him, "GET BACK INSIDE! IT'S A SHOOT-OUT!"

As the fight continued, Russ, bleeding badly from his head wound, managed to crawl across the front seat of O'Ray's cruiser and get to his radio. Under fire, he was able to call Brandon RCMP telecommunications.

"Hello, Brandon," he yelled into the handset. "We got a 10-33 (emergency) here at the Countryside Inn at Virden. Shots are being exchanged. I've been shot. We need help! We need help!"

Runa Dalik, a twenty-four-year-old civilian radio operator received the call in Brandon at exactly five seconds after 1:00 a.m.

"10-4, Virden," the dispatcher replied. "Who should I call?"

"Call Joe MacDougall . . . then call anyone else you can."

"OK, hang in there," she said. "Help is on the way."

The dispatcher immediately called Joe MacDougall and then began her fan-out call to the other members of the Virden Detachment. First on the list was the detachment commander, Fred Westerson, then the corporals, then the rest of the detachment members. After Virden she phoned the Brandon personnel one by one. Then, this capable young woman who had only six months experience on the police radio began to alert the surrounding detachments. She called Moosemin, Souris, Reston and Hamiota and got them rolling. Always her message was the same: "We've had a shooting in Virden. One of our members is down. We have no description of the gunman. Get all cars out on the highway and stop anything that's moving." Then she called the detachments close to the American border in Boissevain, Melita and Deloraine and ordered them to close the border to all outbound traffic. Throughout it all, Runa didn't panic; she was far too busy to lose her composure.

While reinforcements were being mounted elsewhere, the gunfight still raged on at the motel. When Hornseth opened the cruiser door, the interior light went on, signalling to Archer that he was radioing for help. Now Archer was determined to kill him. He grabbed his .308 rifle and tried firing at Hornseth directly through the hood and fire wall of the car. Luckily for Hornseth, one of Archer's first shots caromed off the big steel hinge that raises the automobile's hood. When Russ heard the louder crack of Archer's new gun, his experience as a hunter told him the distinctive sound meant that Archer was using heavier fire power. Suspecting Archer's rifle could pierce the front end of the car and kill him, Hornseth immediately squirmed his way off the front seat and out of the cruiser. He knelt behind the rear of the car. While he was in this position, Archer tried to glance a shot off the pavement underneath the car so it would ricochet up and hit Hornseth on the other side.

Russ kept thinking if he only had a shotgun, he would take his chances and charge the room. He figured if he could get close enough to Archer, the spread and the power of a shotgun would put him out of commission. Hornseth was not about to rush the room armed only with his service revolver. That would have been sheer suicide.

As soon as Fred Westerson got the call from Brandon, he called Syd Barrie. Barrie was a heavy sleeper so his wife, Vivian, answered the phone. Westerson was very brief. "Vivian," he said, "Syd's got to get over to the Countryside Inn. There's trouble there. Tell him I'll meet him there."

When Vivian told her husband about Westerson's message, Syd got up and dressed. In less than ten minutes he was gone from the house. Vivian was upset. She wondered what kind of trouble could be happening at the motel at this time of night that required her husband to be there. It didn't sound good to her and she couldn't go back to sleep.

For Hornseth at the motel, things weren't going well. He had retreated to the rear end of the cruiser for safety but now he was beginning to feel woozy. Looking for some help, he called out in O'Ray's direction.

"Who's out there?"

"It's O'Ray," John replied. "I'm over here," he called out from his position beside the house on Nelson Street.

"Get over here, John, I'm in trouble." Hornseth ordered.

Then Russ called to Candy, "Candy, he doesn't know you're there. Don't move."

Russ changed his plans with O'Ray. "John," he called, "I'm just about done. I think I'm going to faint. Meet me out on the

149

frontage road."

"Can you make it out there?" O'Ray asked.

"Yeah," Hornseth replied. "I can make it that far. Meet me out there."

"OK," John replied.

John crawled along the side of the house that he had been using for cover and then ran out to Nelson street and towards the frontage road.

Hornseth, in turn, dashed from behind the cruiser to the cover of the corner of the motel. Then he painfully stumbled along the motel's front driveway towards the frontage road.

Once Tom Schmidt had been warned there was a gunfight taking place, he had run back into his room and lay on the floor by the window listening to the turmoil outside. Dave Melia joined him there and, although they were both frightened by the yelling and the gunfire outside, they managed to gingerly take turns peaking out the window into the parking lot.

Lots of folks on nearby Nelson Street had heard the shoot-out too. They couldn't believe something like this was taking place in their own back yards, in little old Virden. Alex Barron who lived at 538 Nelson Street saw flashes of fire and heard several loud cracks. When he realized what was going on, he told his wife and daughter, "Shut the lights off and stay away from the windows. There's a war out there." But he didn't heed his own warning. He went outside to see for himself what was happening.

Marilyn Stinson, who lived across the parking lot from the motel, was awakened by the gunshots and at first thought the noise was coming from her hot water heater. Then she heard all the screaming and yelling and looked out her bedroom window to see what was going on.

During Hornseth's exchange of fire with Archer, Candy Smith had remained in a low crouch position against the motel wall, waiting for a chance to get off a shot. But all she ever saw was the momentary protrusion of Archer's gun barrel from the motel doorway and the reddish orange flame that leapt from the breech when he fired. Not realizing that Hornseth had departed to meet O'Ray on the frontage road, she was surprised when the gun fire ceased abruptly. Everything went strangely quiet.

Candy tried to assess her position. All she could see were

Dennis' feet protruding ominously from behind the other side of the white truck. She didn't know where John O'Ray was and she didn't know why Russ had stopped shooting.

Archer was equally puzzled. He had seen Hornseth and Onofrey at the door and saw O'Ray fall when he was running but he had no idea that Candy was sitting on her haunches with her gun drawn waiting beside the motel wall for a chance to shoot him. Archer figured he'd either wounded or killed the first cop and had chased the others off with his heavy duty gunshots. He waited and listened. Hearing nothing, he decided to step outside the motel door and check things out.

Because Candy's legs were cramping in her uncomfortable position, she looked down at her feet while she changed her stance. When she looked up, she was startled to see Archer standing twenty feet away in full view on the sidewalk outside his room. He was holding his shotgun and looking around. It was obvious to her that he had no idea she was there. Although it was a difficult thing for her to do, she knew she had to shoot him. She was also painfully aware that if she missed, she probably wouldn't get a second chance. Pointing her gun at him, she shouted, "DROP IT!"

In a flash of reflex, Archer was back in his room. As he disappeared, Candy fired. It was too late. Now that he knew she was there, Candy realized her position was terribly vulnerable. She had no cover and a long, open run to safety.

As Archer tried to peek out and determine her location, Smith got two more shots off at him. Then very quickly, Archer stuck only the barrel of the shotgun out the doorway and pointed it in her direction. He fired blindly along the wall in her direction.

Candy saw Archer's gun come out. Then she saw the flash and heard the loud report. Immediately she felt a very heavy blow on her upper right thigh and groin. The impact knocked her away from the wall and down on her butt on the sidewalk. Stunned and in terrible pain, she waited with her gun still trained on the doorway. This time Archer stuck the .308 out the door in her direction and fired again. The bullet ricochetted off a downspout on the wall and was beginning to spread when it tore into her thigh. Splinters of bone and bullet ripped into her abdomen. She fell back in horrible pain and rapidly began to lose consciousness. The last thought that went through her mind before she passed out was,

151

"If this is death, it's not too bad. I can handle this." Then she blacked out.

After Archer had hit Candy the second time, everything went quiet again. Not wanting any more surprises, Archer listened intently for any indication that another police officer might be outside. Hearing nothing, he was now convinced that the gun battle was over. Cautiously, he once again stepped out of the room to assess the situation.

During Candy's gun fight with Archer, O'Ray was meeting Hornseth on the frontage road north of the motel. At this point, neither of them knew that Dennis was dead nor that Candy was under fire. Both of them were under such stress, the sounds of the gunshots coming from the motel didn't register.

As they spoke, John tried not to let on but he was shocked to see the terrible condition of Hornseth's face.

"I got to get to the hospital," Hornseth said.

"Do you want me to take you there?" John replied.

"No", Russ said, "I think I can make it. Candy is O K. You go back and stand where I was standing and pin that bastard in the room down until help arrives. He won't try to go by the truck because Dennis is there."

Russ was getting so dizzy, he had to stop to collect his thoughts. "He's got a shotgun, John, so be careful."

"OK," John replied, staring at the corporal's appalling wound.

With that Hornseth turned and staggered off towards the hospital two blocks away. Along the way he hurried past a young man who was walking towards him. "What happened to you?" the lad asked.

"There's been a shoot-out at the Countryside Inn," Hornseth replied.

The youth didn't know if Hornseth was kidding or not, but by the look of the policeman's face, he wasn't about to ask any more questions and hurried on his way.

When Russ got to the hospital, he had to ring the night bell to get someone to let him in. As soon as the nurse who opened the door saw his face she called for some assistance. "We've got a car accident here," she called out. When they got him up on an examining table, it took Russ a while to explain exactly what had happened to him. While the doctor worked on him, he told him of the storm of violence that had broken out at the Countryside Inn.

After Archer saw that he had finished off Candy Smith, he carefully stepped out of the motel and checked on Dennis Onofrey. Seeing he was either dead or badly wounded, Archer removed the revolver from his hand. Then he walked over to Candy Smith and did the same. Although she wasn't completely unconscious, Candy had only a vague awareness of his huge shadow standing over her. Then, without hurrying, Archer went back into the motel room and spoke to Dorothy.

"The coast is clear," he said. "We're leaving."

Malette who was badly shaken wanted to take her suitcase with them but Archer said, "There's no time for that. We're taking a police car."

Dorothy was afraid and appeared hesitant.

"I'm going out first," Archer said, "and when I yell 'run' you follow me."

"What about our clothes and . . . "

"Clothes won't do us no good. Get your coat on and get into that far police cruiser out there."

As Dorothy went for her coat, Archer began gathering up his arsenal and his remaining ammunition.

After John O'Ray and Russ Hornseth had parted on the frontage road, John ran back to the west side of the motel where all the cruisers were parked. He still had no idea that Candy had been shot. With his gun drawn he was cautiously moving along the west wall of the motel when he saw somebody run towards Hornseth's cruiser, parked behind the white van. John could see that its motor was still running because there was condensation vapor coming from its exhaust pipe.

O'Ray couldn't make out who the figure was but he appeared to have a rifle in both hands. For a moment John was confused. He was convinced that whoever he saw running was not a police officer but he couldn't understand why Onofrey or Smith weren't firing at this person or at least yelling at him to stop. When John saw the unidentified figure get into the driver's side of Hornseth's car, it became clear to him that this was the gunman trying to make his get away. Then another person, who turned out to be Dorothy, came running past the white van and went around the back of Hornseth's car heading for the passenger's door. Now John opened fire.

His first two shots blew holes in the trunk of the cruiser. His third shot hit Dorothy square in the back puncturing her fifth rib. She let out a scream, but managed to open the car door.

"I've been hit," she yelled.

Archer said, "Get in!"

As she did, she yelled, "Drive!" and the cruiser sped off with its tires throwing snow in the air. It careened wildly around the south end of the motel, turned back towards the frontage road then disappeared heading east on the Trans-Canada Highway.

While it was speeding away, O'Ray saw someone lying near the face of the motel. He ran over and discovered it was Candy Smith. Kneeling down beside her, he called "Candy! Candy!" When she didn't respond he ran over to his cruiser to chase the escaping fugitives. As he drove by the white van, he saw the body of Dennis Onofrey, lying in a pool of blood on the motel sidewalk Swerving around the end of the motel he called Brandon telecommunications. "I'm at the Countryside Inn. Two of our members are down and we need an ambulance. The fugitives have headed east on number one highway in a PC and I am in pursuit."

Brandon acknowledged receipt of O'Ray's call and recorded the time as 1:10 a.m. All this horror had taken place in just ten minutes of time.

While the last stages of the gun fight were taking place, Joe MacDougall and his wife were fast asleep in bed . Shortly after 1:00 a.m. the fan-out call came from Brandon. As Joe groggily answered the phone, Elaine watched his face contort in agony. He only spoke on the phone briefly but, for one of the few times in their marriage, Elaine saw tears come into Joe's eyes. When he hung up, she said, "What's the matter?"

"There's been shots fired at the Countryside Inn," he replied. "One of our members is down. I got to get over there."

In a flash Joe had on his boots and was dressed in his civvies. With his shirt-tail hanging out, he grabbed his shotgun and service revolver and, without saying good-bye, was out of the house and into his Oldsmobile. He was gone before Elaine could tell him to be careful.

Out on the highway, O'Ray soon realized his car couldn't continue the pursuit. He had no headlights, the punctured radiator was throwing coolant up on the windshield, and besides, his left front tire was flat. He had no choice but to radio Brandon that he was giving up the chase and going back to help the wounded at the scene.

Back at the motel, Candy Smith had regained consciousness. A voice inside her head told her she didn't have to die here in the snow. It urged her to crawl and find somebody who could help save her life. Although she was in terrible pain, she began crawling along the sidewalk towards the motel office, her arms straining to pull the dead weight of her legs. Every inch she moved was agony but she was determined not to die without a fight.

When John O'Ray got back to the motel, he found Candy Smith crawling along the motel sidewalk toward the registration office. Seeing she was badly wounded, he picked her up and began putting her on the back seat of the cruiser. She was in terrible pain.

Meanwhile things began to heat up as Brandon continued its fan-out call. When they phoned Debbie MacLean at home and told her what was happening, she borrowed one of her roommates' cars and drove to the detachment office so she could pick up a cruiser and monitor what was happening on the radio. Then she headed for the Countryside Inn. On the way she passed another member, Len Gaudet, in his own car, and flagged him down. He had been driving by the Countryside Inn and saw the commotion but didn't know what was happening. Debbie told him she was going to the motel and asked him to go to the detachment office to man the radio and the phones. Gaudet agreed and they went their separate ways.

At the motel, just as John O'Ray had gotten Candy into his cruiser, Joe MacDougall came roaring into the parking lot and ran across to help him.

"I'm all right here, Joe," John said. "You go over and give Dennis a hand."

"Where is he?" Joe asked.

John pointed toward Archer's vehicle. "Over there, on the other side of the white truck." Then John climbed behind the wheel of his car and started for the Virden hospital.

Following John's directions, Joe pulled his gun and proceeded cautiously behind Archer's truck towards the place where John had indicated he would find Dennis. The acrid smell of cordite still hung in the air. As he carefully peered around the end of the truck, he saw Dennis lying face down in a pool of blood. He ran to him.

155

"Dennis! Dennis!" he called out. Checking him over, Joe found there was no pulse or body movement. His friend was cold and his eyes and mouth were open. "They've killed him," he cried, "they've killed him!" Then Joe began to weep.

Knowing his friend was a devout Roman Catholic, Joe recited an Act of Contrition over his lifeless body: Trembling inside and with tears streaming down his face he whispered, "Oh my God, I am heartily sorry for having offended thee and I detest all my sins because I dread the loss of heaven and the pains of hell . . . " With his head bowed and his eyes closed, Joe continued the prayer but towards the end his voice trailed off to a whimper.

Joe was covering Dennis' body with a blanket when Staff Sergeant Westerson arrived and took charge of the crime scene. He had already called Clem MacInnis. After telling him what had happened, he ordered him to report to the motel. Not long after Westerson arrived, Syd Barrie and Larry Keyes pulled in. They were shocked to see Dennis laying dead, face down in the snow. Westerson put Barrie in charge of the murder investigation from the Virden end. He told Keyes to keep the number of Virden personnel at the crime scene to a minimum because he knew that everyone who showed up there would probably be called to testify at the subsequent trial. He asked Clem MacInnis to be in charge of exhibits at the murder scene and to stand guard over Dennis' body.

It wasn't long before Debbie MacLean pulled into the parking lot, followed by John O'Ray who was returning from the Virden Hospital where he had taken Candy. For John the initial numbing shock of the incident was beginning to wear off and the impact of the situation was starting to sink in. He was rapidly becoming emotionally distraught. Debbie watched John as he wandered around in a daze, talking to himself. She couldn't make out everything he was saying but it was clear he was devastated by Dennis' death and horrified that Candy and Russ had been so badly injured. He kept mumbling, "I did my best . . . I tried to follow them . . . I really tried but my radiator blew up and fogged the windshield . . . I couldn't keep going." Westerson assured him that he had done the best he could but now he needed him to write up the incident while it was still fresh in his mind. He asked him to get away from the scene, go back to the detachment office and write down as many details as he could remember. He told him to start at the beginning, take his time, be as thorough and accurate as he could be and work his way through the entire incident. John departed for the office.

As he left, the medical examiner, Dr. Elliot, came on the scene. Very quickly he ascertained Onofrey's condition and determined that he was, in fact, dead. It was a particularly difficult task for him, since he also served Dennis and his wife as their family doctor. After the doctor was finished, Clem MacInnis, according to policy, was required to identify Dennis' body. He did this by tying an identification tag to the zipper of his friend's boot. This was one of the most difficult tasks he had ever been asked to perform. Dennis' face was caked with blood and the wadding from the shotgun blast was protruding from the hole in the upper portion of his storm coat. Clem's hands shook while he tried several times to thread the string from the identification tag through the eye of the zipper.

While they waited for the ambulance, Clem did a preliminary walk-through of the motel room. It still retained the bitter tang of gunpowder and a hint of cologne. There were traces of fresh hair clippings in the sink. He found Maurice Crystal's credit cards and several pieces of identification, and also identification items for several other individuals. When Clem did a cursory examination of the back of Archer's truck, among the furniture and clothing, he found a box containing albums of pornographic photos and magazines. Everything he knew about this case led him to believe that there was more to it than just a stolen vehicle.

At 1:30 a.m. the ambulance arrived but there was little for them to do. Dennis' body was to be held at the Countryside Inn until an RCMP investigator arrived from Brandon to officially release it from the crime scene. Only then it would be escorted to Winnipeg for an autopsy.

Just after the ambulance got there, Staff Sergeant Westerson told Debbie MacLean that he wanted her to go over to Paula Onofrey's and apprise her of Dennis' death. Debbie wasn't pleased with this directive. She resented it because she thought it was his job to do. But Westerson felt it was more important that he remain at the motel and manage the crime scene. His insistence that she go was frightening for Debbie because she had never done anything like that before in her life, especially to a friend. Her first instinct was to find the Onofreys' parish priest, Father Ken Foran but she quickly found he was away from town and unavailable. So Debbie turned to Doctor Elliot for support. When she asked him if he would come with her, he agreed, thinking it was a good idea considering the fact that Paula was pregnant.

Joe MacDougall drew the assignment of going to Hornseth's house to tell Kim that Russ had been shot. As soon as Kim saw Joe at the door, she knew something had happened to her husband. She held up very well as Joe told her that Russ had been wounded and was on his way to Brandon for surgery. She was devastated when she heard about Dennis and Candy Smith. Joe called the Needhams, explained the situation and asked them to come over and stay with Kim. Then he told Kim he had to go because they needed him to check out a small airport north of town to make sure it wasn't used for a getaway by the fugitives. He apologized for leaving so abruptly. Kim said she understood and they parted.

Paula Onofrey had spent an uncomfortable night trying to get to sleep. That rarely happened to her but this Sunday night she had tossed and turned and had completely awakened to see the red numbers on her bedside digital clock read 1:11 a.m. At the end of the bed she saw her husband's red serge Mountie tunic through an open door in her bedroom closet.

The uniform appeared to be coming out to meet her.

Shortly after that, the phone rang. It was Runa Dalik, the dispatcher from Brandon. She was doing her fan-out call to get some help over to the Countryside Inn and didn't know that Dennis was working that shift. She certainly had no idea that he had been killed.

"Is Dennis home yet?" Runa asked.

"No," Paula replied, "he should be home soon."

"Thanks. Sorry to bother you." The dispatcher hung up.

Paula had detected the urgency in her voice. She thought the call was curious but got back into bed and slowly fell back asleep.

When Debbie and Dr. Elliot got to Paula's house, they went around to the back. As soon as Debbie pushed the doorbell, the Onofrey's little cockipoo started yapping and scratching at the kitchen door. Debbie took a deep breath and rang again. The dog continued barking. The wait seemed interminable.

Paula, deep in sleep, faintly heard a doorbell ringing somewhere far off in her dreams. Ever so gradually the sound came closer and closer until it wakened her and she realized it was coming from her own back door. Awkwardly she struggled out of bed, put on her housecoat and opened the door. When she saw it was Debbie MacLean in uniform, her heart began to pound.

To Debbie, Paula looked confused, as if she sensed there was a problem. She opened the door and said, "Hi, Debbie, what are you doing here so late?"

Debbie stepped inside. Dr. Elliot remained on the porch out of sight.

"There's something I have to tell you."

"What?" Paula asked.

"Let's go in the living room and sit down."

Now there was a hint of dread in Paula's face. "No . . . I don't want to go inside. What's wrong, did Dennis forget something?"

"No . . . that's not it," Debbie murmured.

"Well what then? What is it? Tell me, Debbie."

"Paula, I'm so sorry. But ... there's been a shooting."

Now Paula knew it was something bad. "Oh no," she cried. "Oh no."

"I have to tell you that Dennis is gone."

At first Paula just stood there stunned and limp. Then Debbie put her arms around her and they hugged each other very firmly face to face.

Debbie whispered in her ear, "Dr. Elliot will be here in a minute."

Now Paula was crying but not hysterically. She fought her inclination to scream, to sob, to collapse. She had to be calm for the baby. She sat down on a kitchen chair and wept. Dr. Elliot stepped into the kitchen from the porch and immediately administered a hypodermic sedative that took effect very quickly. Then Debbie and the doctor helped her to the couch in the living room where she fell into a semi stupor where nothing registered. No memory, no pain.

Debbie, realizing that Paula could not be left alone like this with little Corey, went over to Orville and Eileen Sheane's. She knew how close they were to Dennis and Paula and was positive they would want to help. When Orville answered the door, Debbie said, "Hello, Orville. I'm sorry to disturb you so late but there's a problem over at the Onofreys.'

"Oh, really, " Orville answered. "What's up?"

"Can you go over there and stay with Paula and Corey for a while?"

"Sure I can. What's the problem?"

"There's been a shooting."

"What do you mean, what shooting?"

"It just happened," Debbie explained. "At the Countryside Inn."

"Really!" Orville said. "What happened over there?"

"I can't go into all the details right now . . . but . . . all I can tell you is that Dennis is gone."

Orville was puzzled. "Gone where?"

"He's been killed."

Orville stared at her with his mouth open.

"By a stranger at the motel."

The blood drained from Orville's face. His complexion went as white as his hair. "Oh my goodness, oh my goodness, " he repeated over and over.

Debbie was afraid he was going to have a heart attack. She led him to a chair and stayed with him for ten minutes or so while he told his wife. Then Orville and Eileen got ready and went to Paula.

While Archer and Malette fled down the highway, the agony he had caused was spreading like terrible ripples in the water. Further down the road more pain was yet to come.

FLIGHT

When Archer and Malette turned onto the Trans-Canada Highway in Hornseth's police cruiser, he rammed the accelerator to the floor. The car fish-tailed momentarily then roared down the road like a racing car. Archer was frantic. Every nerve in his body seemed to be throbbing and his eyes darted continuously from the road ahead to the rear view mirror. So far, there was nothing behind him but he knew it was only a matter of time.

The shot that Dorothy had taken in the back had hit her in the ribs on the right side. As the police car sped along, she moaned and made little gasping sounds because it hurt her to breathe.

Although Archer's mind was racing, he was very clear headed. He figured since it was so early in the morning and three police cars came to the motel, there wouldn't be another car on duty in the immediate area. He didn't know if the police had tried to follow them from the motel but he was sure that the cop who was firing back at him from behind the cruiser had made it to the radio and called for help. He felt positive there would be a number of police cars on their way from somewhere, probably Brandon. He knew he had only a few minutes to get rid of the police cruiser they were driving.

"We gotta ditch this thing . . . and fast."

Dorothy moaned in agreement.

Bruce kept looking for a likely place. All the houses were in darkness so he looked for a barnyard light.

After driving about five miles they went speeding past a road sign that read Routledge. Here the Trans-Canada began to take a big curve to the left.

"Good," he thought to himself, "if there's anybody behind us, they'll lose my tail-lights."

Once he finished the long sweep of the curve, he was even more relieved to see that Routledge wasn't a town or a village. The sign referred to a rural area, nothing more than a crossroad on the main highway. The last thing he wanted right now was to go through a built-up area. He needed an isolated location. As the car raced along, his eyes intensified their search for a haven.

When he spotted a yard light up on the left, it was too late to turn in. The road was covered in black ice and he couldn't slow down to make the laneway. The car shot past the house and it took Archer another 300 yards to get it to stop. Then he carefully made a U-turn and went back. From this direction he could make out a small, white frame house with several farm buildings behind it. Archer slowed the cruiser, turned right onto the laneway and parked it tight against the side porch of the house. He honked the horn several times. Then grabbing one of the police revolvers, he got out of the car, went up on the side porch and began banging on the door with his fist.

Inside the house, forty-two-year-old Dave Penny was fast asleep. The first thing that he heard was his dogs barking and then some heavy banging on the side door. Dave got out of bed and put his pants on. When he went into the living room, Archer had broken in and was standing in the living room pointing a revolver at him.

"Stand right where you are and do what you're told and you won't get hurt," Archer said calmly. "My wife's been hurt. I need you to help me carry her into the house."

Even though he wasn't sure what was happening, Dave Penny didn't attempt to argue. He tugged on his boots and followed the armed stranger out to the car. When Dave saw it was a police cruiser, he was further puzzled. However, he was immediately preoccupied with following Archer's orders and helped him to ease Dorothy gently out of the front seat. Once she was removed from the vehicle, she moaned in agony as they carried her up the steps and into the living room of the house.

Dave's eleven-year-old daughter Cherel had been sleeping on the chesterfield. Now that she was awake and saw what was going on, she started to cry.

As Penny tried to console her, Archer made things much more tense by ripping the phone off the wall.

"I've killed two policemen," he said, "and I won't hesitate to use this gun again if you don't do what I say."

Penny, a big, slow-moving man, thought it was all a bad dream. Everything was so confusing. He was too numbed to be afraid. But his daughter was terribly frightened. While he hugged her and tried to comfort her, Dave's wife, Irene, came out of the bedroom rubbing her eyes. She saw Archer and Malette armed with revolver and rifle. Irene, like her husband, was astounded.

Archer ordered the three Pennys to sit together on the couch.

Dorothy watched the proceedings momentarily, then found herself a chair. She was clearly in pain, but not quite doubled over. Dave thought she looked nervous, kind of jumpy. She sat pointing the revolver in their direction as Archer spelled out what he wanted.

Archer told them, "I don't want to hurt anyone." To Dave Penny he said, "I need your gun, some medical supplies and either your car or your truck. I got to get rid of this police car."

Dave calmly indicated he could provide them with these things.

"I also need a pair of socks," Archer said.

Dave and Irene could see he was wearing none.

"And I need a parka," Archer said, "so I can use my own coat to keep my woman here warm."

Dave's intention was to cooperate in every possible way in order to get these two fugitives out of his house and away from his family. Although Dave found Archer behaved decently with him, almost reasonably, he was wary of him. Archer made him give up the small amount of cash he had, his credit card, his rifle and the clothing he requested. Dave also offered him the keys to his pick-up truck.

Archer took the keys and said, "You're coming with us."

That sent a shiver of fear through Irene but Dave told her with his eyes that it would be all right. Dave Penny was a quiet, gentle man of the Bible who trusted in God. He didn't want to be separated from his family but he was willing to go without a fuss to get the armed intruders out of his house. Once they were away, he figured he could fend for himself.

Archer tied up Irene and Cherel with some electrical cords and left them sitting on the couch. Then Archer, Malette and Penny went out and got into the red pick-up truck. Bruce got behind the wheel and backed it out onto the highway. Then, as the truck lurched ahead on the slippery road, he lost control and it slowly drifted into the snow bank along the shoulder.

In his haste, Archer tried to gun the motor but it only made things worse and the small vehicle settled firmly into the deep snow of the ditch. With the seconds ticking away in his brain, Archer knew they didn't have time to dig the truck out.

"Let's go," he said. "We got to use the police car."

The two men helped Malette back into the house and Archer devised a new plan. Dorothy would stay and hold a gun on Irene and Cherel, while he and Dave went to get another vehicle from a neighboring farm. Dorothy sat in a chair in the living room with a revolver in one hand and a shotgun in the other.

"Don't be afraid to use them dear," Archer told her.

"No dear," Malette replied. "Don't worry."

Penny didn't like the idea of leaving his wife and daughter with this armed woman, but he had no choice. Archer followed him outside with a rifle and together they climbed into Hornseth's cruiser and went looking for a side road where they could swap it for another car.

Meanwhile in the Virden Hospital, Dr. Alan Nixon had patched up Russ Hornseth's facial wounds. He could see that extensive damage had been done to his eye and planned to transport him to Brandon General where they had more sophisticated equipment and where Russ could be seen by their specialists. He had no sooner finished dressing Hornseth's face when John O'Ray brought in Candy Smith. Her wounds were much more serious. Nixon knew it would be touch and go to save her life. Immediately, he ordered that intravenous lines be started in all four of her extremities to prevent the danger of vascular collapse from blood loss. Both Russ and Candy were fortunate with the initial treatment they received from Dr. Nixon. He was particularly effective in dealing with their injuries because of his training. Before coming to Canada, he had gained comprehensive experience with gunshot wounds as a medical resident in his native Belfast.

As he cleaned and packed Candy's wounds, he ordered an ambulance to take both of them to Brandon General Hospital, where she could receive critical major surgery as soon as possible. The doctor also directed a Virden nurse go along to care for them in the ambulance.

With everybody in the Emergency Room on the run, Hornseth and Smith were put on board the ambulance and within minutes it was pulling out of Virden, siren screaming. A few miles down the road it roared by Dave Penny's tranquil farm. Inside the house sat Dorothy Malette with a police revolver trained on a frightened Irene Penny and her trembling daughter, Cherel.

164

As the ambulance wailed through the night, the nurse hovered over Candy Smith repeatedly telling her, "Hang on, you're going to make it. Just hang on. Hang on!" Further east at Griswold the ambulance had to stop for an RCMP roadblock that had already been set up on the highway. The ambulance driver told the police that he had the two wounded officers on board and was heading for Brandon General. The police insisted they had to check the back. When they saw Hornseth still in his uniform pants and the nurse working on Candy, they were convinced. Slamming the back door, one of them yelled to the driver, "OK, get going."

By now Runa Dalik at the Brandon telecom centre had been advised that the female fugitive at the Countryside Inn had been wounded. In response, she called the emergency wards of all the little hospitals in the surrounding area—Wawanesa, Souris, Reston and Virden—to warn them the fugitives might come seeking medical attention. Runa also asked each hospital to call their doctors at home and advise them of the situation. None of the doctors in the area was to respond to an emergency call without first notifying the RCMP in Brandon.

About this same time in Winnipeg, Rose Onofrey was sound asleep in her small apartment when she heard a knocking at her door. Rose looked at her clock and saw that it was after 2:00. The knocking persisted so Rose got up to answer it. As she walked to the door, she was sure someone had the wrong apartment.

"Who is it?" she called.

"Is this the apartment of Mrs. Rose Onofrey?"

"Yes," Rose answered. "Who's there?"

"It's a police officer."

When Rose heard him say that she knew something had happened to her son.

"What happened to Dennis?" she asked, her voice in pain.

"Can you open the door, Mrs. Onofrey, please?"

Rose's hand was shaking as she undid the chain and the lock. When the door was open, she asked again, "What happened to Dennis?"

"I'm sorry to have to tell you this but there's been a shooting . . . Dennis has been killed."

Such a rush of terror gripped her that she became unaware of time and space. Her mind focused on only one possibility. This must be a bad dream. If she tried hard enough she could wake up and it would all go away. But it didn't happen. She collapsed in her chair and sobbed. The visiting policeman tried to soothe her but she didn't hear a word he said. She was numb. She couldn't think; she couldn't act. It would be over an hour before she could function, to call Jerry and her mother and her brother Stan. With that late night knock on her door, she felt as if her life had ended.

While Rose sat grieving, Archer was busy trying to find another car as quickly as possible. The farm that he decided to stop at was only a quarter of a mile away from Penny's place. It belonged to fifty-eight-year-old Wally Graham and his wife Irene. After pulling into the laneway, Archer followed Penny to the Graham's front door. When Wally Graham answered the door in his pajamas, Penny said to him, "We've got big trouble over at my house, Wally. Please do what this man says."

"I'm with the police," Archer said. "I need to search your house."

Wally saw the stranger was packing both a rifle and a revolver so he let him in. Archer did a cursory search of the house. Then he came out into the living room and said, "I've shot two police officers and my wife is badly hurt. I have to have a vehicle to get out of here."

Wally Graham tried not to show how upset he was. His wife, Irene, began to cry.

"There's a big car out in the garage and I want it," said Archer.

"That's the Chrysler and I don't have the keys to it," Graham lied.

"Don't give me that baloney," Archer said.

Wally stood firm. "I'm telling you the keys aren't here."

They argued briefly but Bruce was satisfied when Wally offered him the ignition keys to his 1971 Renault. Penny was told to wait in the living room. Then Archer destroyed the phone lines and tied Wally's hands behind his back and his feet to a table leg in the dining room. Archer ordered Irene Graham into the bedroom. There he tied her up and left her lying on the bed. In the process of doing this, a telephone fell from the bookcase headboard and grazed Irene's skull.

Archer patted her head and apologized.

"That must have hurt," he said. "I'm sorry."

The vulnerable positions the Grahams were in heightened their fear. They had no idea what this man would do to them but

166

remembering stories in the newspapers of intruders and the terrible things they did to their captives, the Grahams feared for the worst.

Then that strange pair of men, Penny the gentle farmer and Archer the violent fugitive, left the house as quickly as they came. Archer parked the police cruiser inside Graham's garage, waved his rifle at Dave and told him to get in the other car and drive, then slipped in beside him. At first neither of them could figure out how to turn the headlights on but once they did, they pulled out of the garage and headed back to Penny's place.

As soon as they left, Irene Graham untied herself and then her husband. Cautiously Wally went out to see if the intruders had left. He was surprised to find a police cruiser in his garage; his Renault was gone. He and Irene got dressed and waited five minutes or so to make sure the gunman wasn't lurking somewhere around the house. Then they got in their Chrysler and drove to the Virden RCMP detachment office. When they got there, Wally still had green electrical cord wrapped around one of his wrists. They reported Archer's whereabouts to Constable Len Gaudet who relayed the information to Brandon. With this valuable information, the NCO in charge at Brandon began to give the dispatcher orders on where to set up the police road blocks. By then, every working RCMP member in both Virden and Brandon had been wakened and sent out on the road. Their manhunt was now focused on the area between Virden and the area east to Oak Lake.

While Archer and Penny were at Graham's place, Malette discovered there were two other people in the Penny household. One was seventeen year old Cindy Penny who was sleeping in a bedroom. The other was a family friend, twenty year old Derrick Chippeway who was sleeping in another room. They had remained concealed until Archer and Dave Penny left. When they came into the room, Dorothy made them sit down. She told them she had a hunk of lead in her.

Brandishing the revolver in their direction, Dorothy said, "If I faint, you two will be the first to go. We've already shot three cops and I'm not afraid to use this. We have nothing to lose."

Derrick attempted to make pleasant conversation with her but she would have none of it and cut him off. Her manner made everyone fearful.

By the time Archer and his hostage got back to Penny's farm,

167

things had become more complicated. Not only were there two more captives to contend with but Dorothy's pain was much more severe. There was little colour left in her face and Archer was concerned about her condition. He knew he had to get her to a doctor. After tying Cindy and Chippeway up like the others, he and Dorothy discussed their next move. One of the things they considered was getting her to the Brandon General Hospital. Archer rejected that because if they tried to get in there, he knew they'd be caught for sure. He decided that somehow they had to find a country doctor to patch her up.

As they talked, Dave and Irene Penny wondered what they would do with their family. Neither of them really feared Bruce Archer. He didn't seem to be a cruel person and it was obvious that he didn't want to hurt anyone. At times he even appeared to be apologetic to his captives. It was Dorothy who appeared to be mean and hard. It might have been because she was suffering physical distress but, nevertheless, the Pennys were afraid of her. When she gave orders with the gun, she snarled. Chippeway didn't like the way she brandished her revolver.

Finally Bruce and Dorothy made up their minds that they were going to search for a place to call out a country doctor. They shocked Dave Penny when they told him they were going to take some hostages with them.

"Your wife and the young girl are coming with us," Archer said.

Dave felt sick inside. His worst fears were coming true. "No. Please don't do that," he begged. "Please take me instead."

At first Archer wouldn't agree to Dave's suggestion. But the tranquil farmer continued to reason and plead with Archer, especially about his daughter. Archer seemed sensitive to Dave's concerns where the young girl's safety was involved. Dave suspected that Archer might have a daughter of his own. Finally Archer consented to his request. He knew he didn't have time to waste. With the cops closing in he had to get moving. In a matter of minutes he, Dorothy and Penny were on their way. It was 2:45 a.m.

Just before they left Penny's place, two members of the RCMP went rolling past the Penny farm in an unmarked cruiser. One of these policeman was Corporal Ken Bullock, an Ident officer from Brandon, who was on his way to the murder scene at the motel. As he and his partner drove past the farm, they noticed Penny's red pick-up truck stuck in the snow of the ditch. They speculated that the truck might have something to do with the fugitives' escape and wondered if they should stop and look into it. After a brief conversation they decided it was highly unlikely and pushed on to the Countryside Inn where Bullock knew there was a big job to do.

As Archer's vehicle sped through the night, he tried to think his way through the problem he had created. He was sure that the cop who had fired at him from the police cruiser at the motel had made a radio call for help. That meant by now the police would be out in force and on the chase. Suspecting they would set up roadblocks on the Trans-Canada Highway, he had ordered Dave to head south on the back roads. As Dave drove, Archer kept his shotgun on him. Dorothy was piled uncomfortably in the back seat of the small Renault.

Dave Penny was tremendously relieved to have them out of his house. Only when they got a fair distance away from it did he think of jumping out of the car and trying to make a run for it.

Archer almost read his mind.

"If you're thinking of jumping, don't try it."

That was the last of Penny's thoughts about escaping. He knew it would have been very unwise because he had noticed how easily Archer handled his gun. He was obviously very good with it. Besides, if he jumped out of the car, he would be a sitting duck for Archer's rifle. There was nowhere for him to hide in the open snow-covered fields. Dave made up his mind that he was with them for the duration even though he had no idea what these two desperate people might do.

Archer broke the silence by saying to him, "We gotta find a place to hole up."

Penny nodded that he understood.

The first place they turned into was no good. It was a trailer home on a permanent foundation and it was too low to suit Archer. He wanted a "double decker" house where he could defend himself from upstairs. Further down the road he spotted one and they drove in to examine it.

It was no good either because it was a frame place.

"I need a sound two-storey stone house," he told Penny.

Obviously Archer was thinking of a standoff. When Dave heard he and Dorothy make a pact with each other to save two bullets for themselves, he was convinced that Archer was ready to shoot it out with the police. They were prepared to kill themselves rather than surrender.

As the trio searched the back roads for a place to hide, a key figure in their future, Corporal Gerry Coulter, was being wakened in his bed in Brandon. On the phone was the section NCO, Staff Sergeant Don McDonald.

"Gerry," McDonald said, "one of our members in Virden, Dennis Onofrey, has been murdered at a motel out there. I want you to come into the office as soon as possible. We're sending you to Virden to investigate the homicide."

It was stunning news to Coulter but, remaining composed, he replied, "OK Don, I'll be right in." Still groggy from his interrupted sleep, Coulter packed his shaving kit and an extra change of clothes and departed for Virden at 3:00 a.m.

McDonald had made the right choice. Although Coulter was only thirty-one, he had twelve years experience on the Force in a wide variety of postings that had prepared him well for his work. Low key and meticulously thorough, Coulter was a wily investigator who would prove to be a major factor in the drama that was unfolding.

About the same time that Coulter got the phone call, Vivian Barrie was arriving at Paula Onofrey's. When Syd Barrie left for the Countryside Inn, Fred Westerson had called Vivian back and told her that Dennis had been killed and Candy and Russ were badly wounded. Vivian immediately volunteered to go over to Paula's. She was prepared to stay with her as long as necessary. Paula was resting comfortably now but there were worse times ahead and Vivian was determined to see her through it.

Meanwhile Archer and company were continuing to search for a place to hole up on the back roads east of Virden. Suddenly, he came upon a farm that he thought would suit his purposes. About six miles south of the village of Oak Lake he spotted a large beige sign at the side of the road that advertised *Pleasant Dawn Farms— Polled Shorthorns, Registered Charolais*. The sign also indicated this was the home of Lloyd and Wilma Hatch. Archer nudged Penny and indicated he should turn in here.

Archer had no way of knowing but he was driving into the farm of a highly respected cattle farmer who was known for his iron will and his stubborn ways. Lloyd Hatch was not a man who would readily accept people bursting into his home in the middle of the night. At sixty-three-years-of age, Hatch was still trim and stood ramrod straight. He owned one of the most successful cattle farms in the Oak Lake region. It sat on 1600 acres of grazing land and produced some of the finest purebreds in the province. Lloyd was so good at what he did that he was often chosen to judge cattle at agricultural fairs cross the country. He was not a man to trifle with.

Penny carefully steered the car down his laneway. It was 300 yards long, curving through almost a quarter section of land towards the nest of buildings and trees that made up the farmstead. Once they pulled up in front of the house, Archer sprinted to the front door and opened it. Lloyd Hatch never locked his doors at night. None of his family had since the time his grandfather built the house in 1882. No one had bothered the home in all the years since then.

This would be the first time. As quickly as possible, Archer felt his way through the furniture in the living room and headed up the stairs where he knew the bedrooms would be. He went into the Hatch's room and turned on the light. When Lloyd Hatch opened his eyes and sat up, he saw Archer standing in his bedroom doorway with a gun in his hand. It was 3:20 a.m.

"There's been an accident and my wife's been hurt," Archer said.

Lloyd pulled on his pants and Wilma put on her housecoat and they followed him downstairs where they found Dorothy sitting on the couch and Dave standing nearby. It took Lloyd and Wilma a while to understand that Dave was a hostage of the other two.

Archer told them, "I've been in trouble with the police and I've shot two cops." Then he showed them the two service revolvers he had taken from the police.

"Sit down," he said to Lloyd Hatch. "I want to talk to you."

"I don't care what you do, you can tell me while I'm standing up," Hatch replied defiantly.

Wilma could see from the look in her husband's eyes that there could be trouble between him and Archer. She knew Lloyd could be feisty when he was pushed too far. He was a tough, old farmer and he wouldn't sit down, not even for a stranger with a gun. Archer measured his defiance and let him remain standing.

The confrontation made Dave Penny very uneasy. He saw that

Hatch wasn't afraid of Archer and was concerned that the big farmer might get the gunman riled up and precipitate something. Dave deplored violence. One of the reasons that he had ruled out trying to jump Archer was that he felt Archer was so desperate he wouldn't give up until someone killed him. As big and strong as Dave Penny was, he knew he could never bring himself to kill another human being, including Archer.

Wilma Hatch wasn't afraid of Archer but she too recognized that he was desperate. He told her he wanted to get himself and his female companion out of the country as soon as possible. As he stomped around the room, he said, "I'll kill five or six more cops if I have to. I've killed now and it doesn't make any difference."

Wilma didn't think he was crazy or anything like that, but he did seem very agitated. He never stopped talking and she wondered if he was high on drugs.

All through his diatribe, Archer kept up a constant harangue against the Mounties. He said he hated the police, especially the way they treated him when he was in jail. At that Wilma quietly moved a vase of flowers in front of their son Fred's picture on the table. It showed him dressed in the red serge of the RCMP.

"Who's the local doctor?" Bruce demanded. "Call the doctor and get him out here."

"No," Lloyd replied. "I'm not calling the doctor. Not at this time of night. He's not going to come out here."

"What's his name?" Archer demanded.

"His name is Scherz. He's an elderly fellow. He doesn't even make house calls. I'm telling you he won't come out here at this time of night."

"Get on the phone and give him a try," Archer insisted.

"No, I won't," Lloyd said. "If you want to call him, call him yourself . . . but I'm not doing it."

Archer's eyes flashed angrily back and forth between Dorothy and Hatch. He could plainly see that Lloyd was not going to budge.

Sensing Archer's loss of momentum, Hatch went further and tried to convince Bruce to surrender. "Why don't you give yourself up? You'll never get away with it. Why don't you just give up?"

Archer wouldn't listen. "I've been to prison and I'm not ever going back. I'm going to go out fighting."

In the middle of their argument, a young hired hand name Ralph Molderink came up from his sleeping quarters in the basement. He'd been awakened by the loud voices.

"Go back downstairs, Ralph," Hatch ordered, trying to protect the boy.

Molderink did as he was told. Without a word, he turned around and went back down the stairs. Strangely enough Archer let him go without any bother because, at this time, his primary attention was diverted to Dorothy. The pain was starting to get to her and she was moaning.

"Oh my God, I feel awful," she said.

Penny said to Archer, "I know where the doctor's office is. Let's drive her in there."

Archer thought it over briefly. He knew it was the right thing to do. But Wally Graham's Renault was too small and uncomfortable for her.

"What kind of car have you got?" he asked Lloyd.

Lloyd was now prepared to cooperate with him, anything to get him out of his house. "There's a 1975 Pontiac outside in my garage. You can use that."

Archer pointed his revolver at Lloyd and Dave. "You two come outside with me and help me get it out of the garage. If we get it out, we'll leave here and I'll leave you both alone."

Before they left the house, Archer gave his wife a gun. "Keep them quiet," he said. "Use the gun if you have to."

"Don't worry, honey, I will." There was a fearful intensity in Malette's voice and in her eyes. The Hatches had no doubt that she would shoot. While the men were gone, the two women had little to say to each other. At one point Malette moaned and grunted, "God, I'm in awful pain." A little later she said, "You have lovely furniture. I hope I'm not getting blood all over your chesterfield."

To Dave Penny, the two fugitives seemed like a strange combination. Archer appeared to be the leader and Dorothy his devoted follower, yet, even though Archer was the one who made the decisions and gave the orders, Dorothy appeared to be the strength behind him. Alone Archer seemed to have a soft side and Dave felt he could talk to him and reason with him. But Bruce suddenly became harder and more difficult when Dorothy was with him. Penny felt a lot safer when Bruce and Dorothy were apart.

"Let's go," he said and the three men went outside.

When Corporal Gerry Coulter arrived at the Brandon RCMP office, there was tremendous activity in the building. The phones were ringing, members carrying shotguns were coming and going, some in plain clothes like Coulter, others in uniform. The dog master and his animal were pacing about, waiting for orders. Coulter was told that they knew the killer had taken a police car but, as yet, it hadn't been located.

The Brandon radio operator, Runa Dalik, was busy calling every member of the Virden and Brandon detachments in for duty. Repeatedly Coulter heard her use the phrase "one of our members has been killed." Besides the calls to members, the operator was taking direction from Staff Sergeant Ken Elliot who was setting up the roadblocks and coordinating the manhunt. Before long she would be calling members from neighbouring detachments to assist in the search. Dozens of heavily armed police would be involved. When daylight came, helicopters and assault teams would be brought into action. Although no one knew Archer's whereabouts, they were convinced it would just be a matter of time before they ran him down. They were very determined to do just that.

Archer didn't have a chance of escaping. It may or may not be true that the Mounties always get their man but it is a fact that the Mounties always get the man who got a Mountie. In that one self-indulgent moment, when Archer killed a member of the RCMP, he had brought down the wrath of God on himself. He was about to find that out.

At Hatch's place Archer helped the other two get Lloyd's car out of the garage. Then all three of them went back to the house. As soon as they got inside, Archer said he wanted some money. He asked Lloyd where he kept his wallet and the farmer told him it was upstairs. When Archer found it, he brought it back down and started to rifle through it. As he did, Hatch said with disgust, "Just take the money and leave the rest of the stuff alone."

Once again Archer complied. Then he tore out the phones and began tying everyone up including the hired hand, Molderink, whom Archer had summoned from the basement. As Archer tied them up, he made Lloyd and Molderink lie down on the living room floor. Wilma was tied up sitting in a chair.

174

While working on Lloyd, Archer struggled with the nylon rope. "I'm not a professional at this," Archer said. Lloyd could tell that he wasn't and held his hands apart so that he could slip the bonds off quickly once Archer was gone.

"This is pretty uncomfortable for people our age," Lloyd complained.

"All right," Archer agreed. Then to Penny he said, "Pass me those pillows." Archer tucked them under Lloyd and Molderink's heads.

When Bruce was tying up Ralph Molderink, he even gave the young labourer a lecture on the evils of drugs and debt. Archer used his own fugitive circumstances as a dramatic example to underline his text.

Then Dave and Bruce carried Dorothy out the door and put her into Hatch's car. Archer went back and took Lloyd's .30/30 rifle, his 12-gauge shotgun and all the ammunition he could carry and started to return to the car. As he was going out the door Lloyd Hatch called to him and asked him to turn off the water that had been running in the sink and then added one more thing.

"Close the door when you leave."

"I will," he said. "But don't get too comfortable. If I have any trouble, I'll be back." Then he closed the door and moments later the three in the house heard the other three drive away.

What Archer didn't realize was that the Hatch's son, Tully, and his wife Arlene lived across the yard on the same homestead. Tully had heard his German shepherd barking when the fugitive car drove in but he didn't think much of it. Tully and his dad had just butchered a cattle beast the day before out behind the trees. They had tied it to the bucket of a front-end loader, killed it, skinned it, gutted it and then cut up the carcass in the implement shed. The internal organs had been thrown into a forty-gallon drum and left in the shed. This tended to attract coyotes and Tully thought his young dog was barking to scare them off. Later he did hear a car drive out of the yard but he wasn't alarmed by that either.

He did, however, wake up and get moving when he heard his dad banging on his front door, yelling for him to wake up. When Tully let him in, Lloyd told him the whole story from beginning to end as quickly as he could. He ended with, "The guy said `If I have any trouble, I'll be back.'" Since the phone lines to both their houses were out of service, Lloyd told him to take his snowmobile

175

and get to a phone so he could call the police and advise them of Archer's whereabouts. It was now 3:30 a.m.

Tully dressed as fast as he could, got on his snowmobile and raced over to Wayne Heape's place, the first farm to the north. It was easy traveling on that bright, moonlit night. After getting Wayne out of bed, Tully went through the story with him, adding that Archer was "a crazy man who says he'll come back if there's any trouble."

Heape handed Tully the phone and he called Brandon RCMP. The call was taken by Staff Sergeant Don McDonald. Tully went over his dad's story once again and advised McDonald that Archer was on his way to Dr. Scherz' place in Oak Lake with a hostage. From there, under Staff Sergeant McDonald's direction, the great police dragnet began to close in on Archer and Malette and their captive passenger. At 4:14 a.m. a description of Hatch's vehicle and the fugitives' intended destination was broadcast to all working police vehicles in the Brandon Sub-Division.

After Tully Hatch got off the phone to the police, he jumped on his snowmobile and roared back to his house. Then he and his father got out Tully's rifles and stood guard, in case Archer came back as he had threatened.

Back at the Countryside Inn, Corporal Gerry Coulter was just arriving to do his investigation. His primary job was to make notes on the crime the scene and to preserve whatever evidence that was there. He immediately observed that there were a few people on the scene, such as an RCMP officer who was home in Virden visiting his family, who had no business being there. He pointed this out to Westerson and the Staff Sergeant ordered them to leave.

Ken Bullock was busy photographing the crime scene both inside and outside the motel. His most gruesome task was taking pictures of Dennis' lifeless body. It was doubly difficult for him because Ken knew Dennis personally and his death brought back horrible memories of Ken himself being shot. A few years back in Minnedosa, Manitoba, a disturbed teenager had shot Ken from a distance with a rifle. The bullet tore through his cheek and exited out the back of his neck. The same night this happened, the teenager turned his gun on himself and died.

Although Bullock was off work for months and lost some hearing as a result of his wound, he had, by now, put the experience behind him. The sight of Dennis prostrate in the snow brought it all back and reminded him of the dangers of the job. He was equally disturbed when he photographed Candy's fur hat and her gloves lying beside another deep red blotch on the motel sidewalk. As Bullock took his pictures, Gerry Coulter made notes on everything of significance. Outside the motel he had found Hornseth's flashlight, several shotgun wads, the fur hat and gloves of Candy Smith. A blood trail traced Hornseth's movement from the car to the corner of the motel to the frontage road. The only two vehicles in the parking lot besides the hearse from Carscadden's Funeral Home in Virden and the Ident car were trucks belonging to Archer and Melia and Schmidt. The wall around the door to room 20 was pocked with bullet marks.

For continuity of evidence, Coulter had Clem MacInnis, who had been standing guard over Dennis' body, identify the corpse to Brandon Constable Gary Harrison so it could be removed from the scene. At 3:25 a.m. Harrison climbed on board the hearse to escort the body to Deer Lodge Hospital in Winnipeg for autopsy.

Inside the motel, Coulter and Bullock found the room a mess. There was a bullet hole in the door and two holes in the wall. Ten 20-gauge shotgun shell casings were scattered on the floor. The gun cases for Archer's rifles were near the bed. It appeared that almost everything the occupants owned was still there: two open suitcases, clothes hanging on the coat rack, women's undergarments, socks hanging to dry on the bureau drawer, Archer's eye glass case, toilet items, deodorant, pop cans, chocolate bars. It was obvious they left in a hurry. Coulter noted that when he entered the room the lights were off, the front window was open and the screen had been slashed with a sharp object. Two hunting knives were found along the base of the front inside wall. There was also a can of white spray paint that Coulter turned over to Ident for fingerprints. Corporal Coulter's investigation took more than four hours to complete. Bullock's photography work kept him on the scene for over twenty-four hours.

As the police were investigating the motel, Archer, Malette and Penny were racing north to Dr. Scherz' place. As they drove, Dave Penny tried to talk to Dorothy about the Lord. She looked so pale and drawn, it appeared to Dave she might die and he believed if Dorothy were to die the way she was, she would go to hell. Dave told her he had found Jesus some fifteen years ago, when he was twenty-seven. Not only did he want to comfort her and share the love and warmth he felt from God, he told her that he was truly concerned for her immortal soul.

Dorothy's only response was anger. "Don't preach to me," she gasped between moans.

Archer softened this with, "Just get us to the Doc's house, Dave."

They rode in silence for a while until Dorothy asked, "If the cops catch up with us, will you shoot it out with them?"

"Yes," Bruce replied. "I'm not going back to jail."

"If that happens," she went on, "I want you to kill me first. I don't want to live without you."

"If it comes to that, I will," he said flatly over the drone of the motor.

Again there was silence, everyone thinking their own thoughts. All of them knew the net around them was tightening. Within minutes they were in the tiny village of Oak Lake driving along North Railway Street beside the Canadian Pacific Railroad tracks which ran through the heart of the community.

"I know it's along here somewhere," Dave said. "Maybe another block or two."

As they came to the corner of Second Avenue, Dave spotted the doctor's gray insul-brick two-storey house. "That's it," he said, "his office is around the back."

"What door do we use?" Archer asked as he turned left down Second Ave.

"The side door, I guess," Dave answered. He pointed down a sidewalk that ran from the doctor's car-port to the office. The walkway had been shovelled clean and snow was piled high on either side of it. "That one there."

Archer pulled the car over. All three of them studied the house.

"All right," Archer said to Penny, "let's get her in to the doctor."

OAK LAKE

Oak Lake is located just south of the Trans-Canada Highway about one third of the way between Virden and Brandon. It's a quiet little village with a population of 360 that straddles the same CPR main line that runs through Virden. In 1978 one of the few amenities it offered was the services of a Polish-born physician named Markus Scherz. He received his medical degree from the University of Brussels in 1941. After the Second World War he was awarded a citation for his service with the Belgian Resistance. Enduring great hardship he emigrated to Canada in 1951 and struggled to obtain his medical licence and hospital privileges in Manitoba.

At sixty-three, bespectacled, balding and slight of stature, he looked like a kindly, old gentleman. But with his blunt manner and abrupt approach, he was sometimes judged to be arrogant and difficult by the villagers. Although the little doctor accepted anyone who came to his door for help, many in Oak Lake had not fully accepted him and would only go to see him in an emergency. Most of Dr. Scherz' practice was made up of natives who came to him from the Sioux Valley Reserve ten miles northeast of the village. He got along well with the natives who had great faith and trust in him. Only twenty percent of his practice came from people in the village and local farmers. These folks found that once they got past his gruff exterior, there was a conscientious and caring person wanting to help them.

Stefanie Scherz, in contrast to her husband, was friendly, refined and gentle. She was highly regarded by her friends and neighbours. Certainly her appearance was pleasant, strong eyes peering out from behind spectacles worn over chubby cheeks and a ready smile. She too was of European extraction and, although she had been in Canada for almost thirty years, she still retained the slightest hint of a German accent.

Dr. Scherz had not been warned by the Virden Hospital about Malette needing medical attention because they knew he was semi-retired and didn't want to disturb him so early in the morning.

179

Scherz and his wife slept soundly in their room, unaware of the shattering experience that was about to envelope them.

When Archer and company pulled into the doctor's carport, it was 4:20 am. After Dave Penny turned off the ignition, he and Archer locked hands and made a chair with their arms to carry the heavy, wounded woman to the side door. Archer banged on it loudly and in a few moments a light came on upstairs.

As Archer was rousing the doctor from his bed, the RCMP were quietly and cautiously making their way into Oak Lake in unmarked cruisers. The first to arrive was Staff Sergeant Bart Hawkins, the west section NCO out of Brandon Sub-Division who was in charge of this district. Riding with him was Fred Westerson from Virden. The two senior Mounties had been tracking the fugitives' car for miles.

After Wally Graham reported Archer's break-in at his farm to Len Gaudet in Virden, Gaudet relayed this information to all units. Hawkins heard Gaudet's report at the Countryside Inn. He had raced to the motel from Brandon, his trunk loaded with shotguns, rifles, heavy duty vests and tear gas. After hearing Gaudet's radio message, he and Westerson decided to go to Graham's place and see what they could find out. They discovered that Graham's Renault made a distinctive narrow tire mark in the snow and decided to follow it. Their pursuit was slow-going because they occasionally lost the car's tracks in the blowing snow but they managed to follow them back to Penny's place. From there the car's tracks went south. Hawkins and Westerson thought the fugitives might be heading for the hospital at Souris.

They followed the tracks as far as Oak Lake Beach, a small resort area on Oak Lake well south of the village of Oak Lake. It was here they heard, as a result of Tully Hatch's phone call to Brandon, that Archer was heading for Dr. Scherz' place in the village. They raced for the doctor's home but when they got to the village, didn't know where his house was located. Using his radio, Hawkins asked for directions. Debbie MacLean came on the radio and, since Dr. Scherz was her personal physician, she was able to give them directions.

Dr. Scherz was accustomed to being wakened in the middle of the night but he never came to like it. As he worked his way downstairs, Archer kept banging on the door.

*Lloyd and Wilma
Hatch
in 1978
demonstrating
how they were
tied up by
Bruce Archer*

The Brandon Sun

Candy Smith's grad photo from Depot, taken six weeks before the shootout

Dr. Markus Scherz

The Brandon Sun

Dave Penny in 1987

Dr. Scherz' house, car port and garage in Oak Lake, taken during the siege

RCMP aerial photo of Oak Lake

Oakland Hotel

Bert Fuller's

Dr. Scherz'

the Command Center

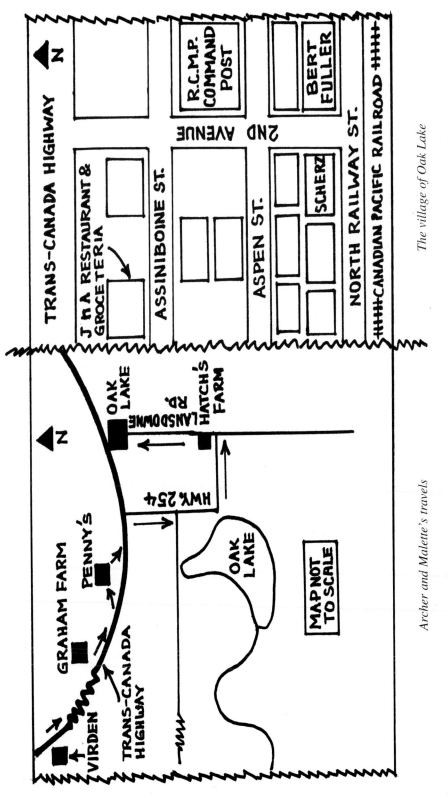

The village of Oak Lake

Archer and Malette's travels

Sketches by Peter Fillman

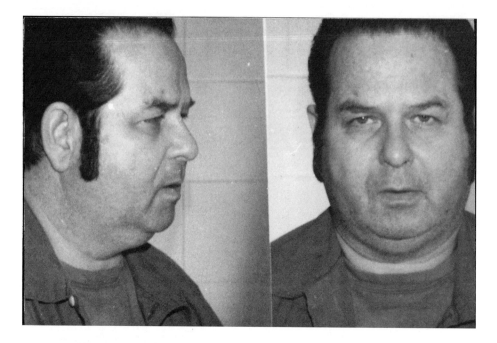

Herbert Bruce Archer at the time of his arrest

Archer's arsenal at the time of his surrender

RCMP Cpl.
Gerry Coulter
in 1987

Bruce Archer
in
Warkworth
Penitentiary,
1989

Photo by
John Shoveller

Rose Onofrey holding a portrait of her son

Photo by Robert Knuckle

Troop 27's graduation program from Depot Division. Dennis Onofrey's signature is in the top left corner

Courtesy of Sgt. Gerard Hebson

"What do you want?" Scherz called out in a strong voice behind the locked door.

"My wife is badly injured," Archer replied.

"Take her to a hospital," the doctor said.

"She's bleeding to death," Archer yelled.

There was a silent pause and the door opened.

"Well, bring her in and I'll have a look at her."

As Hawkins and Westerson eased their way along North Railway Street, they came upon a second police cruiser that was searching for the doctor's house. In that car was dog master Corporal John Coagie with his police service dog Buzz. Within minutes all three men spotted the doctor's residence. Both cars drove by quietly. When they were well past the house, Fred Westerson got out and went back to survey the scene. After he identified Lloyd Hatch's car in the doctor's carport, he returned to the cruiser and confirmed Archer's presence at Scherz' place to Brandon telecom. Under Bart Hawkins' direction, police cruisers began to secure the roads leading into Oak Lake. It was 4:33 a.m.

Stefanie Scherz stood watching in the doorway of her husband's examining room as the men got Malette up on the examination table. Then, while the doctor checked her over, Archer gave Malette a hand gun and went back out to the car.

Both Dr. Scherz and his wife were puzzled by this but the doctor continued his examination. When Malette asked for something for the pain, the doctor refused to give it to her because of the severity of her bleeding.

"What happened here?" Dr. Scherz asked. "This woman has been shot. It's a very bad injury."

Neither Malette nor Penny answered.

When Archer came back into the surgery with several rifles, the doctor knew something was terribly wrong.

"What is going on?" he asked in his clipped European accent.

"My wife has been shot by an RCMP. I think I shot one of them."

"What do you need guns for?" Stefanie demanded from the doorway.

"Because they're coming after us right now."

"Well, don't point your guns at us," she insisted.

At that point Archer took some white surgical tape and indicated he was going to tie up the doctor's hands.

"What are you doing?" Scherz demanded. "I am a doctor. You want me to look after your wife or don't you want me to look after her?"

Archer reconsidered and Scherz continued his examination.

"She needs surgery in a specialized place," Scherz advised.

"I want you to treat her here," Archer insisted.

"No, I can't. You might need an x-ray, blood transfusion, an intensive care unit." He explained that Malette was bleeding internally and that she needed a surgeon and the sophisticated technology of a major hospital like Brandon General. Denied this treatment, the doctor said she would be dead within two hours. Dr. Scherz insisted she be taken to a hospital.

Archer knew the doctor was right and began to make preparations to get her back into the car so that he and Penny could take her to the hospital. The doctor disagreed with this plan. He suggested that she should be taken by ambulance. He said Archer could remain at Scherz' until he found out how she was doing. This way she would receive immediate medical attention from the drivers and, for Archer, there would not be the danger of another confrontation with the police.

"Let me call the local ambulance," the doctor urged.

"No, just a minute, Archer replied. "I got to think this over."

While Archer was contemplating this problem, the police presence was thickening in the village. At 5:00 a.m., a thirty-year-old railroad employee by the name of Donald Gomph was leaving home for the long drive to his job site in Saskatchewan. Donald lived with his parents, Edith and Elmer Gomph, on a 460 acre farm located on the eastern fringe of the village about three blocks from Dr. Scherz' residence. As Donald drove his car to the bottom of the farm laneway, he was brought to a stop by a solitary policeman in an RCMP cruiser.

After both parties identified themselves, the officer asked, "Is there a private telephone line going into your parents' house?"

"Yes, there is," Donald replied. "Why, what's going on?"

"I can't say very much right now," the officer responded, "but thanks for your help." Then he added, "You can go ahead on to work now." The policeman turned away and got back into his cruiser.

By 5:30 a.m. the Gomph farmhouse was swarming with thirty uniformed RCMP who had received permission to use the house as a temporary headquarters for their operation. None of the police were from the Virden Detachment. A decision had been made to keep them away from Dr. Scherz' place because of the emotional trauma they were suffering related to Dennis' death and the wounding of their two colleagues. There was little chance that one of them would snap and do something erratic, but the RCMP didn't want to take any chances. Besides, many of them were busy helping out at the murder scene and those who weren't had their hands full policing the detachment.

At Scherz' place Archer had made up his mind that he wanted Malette to get medical treatment in a hospital. However, after she was treated, he wanted her released from the hospital and returned to him so they could escape together. To accomplish this, he called the Virden Detachment where he spoke to Constable Len Gaudet. Identifying himself as Donald Archer, he advised he had three hostages at Scherz' place in Oak Lake. He said he was sick of fighting and would kill his wife, the hostages and himself if the police stormed the doctor's house. "I know I've shot two cops and I'm concerned about them. I have six guns and a number of rounds of ammunition. Don't push me, my number is up," he said. He also said he wanted a chance to negotiate with the "Chief of Police of Manitoba." He asked Gaudet to send an ambulance for his wife.

Len Gaudet told him he would have someone in authority call him back at the doctor's residence. When Gaudet hung up, he did not act on Archer's request for an ambulance but advised Brandon of the specifics of the phone call. Now that the police knew what Archer wanted, they had time to put all their pieces in place. There was no need to rush and meet his demands.

By this time other RCMP who had been arriving from Brandon, Boissevain, Souris, Virden and Shoal Lake, had surrounded the village and had isolated the Scherz' residence. Prior to Archers' phone call, they didn't know exactly what was going on inside the house. Now that Archer had confirmed their worst suspicion, the police realized they were facing the menacing prospect of a hostage-taking.

Accordingly every entrance to Oak Lake was blocked off by police cruisers and the RCMP began to evacuate an area two blocks square around Scherz' house. At the Gomph farmhouse, Edith served breakfast to the policemen while sixty-six-year-old Elmer went out and did his farm chores. Having so many people in the house didn't bother the Gomphs because down through the years they had raised well over 100 foster children. Five of them were sleeping upstairs now as the police went quietly about their business in the house. Even though the Mounties tried to be polite with her as she fed them coffee and toast, Edith could feel the tension among them. Although they made it clear they couldn't say much about what was happening in Oak Lake, Edith knew it was serious because she overheard one of the officers whisper that some shooting might be going on.

The police patiently waited until everything was in place before they returned Archer's call. There was no hurry because time was on their side. This knowledge controlled their game plan right from the first.

At 5:50 a.m. they made their first telephone contact. Archer's primary concern was getting Malette medical attention. He wanted an ambulance to take her to Brandon General. He said he would hold the hostages at Oak Lake until she was well enough to travel. Then he wanted clearance so that they could both leave Canada and go to a country from which they could not be returned by extradition. He also demanded $100,000 in cash. With these unrealistic demands, Archer was exhibiting the customary rush of power that a captor usually feels in holding other people's lives at stake. Those of the police who were experienced in hostage situations knew his demands were part of a fantasy that, in time, would diminish and fade. In the meantime the RCMP placed an ambulance on standby. But they purposely held it back, tightened their security and waited.

Back at the Countryside Inn, John O'Ray had returned to the motel to give his account of the incident to Gerry Coulter. He was still badly shaken and kept saying, "I did my best. I tried my best."

Gerry told him, "John, don't worry about it. You did a good job."

Then Syd Barrie came over and said, "Gerry, they've tracked him down at Oak Lake. He got hostages." Although the information was alarming, Gerry knew his colleagues would have the situation well contained in Oak Lake. His only concern was the amount of damage the fugitives would do before they were taken into custody.

Gerry had to remain focused on the scene. His primary

responsibility was to make sure his investigation would prove the case against the murderer of Dennis Onofrey in court. Considering the evidence at hand, Coulter was convinced there was much more to the situation than an overdue rental. From the number of spent shells that littered the room, the occupants had been prepared for a fight.

In the motel Coulter found a number of cards and credentials belonging to Maurice Crystal. These included his personal business cards, his driver's license, cards for Blue Cross Medical, Social Insurance and the Calgary Public Library. There were credit cards from American Express, Visa, MasterCard, Eaton's, Simpsons, Imperial Oil and Shell Oil. Coulter also found a Holiday Inn room receipt from Lethbridge, Alberta.

When the back of the Archer's truck was opened, it was obvious that the drivers of the truck were a pair of pack rats. Besides the furniture, equipment and clothes one would expect to find in a moving van, the truck was jammed to the roof with boxes of papers and literature. Some of the boxes contained albums of pornographic photos, advertising brochures for swinging clubs and sexual aids paraphernalia. They only had time to give the contents a cursory examination. Then the truck was closed and sealed for transport to Brandon.

At Sherz's' place, Archer was becoming frantic because there was still no sign of an ambulance. He phoned Gaudet again in Virden demanding that he send an ambulance right away. "If my wife dies," he said," it will be all over."

When the ambulance still didn't come, Archer phoned Virden hospital and asked them to send over a surgeon. They told him that wasn't possible. He then asked for an ambulance. The nurse who answered the phone, aware of the situation, only reported his requests to the RCMP in Brandon.

When the first incomplete news of the fatal gunfight at Virden began to break on the radio, it caused consternation across the country. Some people in Virden thought it was John O'Ray who had been killed and called Marion to offer their sympathy. Relatives and in-laws of Virden members from as far away as Calgary phoned to see if it was their brother or sister who was injured in the gunfight. Elaine MacDougall had to call her husband's parents in Cape Breton Island to assure them that Joe was all right.

185

Ralph and Sonja Mahar were spending his weekend off at her parents' farm near Manitou when Sonja's mother came knocking at their bedroom door early in the morning.

"Something terrible has happened in Virden," she said.

"What is it?" Ralph asked.

"There's been a shooting and a policeman's been killed."

Ralph hopped out of bed and went to the phone in the garage where he could speak in privacy. He began to dial Dennis' number but then thought better of it since the incident might have involved him. He hung up and called the Virden office where Morris Cameron gave him the news. Both he and Sonja were crushed by Dennis' death. They packed immediately and left for Virden. As soon as they got home, Sonja went over to Marion O'Ray's to comfort her. Carolee Keyes and Elaine MacDougall were there too. All of them were badly shaken.

At 7:00 a.m. the police evacuation team knocked on Bert Fullers' door. He lived in a big old house about fifty yards east of the doctor's place, directly across Second Avenue where the doctor's carport was located. Much to the surprise of the police, Bert Fuller refused to move out. Even when they advised him of the danger of the situation and told him they wanted to set up sharpshooters in the windows on the west side of his house, he refused to budge. Bert told them they could come in and do what they wanted but he wasn't moving.

"We've got to use your house," one constable said, "because it overlooks all the side exits of the doctors place."

"I don't care," the seventy-seven-year-old widower said. "You can come in and use my place but no way I'm moving out."

The RCMP should have known better than to argue with Bert Fuller. He may have been old and wrinkled but he was still a powerful man of spirit who had honed his stubbornness with years of hard work handling teams of horses. Furthermore, he had a personal interest in the well-being of Doctor Scherz because he had chauffeured him around the county in years gone by.

No matter what tack the police took, Bert was adamant: "I'm not afraid and I'm not moving." As a matter of expediency the officers decided to stop arguing with him and let him stay as long as he promised to keep out of the line of fire. One group of RCMP put mattresses up against the inside west walls of the parlour and manned their rifles at the parlour window. Another group did the same thing upstairs in his daughter Cheryll's room. She was away studying in Oklahoma City. In her room the police pulled a big chest of drawers over to the window on which to mount their rifles.

While all this activity was going on at Fuller's place, at the doctor's they had moved Malette to an upstairs bedroom. As the clock ticked away she writhed in pain and whispered to Archer, "Honey, I'm dying."

"I won't let you die," he promised. "You mean too much to me."

Archer raced back to the telephone and made numerous frenzied calls to the police. Still, there was no ambulance.

Frantically he phoned a Winnipeg radio station and the Winnipeg Free Press. He told them, "I've got enough hostages to make one hell of a big grave." This time he gave his name simply as Cliff. "I want my wife patched up and I want to get the hell out of Canada." He repeated his money demands to them and finished by saying: "Send out one of your hotshot reporters. I'll give him the full details. I want him to come stripped. I don't want him carrying any weapons."

But all this talk was getting him nowhere and he knew it. It was past 7:30 a.m., Malette was dying right before his eyes and there still was "no goddamn ambulance." His head was on fire. He felt like he was going crazy.

Dr. Scherz was concerned by his erratic behaviour. He was afraid that if the woman died, they would all die. Refusing to wait any longer, he phoned the local ambulance drivers and, in his assertive manner, insisted they bring their ambulance to the house.

Before the ambulance arrived, Archer went upstairs to say good-bye to Malette. Together they devised a code that only the two of them would know. They could use it to signal each other that she was still alive once she was taken to the hospital by the police. They decided to use the name of one of Malette's aunts.

"Annie Laurie Kay" would be their secret word.

Ten minutes later Manual Wiens and Jake Brown rolled their ambulance up to the house. Working quickly they loaded Malette on board and pulled away for Brandon General Hospital.

Immediately after the ambulance left, Archer tuned into another radio report on the gunfight at the Countryside Inn. When he heard about the severity of Candy Smith's wounds, Archer called out in agony, "Oh, the poor little lady, the poor lady." This seems more devised than real on his part. He obviously knew how badly she was hurt when he saw her lying unconscious in a pool of her own blood on the motel sidewalk. How could he possibly think that two rifle blasts at such close range would do any less damage?

This radio report was the first time Archer heard the official news that the RCMP constable, Dennis Onofrey, had died as a result of his gunshot wound. On hearing this, Archer called the police to confirm the radio report. When they told him it was true, he became distraught and wept and moaned at what he had done.

His emotional response was probably an act for the benefit of his captives because he had surely seen that Onofrey was dead when he examined him in the parking lot before relieving him of his service revolver. If his reaction were genuine, it was only because he finally realized what a ruinous thing he had done. He'd been in petty trouble of one kind or another for the last few years but this time it was serious and irreversible. He knew he wasn't going to run away from this one.

In the midst of his crying jag, he yelled out, "It was him or my wife. He was gonna shoot my wife, what could I do?" It was a pathetic attempt to win sympathy and excuse his murderous act.

But he had their attention. Archer carried on so much at the news of Dennis' death that the hostages thought he was going to snap. As Archer sobbed, Dave Penny put his arm around him and prayed with him. He asked the Lord to help them all. When Dave was finished praying, Archer thanked him for his kindness.

When the ambulance pulled away from Scherz' with Malette on board, the police were taken completely by surprise. They had no idea the doctor had phoned for an ambulance on his private line. When it began to roll down the street with Malette on board, there was a jumble of police radio activity from car to car and post to post as they tried to figure out what was going on.

While these radio messages were crackling back and forth, Gerry Coulter and Sergeant Arlie Corbett were leaving the Countryside Inn and driving towards Oak Lake. When they heard that the woman fugitive was being taken away from the doctor's place in an unescorted ambulance, Coulter ordered all traffic off the radio and sent out a message that the ambulance was to be stopped and held until he got there. "Be careful," Gerry warned, "extremely careful."

One of the Brandon members who heard Coulter's warning was Constable John Williams who was positioned in his cruiser on the eastern edge of Oak Lake. A few minutes after the radio alert, he spotted the ambulance pulling out onto the Trans-Canada Highway. He went after it and pulled it over about four miles east of the village. With his gun drawn, Williams directed both ambulance attendants to step out of the vehicle and come back to his police car. Then he radioed Coulter his position and waited for him and Corbett to arrive. Once they got there, Corbett carefully opened the back of the ambulance and found Malette lying on a stretcher, wondering what was happening. Corbett ordered her to pull her hands from under the blankets and show them to him. Then he searched her and the interior of the vehicle to make sure she wasn't armed. Finding she was not, Corbett climbed into the back with Malette and rode into Brandon with the ambulance.

In the village the police maintained their strategy throughout the early morning. They knew that holding hostages can be an extremely demanding experience, particularly for the captor, so their basic plan was to play for time and wear Archer down. They needed to make an elaborate production out of his smallest request. Nothing could be answered on the spot. Everything had to be referred to a higher authority. The police would also attempt to suppress information to the media on the extent of the injuries sustained by the Mounties at Virden as well as the condition of Archer's wife. They knew Malette was their bargaining device and no contact of any kind between Archer and Malette could be allowed.

They also knew that with the passage of time Archer would become more and more familiar with his captives. The better acquainted they became, the more friendly they would become. This would reduce their danger because in hostage-taking cases it is common for the captor and his captives to eventually become close. They end up liking each other. This phenomenon is referred to as the Stockholm Syndrome.

At 9:00 a.m. Dr. Scherz' daughter, Evelyn, who lived in Brandon, showed up in Oak Lake. In her meeting with the RCMP, she emphasized her concern with getting her parents out of the house unharmed. The police assured her they were doing their best to have them safely released as soon as possible. Shortly after Evelyn's meeting with the police, her brother Harold approached one of the road blocks rimming the village and identified himself. He was taken to see Gerry Coulter who was working the perimeter in his police car. Harold asked where his parents were and Coulter told him they were in the house.

Then Harold, a young man in his mid-twenties, said emphatically, "I'm going in there and get them."

Coulter told him that was impossible. He explained Archer's unstable frame of mind and the delicate negotiations that were in progress. Harold was adamant and kept on insisting he was going into his parents' house until finally Gerry said to him, "If you try to do that, I'm going to arrest you." Then Gerry took him out to one of the police cruisers standing guard down the street and said to the two officers sitting inside, "This guy is to stay here with you. If he makes any attempt to approach the house, restrain him."

At 11:30 a.m. Edith Gomph was astounded to see a huge helicopter slowly putting itself down in the lane outside her kitchen. She watched in disbelief as ten men with rifles and flack jackets jumped down from its open doors. They squatted momentarily in the snow and then set out on the run towards the roadway. This was the ERT (Emergency Response Team) from Winnipeg, an RCMP task force of snipers who were flown in to cover Scherz' house. They were running to take up assigned positions at various vantage points around the village. One of these positions was high atop the grain elevator that stood across the tracks from the front of Scherz' house. Another relieved the members stationed inside Bert Fuller's house.

Shortly after the arrival of the Winnipeg ERT, the RCMP moved their command headquarters from the Gomph's farm to the local high school which had been ordered closed earlier in the morning. The school was located in a strategic position just one short block down Second Avenue, the street that ran between Bert Fuller's house and Scherz' place. Besides being the communications centre, the school would serve as the RCMP barracks. The gym was set up to house thirty policemen when they came off duty.

In preparation for a potentially long siege, the Mounties had called the supply office at Canadian Forces Base (CFB) Shilo, ten miles east of Brandon, and requested a long list of equipment. This included cots, blankets, sleeping bags, lamps, powerful exterior flood lights and the generators to run them. When this requisition was being placed, the army corporal who took the order finished the conversation by asking, "Anything else you need?"

The Mountie doing the ordering replied in jest, "Yeah, you can send us a Sherman tank too." Thinking he was serious, the army corporal ordered a tank and reversed himself only when he was told that the policeman had been joking. By that time, the tank was about to be loaded on a flat bed truck for delivery to Oak Lake.

Shortly after noon in Virden, Ralph Mahar supervised the removal of Archer's truck from the Countryside Inn. To preserve continuity of evidence, he was required to ride in the tow truck that hauled it to the police garage in Brandon.

By this time reporters were beginning to arrive in Virden looking for local reaction to the death and wounding of the RCMP officers. They quickly learned that the mood of the peaceful little town was angry and bitter. One man told a reporter, "I hope they get the bastard." Another was quoted as saying, "I hope they get him like he got ours." Many suggested that Archer should be hanged or shot. Bill Bohonis, the owner of the motel, told the Winnipeg Free Press that the local RCMP were very upset about the incident. "The boys are shook up," he said.

Information from the truck rental agency in Surrey via CPIC now identified the man who signed the lease for the truck as Donald Alfred Archer. As soon as this information was received, the RCMP began running that name through the CPIC system to see what information was available on such a person.

From the command centre at Oak Lake the police used two negotiators working alternating shifts. Staff Sergeant Jerry Ferguson and Staff Sergeant Don McDonald slept in the gym and phoned Archer from the school's main office every hour on the hour. Both were NCO's from the Brandon Sub-Division who had taken courses in hostage-negotiating. One of them was always waiting at the phone to deal with Archer at any time of day or night.

The two men had dissimilar styles in the way they dealt with him. Jerry was mild mannered and soft spoken and tended to present himself as pleasant and accommodating. Although he had a great revulsion for what Archer had done, Ferguson did his best to treat him like an understanding counsellor. McDonald was more direct and abrupt and tended to challenge Archer when he was pushing things too far. Their intention was to get Archer to trust them but to realize he was not in control. They wanted to give him some understanding and solace but, at the same time, keep him constantly off-guard and somewhat agitated.

Out on the streets, the RCMP left nothing to chance. Gerry Coulter met with the reeve of the township who supplied the RCMP with maps of the village and the surrounding area. The phone company was instructed to isolate the police line into the Scherz' residence and prevent any other callers from connecting with Archer. J 'n A Groceteria, one of the larger restaurants in the village was ordered closed to civilians and was contracted to serve as the RCMP canteen. The operator of the restaurant was kept busy making coffee and sandwiches that were delivered by cruiser to the members manning the road blocks and the sharpshooters stationed around the village.

Negotiations continued throughout the morning with Archer sticking to his unrealistic demands. At one point, in frustration, he attempted to phone the Attorney-General for the Province of Manitoba. The RCMP made sure his attempt was unsuccessful.

Archer did manage to connect with Tom Mark, a radio host on CFRW in Winnipeg. He was on his best behaviour. His conversation was long and rambling but always polite. Throughout he continually said "please" and "thank you" to the host as if attempting to prove to the listeners that he was a model of decency. Occasionally he sounded bizarre. At one point he reiterated his demands and his threats and then went on to sound like a silly school boy, chuckling at the predicament he had gotten himself into.

"Is there some way we can help you?" Mark asked him over the air.

"Yes," Archer replied. "Get me a lawyer."

As soon as Archer got off the phone, the radio station contacted Hersh Wolch, one of the province's most prominent criminal lawyers. They got a message to him in a Winnipeg courtroom where he was defending another client. When the severity of the hostage taking at Oak Lake was explained to the court, an adjournment was quickly arranged. Wolch was

192

immediately transported the 160 miles to Oak Lake by RCMP helicopter. It touched down on the highway in Oak Lake at 5:00 p.m. From there he was whisked to the local command headquarters at the high school for a briefing.

Wolch's first telephone conversation with his new, unknown client lasted two hours. The lawyer used it as an opportunity to establish rapport and trust between the two of them. Much of their conversation was kept confidential but Hersh did report to the media that Archer "has not hurt the hostages and does not want to harm them, but he is ready to do what is necessary to have his demands met."

He said that his client had described himself as "an average guy in a highly unusual situation" and that the incident was "a fight for survival on the part of me and my wife."

Wolch also reported that he had talked to some of the hostages and that they appeared to be on Archer's side. Dr. Scherz had even offered to appear as a character witness in court on the gunman's behalf. Apparently the Stockholm Syndrome was beginning to take root.

Besides talking to Wolch and several radio stations, Archer also had an extensive telephone interview with George Jacob of the Winnipeg Tribune. Identifying himself only as Cliff he told Jacob: "I am the fellow who's causing the trouble. . .I've resigned myself to my predicament. My wife and I both made the decision. . .either we live or die. If they get me, we die; if they leave me alone, we live. I want my wife released from hospital as soon as possible.

"The doctor is giving me stuff to keep me awake. If you want anything from me you better get it in the next twelve to fourteen hours because after that I'll be all hyped up like a cat.

"We're not real bad types. The cops just came out at me and I panicked. I just cut loose . . . I don't want to take lives or hurt anybody."

Archer went on to say, "I want $100,000, a signed statement that they won't deport me and a plane to take me with the hostages to another country where they will be released." He said he didn't want to give his real name to protect his relatives in Canada.

Then Jacobs asked, "Can you describe how the shooting took place?"

In part Archer replied, ". . . I looked out the window (of the motel unit) and they kept banging with their foot on the door and then they pulled their guns just outside the door and held them over their heads ready to fire. And I seen this and I panicked and I opened the door and right away one of them started to lower his gun toward me . . . And when he did, I raised my shotgun and shot at him . . . and then all hell broke loose."

Archer went on to say, " . . . they had their guns pulled and ready to go. So I figured they were going to kill me . . . and that's all there is to it. Just like back in the 1800's when you're shooting it out with the bad men . . . I just panicked . . . "

To another television reporter from the CBC he made it very clear: "I don't want to harm a hair on anybody's head, believe me. I'm not a crazy man or anything like that. I'm just an average sort of guy who got himself in trouble."

To yet another he said that he had jumped bail in British Columbia, where he had been arrested for writing bad cheques and then rented a truck that he failed to return. He added that he had been imprisoned on the coast for a short time and he could never take life in jail.

Even Stefanie Scherz was allowed to speak to a radio reporter. She told him that their captor was "well spoken and in a very good frame of mind."

She added, "We're not going to do anything foolish." And then emphasized that she hoped that the RCMP wouldn't try to force the issue either.

Other conversations that the police had with both Archer and the hostages weren't quite so pleasant in tone. Archer ranted and raved at them for being so slow and deliberate. He wanted things done right away. The hostages said Archer was disturbed and angered by the police inactivity. They expressed their concern by subtly implying that he seemed unpredictable. From these conversations, the police came to the conclusion that the situation was dangerous and that the unstable man they were dealing with could kill his hostages at any time.

The centre of Archer's operations in the Scherz' house was upstairs in the master bedroom where there was a telephone as well as a television set and a radio. At first Archer tied everybody up and kept them in the upstairs bedrooms so they couldn't make a break for it. But as time passed, he untied them and, allowed them to move about the house. However, he watched their every movement like a hawk.

Around 2:00 p.m. the RCMP in Oak Lake found out about the Crystal murder in Calgary. Gerry Coulter called Calgary and spoke to Sergeant Bob Hay, the detective in charge of the investigation. Hay gave Coulter the salient details: Crystal was a prominent realtor, he died of bondage asphyxiation probably on Saturday, January 21, robbery and sadomasochistic sex were apparently involved, Crystal's wallet and money were missing. Coulter advised Hay of the murder in Virden and the situation in Oak Lake and told him that one of the fugitives paid for the Virden motel with Crystal's credit card. He advised that all of Crystal's credentials and cards had been found in the motel room. They agreed to keep each other posted.

At this point in time the Calgary police had not released Crystal's name to the media. His prominent social position and the peculiar conditions surrounding his death had made them reluctant to give out the details of his death. The media's reaction was predictable. They became irritable and contentious, demanding more information.

At 6:30 p.m. information from CPIC indicated the male fugitive in the house was not Donald Alfred Archer but probably Herbert Bruce Archer, who used a long list of aliases. These included: Herbert Archer, Brian Hibbert Archer, H. Bruce Archer, Bryce Archer, Hibbert Archer, Herbert Bryce Archer and finally Donald Alfred Archer who was deceased.

Herbert Bruce Archer's record was literally longer than his arm. There were a number of charges outstanding against him dating back to Peterborough in 1972. Most of them pertained to writing bad cheques. There was one for assault causing bodily harm in Vancouver. A caution was attached that warned he was very violent. Revenue Canada was after him for some income tax irregularities. The information was valuable in helping the police understand the kind of fugitive they were dealing with. Except for the assault charge, Archer appeared to be nothing more than a petty criminal. His unprovoked murder of Dennis Onofrey only made sense if he was connected in some way with Crystal's death in Calgary.

By Monday evening the town's population of 300 had increased by thirty percent. Besides the police, Oak Lake was inundated with reporters and photographers, most of whom stayed at the Oakland

Hotel just down North Railway Street from the Scherz' place. Once the siege began, only police and the news media were allowed in the hotel. It was designated as the site for news conferences that were to be given daily by Sergeant Arlie Corbett. Civilians were barred from entering the hotel for the duration of the siege.

In turn, police command headquarters was declared off limits to the media. RCMP officers stationed around the village were cautioned by their commanders not to make any comments to anyone about the siege. Banks and businesses were ordered closed for the next day and arrangements were made to bus Oak Lake students to Virden schools for as long as necessary.

At Brandon General all three principals from the Virden gunfight were lodged in the same intensive care unit. Candy Smith, whose parents had already arrived from Sault Ste. Marie, was in a private room at one end of the unit. Dorothy Malette, under heavy guard, was shackled to her bed in another private room at the other end of the unit. In between them in the open ward lay Russ Hornseth. Although Russ' eye was badly damaged and his forehead was peppered with buck shot, the only one among the three of them who was in critical condition was Candy Smith.

In Oak Lake as darkness closed in, Coulter set up the guard around the village and checked to make sure that everyone was at their post and clearly understood their responsibility. At 10:30 p.m. the Special Investigation Unit arrived from Winnipeg with sophisticated equipment to monitor the phone lines going into Scherz' house. Then, around the doctor's residence, Coulter and Corbett set up banks of the huge floodlights and generators that had been sent in from CFB Shilo. This was done by mutual agreement between Archer and the police. Throughout the night, both of them wanted to be able to see what was going on outside the house

Inside the house the occupants prepared to retire.

Archer asked them, "Do I give you a sleeping pill or are you going to bed?"

They all agreed that a pill wasn't necessary. Archer ordered them all to sleep in the upstairs bedrooms. The Scherz were in one room, he and Dave Penny in another.

This was a clever move on Archer's part because the older couple wouldn't know if he were sleeping or not and Archer was so wound up that he knew he wouldn't have any trouble staying awake. Archer was confident that Dave Penny wasn't interested in trying anything. It was obvious Penny just wanted to get some sleep.

Archer was so jumpy that every time he heard a creak in the old house it startled him and he sat up and listened intently for a minute or so. Once he became accustomed to the sounds of the place, he just sat and stared out the window. His mind jumped around a lot and he had to concentrate to block out the horror of his predicament.

When Dave Penny suddenly rolled over, Archer's eyes flew wide open and searched the room. His hands tightened on the barrel of his rifle. Seeing it was nothing, he took a deep breath and leaned back against the wall to once again gaze into the darkness. It soon became clear that his first, long night with the hostages was going to be harder on him than on them.

TUESDAY

Before Gerry Coulter signed off duty at 2:30 a.m. on Tuesday morning, he went out and refuelled the generators that ran the flood lights that lit up the Scherz' residence. When Archer saw him approaching the lights, he thought some type of raid was in progress and rushed around in a panic preparing to meet the police thrust. When he finally realized what was really happening, he went back to his bed and spent the night fighting off his need to sleep.

At 8:00 a.m. the RCMP Emergency Response Team from Regina arrived by plane to relieve the Winnipeg ERT. Now the marksmen could spell each other off for meals, sleep and washroom breaks. Photos of Archer were distributed to all of the sharpshooters so they could identify what the fugitive looked like. The Scherz' children, Evelyn and Derek were called to the command centre and asked to provide a detailed sketch of their parents' house so the police would be thoroughly familiar with its layout.

Also by Tuesday morning, the RCMP had completed their examination of room 20 at the Countryside Inn and had listed all the exhibits that could be used as evidence at a subsequent trial. The contents of Archer's truck were removed and stored in the RCMP rifle range located in the basement of the Brandon Sub-Division. Ken Bullock was assigned to dust them for fingerprints as well as photograph and catalogue all the items that were considered relevant for trial purposes. When Bullock saw the tremendous volume of material that was involved, he requested a small task force be assigned to help him complete the work.

By now the siege at Oak Lake was an international story that was carried on all the major TV networks across Canada and the United States. The morning newspapers covered the hostage taking in detail and featured photos of the squadron of RCMP cruisers that ringed the area immediately surrounding the Scherz' home. Other pictures showed the roadblocks that diverted traffic on the Trans-Canada Highway and detoured it by side road around the small community.

This publicity put Calgary police chief Brian Sawyer in a difficult position. On the one hand he was being pressed for more information on the progress of the Crystal killing by the Calgary media. On the other, he was sensitive about the volatile situation in Oak Lake. He decided to hold back and not divulge any information that connected Maurice Crystal's death with the hostage incident now being played out in Manitoba.

In Oklahoma City, Bert Fuller's daughter, Cheryll, was told about the stand off in "the little Canadian town" by one of her nursing friends who had heard about it on the news. Cheryll never suspected the action was taking place in Oak Lake and would never have believed there were snipers in her father's home aiming their rifles at Dr. Scherz' house. She was far too busy with her studies in the nursing clinic to think about anything like that.

Back in Oak Lake her father was really getting agitated. The police hadn't let him sleep in his own bedroom downstairs because its window faced the Scherz' property. He therefore had spent an uncomfortable Monday night sleeping in his clothes on a living room couch surrounded by a barricade of heavy furniture. Tuesday morning Bert knew he was in for a lot more aggravation when he saw the police bringing in supplies of bread, jam and coffee. All he could do was shake his head and mutter to himself under his breath.

Over at the Scherz' place, the first police telephone call came early in the morning. Because little progress seemed to be taking place in the negotiations, they wanted to stir things up a bit. Negotiator Don McDonald was just the man to do that. He was aware that earlier that morning the CBC had broadcast a television interview with a man who knew Archer through some business dealings with him in Vancouver. The interviewee had been very uncomplimentary about Archer and ended up calling him "the biggest con man he had ever known." McDonald phoned and asked if Archer had seen the telecast.

"Yeah, I saw it," Archer said. "So what about it?"

"Well, I was just wondering if you agreed with the man's assessment of your character?"

"No, I do not," Archer shot back, "not at all."

"Well, I do," McDonald said. "I think he was right dead on about you."

Archer immediately took the bait and blew up. For the next

few minutes, Archer went at McDonald with all the invective he could muster. When Archer finally hung up, he sat down and trembled in frustration and anger. It was just what the police had intended. However, the hostages, seeing Archer beet-red in the face and terribly agitated, were concerned about him being disturbed. Stefanie Scherz talked to him quietly, calming him down and soothing him until his breathing became less violent and he began to stop shaking. Once he was under control she made him some breakfast and fed her husband and Dave Penny too.

While he was drinking his coffee, Archer went back into the living room to watch the TV for more news. This time he turned on the radio too. Although he never saw or heard the offensive interview again, he was irked by McDonald's phone call for hours. Throughout the day most of the news reports were repetitive reviews of the high-lights of the Oak Lake situation up to that moment and contained very little information that was useful to him. He badly wanted to hear about Dorothy's condition but there was never anything about her and this led him to suspect she was dead. He tried to ignore that possibility but every once in a while it would come back to haunt him and that made him increasingly despondent.

As distressed as he was, Bruce was slightly amused by the news reports that indicated the police and the media were still confused about his identity. Both the TV and radio reported that a Vancouver newspaper had positively identified him as Donald A. Archer, a man who had rented a three-quarter ton truck from a Surrey, B.C. agency but had never returned it.

In order to stay awake throughout the day, Archer forced the doctor to keep him supplied with an ample quantity of amphetamines. Dr. Scherz reluctantly complied with Archer's demands but feared that violence might result when Archer combined such a heavy dosage of amphetamines with his prolonged lack of sleep. By this time Archer had slept a little more than one hour in the last two days.

He kept one person with him at all times; usually that was Dave Penny. Because Penny was a stranger in the house, he didn't feel comfortable wandering around by himself. Being a shy man, he was inclined to speak only when spoken to and never did anything in the house without first asking permission. Archer and Penny often watched television together or just sat quietly in each other's company. The two Scherz were allowed to do pretty much what they wanted. Stefanie Scherz usually kept herself busy in the kitchen preparing meals. Dr. Scherz spent much of his time looking at medical journals but he kept an eye on Archer in an attempt to assess his mood swings and anticipate his unstable behaviour.

When anything came on the radio or TV about the shoot-out or hostage-taking, Archer asked the others to leave the room. He was particularly cautious about preventing them from hearing anything about Crystal's death in Calgary.

Gradually the relationship among all four of the inhabitants of the besieged house became quite pleasant. Archer was firm in his orders and directions to his captives, but, other than that, he was usually considerate and courteous. The only thing about him that his prisoners feared was his erratic behaviour. Archer could easily be upset such as when he heard about Onofrey's death or when he spoke to Don McDonald on the phone. At these times he became irrational and melodramatic. This put all the hostages on edge because they did not know what he might do.

Sergeant Arlie Corbett held a press conference in the Oakland Hotel at 10:00 a.m. Since the negotiations with Archer were to be kept confidential, he answered very few questions about their progress. He had little to say other than future press conferences would be scheduled daily in the hotel. When the briefing was over, the reporters grumbled to themselves that having press conferences was of little value if the police were determined to say nothing about the progress of the case.

At 3:00 p.m., Gerry Coulter and Syd Barrie went into Brandon General Hospital and spent some time with the medical personnel telling them how the police wanted Malette isolated. She was to be kept under constant guard with no contact with anyone from the outside. She was to be allowed no visitors, no books, no newspapers. She could neither make phone calls nor receive them. She was not allowed to write or receive letters unless they were first censored by the police.

After checking with her doctors, Coulter and Barrie went in to have their first interview with her in her private room at one end of the Intensive Care Unit. To appear as unthreatening as possible, both Coulter and Barrie wore civilian clothes. When they went in, they found her lying in bed in a blue, hospital-issue night gown with a tube in her nose. As they entered she cast her eyes toward the ceiling and kept her focus there through much of the first part of Coulter's interview. Throughout the interrogation Syd Barrie remained behind Coulter and never spoke.

Coulter started by telling her who he was and introducing Corporal Barrie from the Virden detachment.

She did not look at either of them.

"How are you?" Coulter asked.

"In pain, " she answered coldly.

"Are you eating?"

"No."

There was silence for a brief moment until she resumed, "How's my husband?"

"He's alive," Coulter said. "He's in Oak Lake."

Dorothy didn't look at him.

Coulter read to her the standard police caution saying she didn't have to talk, was entitled to a lawyer and anything she said in the interview could be used against her. Then he said, "We've heard the policemen's side of the story, we'd like to hear your side of the story so we can get an accurate picture of what happened."

"What did my husband say?" Malette droned.

"From what he's told the media, he says that the police shot first."

Dorothy showed slightly more interest in the conversation. "Yes, that's right," she said. "The police shot first."

After that she made it clear she didn't want to talk at all and refused to answer any of his questions.

"Would you care to read what I've written?" Coulter asked.

"No."

"Will you sign what I've written?"

"No."

Since it was obvious the interview was going nowhere, Coulter and Barrie started to leave the room.

In a demanding tone Malette announced, "I want a phone in my room—NOW!"

"We're working on that," Coulter lied, "but it's going to take a bit of time."

Sensing she might talk a little about herself, Coulter asked, "How long have you been married?"

203

She didn't answer.

"Do you have any children?"

"Please," she said with a smirk, "you're making me tired."

Gerry said, "I hope you're feeling better." Then he left the room.

Outside Coulter made some observations in his notebook: she spoke with a strong, clear voice; her words were forceful; her eyes moved from the ceiling to him and back; she appeared calm; there was no noticeable shaking or any indication in her voice or in her actions of fear; she was emotionless, coherent.

Coulter thought to himself that he was dealing with a very tough, dangerous individual. To him it seemed apparent that this was not the first time she had dealt with the police.

As Coulter and Malette were speaking, cards of sympathy and bouquets of flowers from across Canada were flowing into the hospital for Candy Smith and, to a lesser degree, for Russ Hornseth. The public was obviously touched by the grievous wounding this young police woman had suffered in the line of duty. Candy's parents were staying in town and spent most of the day at the hospital. Kim was in to visit Russ every day.

For Dorothy Malette, there were no visitors, no cards and no flowers.

Tuesday afternoon, John Bacon, one of Russ' best friends who had served in the RCMP with him in Flin Flon, came to visit him. When Bacon entered the room, he calmly said hello to Kim and Russ but was alarmed to see Russ with his forehead and one eye swathed in bandages. As he chatted to Russ about his condition, Bacon could tell that he was still under heavy sedation from his recent surgery. After a brief lull in the conversation, Bacon made what he thought was an appropriate comment on the tragedy of the situation.

"It's too bad what happened to Dennis," he said.

Russ had kept himself informed of Candy's condition but he never asked about Dennis because he didn't know that anything had happened to him. "Why?" Russ asked. "What happened to Dennis?"

John said nothing. His quick look into Kim's eyes told him that Russ knew nothing about Dennis' death. Kim and the hospital staff wanted to wait until he was stronger before they gave him such horrible news.

204

"What happened to Dennis?" Russ repeated.

There was no way out for John Bacon. "I'm sorry Russ but . . . he was killed."

Russ cried out, "Oh, God! No!" and threw his head back into his pillow. Then he began to sob.

Both Kim and John tried to console him but it was no use. Finally Kim suggested they leave the room and let him deal with his grief on his own terms for a few minutes. Out in the hall John told her he felt terrible about what he'd said. Kim, in her wisdom, assured John that Russ had to be told sometime and she was sure he was strong enough to handle it now. She said no matter when he was told, it was going to have the same devastating effect on him.

That same afternoon, there was a large turnout at the funeral service for Maurice Crystal at the Jewish Memorial Chapel in Calgary. Rabbi Lewis Ginsburg gave the eulogy and paid tribute to Crystal as both his friend and as a member of his synagogue. At that point no one but the police knew the gruesome details of Crystal's death. Many of the Calgary media attended the funeral and immediately after the service they went to the Chief of Police for an explanation of what had happened to Crystal. He continued to maintain his silence.

That same afternoon seventy-five residents of Virden held a service in town at St. Andrew's Presbyterian Church to pray for the safe release of Dave Penny and Dr. and Mrs. Scherz. Penny, a long-time employee of the municipal water works, was well known in the community. The Scherz were equally prominent because of the doctor's professional position in the nearby village.

When Ken Bullock and his Ident team began to examine the contents of Archer's truck, they were astounded at what they found. Besides the regular clothes and household goods there was a large quantity of erotic literature and salacious material. There were porno films, lurid pamphlets and a box of dildos and other sexual paraphernalia. There were photos of Archer involved in sexual acts with a young girl who appeared to be no more than eight or ten years old. Other photos showed Archer with a dog and a horse whose sexual services he apparently rented out. There were brochures of swingers clubs where couples placed ads to engage other couples in sexual activity. One of them showed a photo of Archer and Malette accompanied by their own

205

advertisement. Bullock found material on Archer's infamous *Double Gators Club* and an address in Vancouver where people could write to join. Some of the boxes contained filing cards and books with addresses of club members. Among the stacks of paper was evidence that Archer had placed advertisements similar to the Calgary ad in other newspapers.

Meanwhile, the informal network among the news media started to communicate information to Calgary about a possible connection between the Saturday murder of Crystal in Calgary, the gunfight at the Countryside Inn and the hostage incident that was unfolding at Oak Lake. As the Calgary media became increasingly suspicious, they began to demand answers from the Calgary police. The police still refused to talk.

As the day progressed, the freedom of movement among the hostages became even more relaxed. The captives had long since given up any idea of trying to escape. Archer had convinced them he was an expert marksman. Besides that he told them his rifle was so powerful, he could shoot right through a window pane and hit them on the run.

Down Second Avenue in the high school, Staff Sergeants Jerry Ferguson and Don McDonald were joined by a significant third party. Dr. Larry Breen, a forensic psychologist, had been whisked away from his criminology lectures in Ottawa and flown by jet and helicopter to the command centre in Oak Lake. From the beginning of the hostage-taking, Breen had been involved in the negotiation strategy by telephone. Now, as the siege dragged on, the authorities had decided to bring him on site so he could be closer to the pulse of the situation.

As soon as he arrived, he began assisting the negotiators whose contact with Archer began to steadily increase. By now Archer preferred to deal with Ferguson and wanted little to do with McDonald. But McDonald kept calling anyway, which seemed to keep Archer in a constant state of turmoil. Sometimes after talking to McDonald, Archer became so irritated, his behaviour tended to make the hostages concerned. During one disturbing phone call, Stefanie Scherz, not understanding the police strategy, took the phone from Bruce's hands and berated McDonald. She told him to stop aggravating Archer and "leave us all alone." Then she hung up.

At other times throughout the day Hersh Wolch and Jerry

Ferguson would also contact Archer by phone. Both of them had a calming effect on him. Wolch would listen to Bruce's complaints and demands and then explain why they couldn't be taken care of immediately. In reply he tried to point out to Archer the advantages of giving himself up so he could be removed safely from the house. Wolch said by doing that and not causing any further harm to anyone, he would have the sympathy of the court and receive a fair trial.

When Ferguson spoke to him, he would listen attentively while Archer repeatedly told him the reasons he had to shoot it out at the motel. Ferguson was sympathetic and understanding and always assured Bruce that he knew the whole business was all a terrible mistake beyond his control. He said everything would work out for the best if Archer would prove his good intentions by either giving up his hostages or surrendering before anyone else got hurt.

But Archer wouldn't budge for either of them. At this time he still felt physically strong and in control of the situation. He adamantly refused to release his hostages unless his conditions were met. Surrender was absolutely out of the question.

As the day dragged on with no sign of progress, Archer became more and more disturbed. He insisted that he be allowed to talk to Walter Dinsdale, a local Member of Parliament, or to Morris McGregor, a Manitoba MLA. As usual, Archer was told that the police would see what they could do. In reality, no attempt was made to contact either of them.

Around 2:30 p.m. Dr. Scherz complained of chest pains and, although Archer was concerned, the doctor assured him it was nothing and he would be all right. Archer watched him closely after that but his primary concern was for Dorothy. Having heard nothing about her well-being, he assumed the worst and demanded the negotiators have a doctor call him from the hospital.

At 4:45 p.m. Dr. Samuels called Archer from Brandon General. He advised that Dorothy was still alive but in critical condition. She couldn't be moved from the ICU of the hospital for a period of ten to fourteen days. When Archer hung up he didn't know what to think. Was the doctor telling him the truth or was Dorothy dead and the story made up to pacify him and keep him on tenterhooks?

Late in the afternoon, the RCMP sent Ken Bullock on an aerial photography mission for the Emergency Response Teams. They were anxious to have an accurate overview of the buildings surrounding the Scherz' place in case Archer attempted to shoot his way out. It was so cold out that when Bullock arrived at the Holmes air strip west of Virden, the pilot, Ron Thompson, had to heat the cowling of the motor with a huge propane torch to get the single engine Otter to turn over. After Bullock photographed the area in question, he flew on to Brandon to develop the pictures in his dark room at the Sub-Division. By the time they flew back to Holmes, it was so dark they had trouble seeing the air strip, which wasn't marked with landing lights. The only way the pilot could bring the plane in was to turn on the aircraft's powerful searchlights. Even then it took some masterful flying to land the plane. Once they were on the ground, the aerial photos were rushed to Oak Lake and distributed among the sharpshooters.

To control both incoming and outgoing phone calls at the doctor's house, the RCMP had disconnected all of the Scherz' telephone lines. Then, to reestablish telephone communication with Archer they arranged for a land line to be sent into the house. Just before dark, Corporal Terry Pukas, one of the marksman who was stationed in Bert Fuller's house, used a bow and arrow to fire a land line at the doctor's office door. The arrow was attached to a fishing line that was attached to a rope that was connected to the land line. Once the arrow hit the door, Pukas watched as a hand came out of the partially opened door and tried to wiggle the arrow free from the wood. When this didn't work, Pukas saw Dave Penny step out of the office. He removed the arrow from the door and pulled the land line into the house, thereby reestablishing contact between Archer and the negotiators. From that time on, Archer had no more contact with the media.

The next precaution the RCMP took was to insure that Archer didn't try to use the hostages as shields to get to one of the vehicles in the carport. At 8:00 p.m. Corporal Pukas, under cover from another sharpshooter, crawled into the carport and flattened the tires on the automobiles belonging to Dr. Scherz and Lloyd Hatch.

By this time Gerry Coulter was back at the command centre reporting his findings on his interview with Dorothy Malette. He said he found her to be very strong and determined. She made no attempt to make a deal or give up. She gave no sign of giving in.

His conclusion was that she had the stronger will of the two and, in his opinion, she was the key to their resolving the hostage situation. Jerry Ferguson tended to agree. He felt that Archer had revealed a soft spot when he professed that he regretted what had happened at the motel. Archer said he thought the officer at the door was going to kill his wife and he just panicked.

To his captives Archer tried to rationalize his violent behaviour at the motel. He told Dr. Scherz he was sorry for what he had done. He wanted him to believe it was more like an accident.

"I killed a man," Archer lamented. "And I'll get life. Even if I didn't mean to do it, they won't believe me."

The reality of his predicament was beginning to depress him. This was compounded by the fact that he was becoming increasingly despondent about Dorothy. Not hearing any news on her condition, he felt sure that she was dead.

In an attempt to determine her condition, he tried to contact her with mental telepathy. While Stefanie Scherz and Dave Penny watched, he sat on a bed swaying back and forth trying to conjure himself into a trance calling, "Dorothy, Dorothy." As he did this, his eyes were rolling in his head and he was perspiring. After a short while he stopped and told them he couldn't reach her.

"They must have doped her," he said. Then, struggling to come out of his trance, he mumbled, "Where am I?"

"In our bedroom," Stefanie Scherz answered.

Seemingly dazed and confused, Archer said, "My mother is dead."

"I know," Mrs. Scherz replied.

"I'm hot, I'm hot," Archer complained. "My other self is coming through. Nobody can do anything but Dorothy. I'm not responsible for what I do."

As Stefanie and Dave Penny helped him out of the bedroom, Archer threw his gun on the bed and went with them like a little lost child. Still talking strangely, he said, "I speak Spanish when my other self comes out."

Then he told Stefanie Scherz, "You'll have to sing me a lullaby." He said that Dorothy sang him a lullaby and massaged his temples whenever his "other self "came through. He told Mrs. Scherz that he had spent seven months in a mental institution but Dorothy had "nursed him like a baby" back to full health again. He advised both of them to tie him up and call the police, "as soon as I am

209

not myself any more." This bizarre behaviour was probably nothing more than a dramatic ruse to gain sympathy from his hostages.

Later he did seem to be seriously despondent about missing Dorothy. He sat on the chesterfield in the living room with the hostages all around him. Then he began motioning at them with the rifle. For the hostages this was the worst time in the entire siege. At that point they truly feared he might kill everyone. "If Dorothy is not alive," he said in a loud shaking voice, "I don't want to live either." He put the butt of his rifle on the floor and the barrel under his chin. As he put his thumb to the trigger, Stefanie walked over and pushed the barrel away and said, "Bruce, you don't want to do that."

Then, almost miraculously, the phone rang. It was Jerry Ferguson who told him that Dorothy had made it through the operation and was going to be all right.

Archer wanted to believe him but was skeptical.

"Is she conscious?" he demanded.

"Yes she is."

"Say 'Annie Laurie' to her and tell me what she says in return."

Ferguson relayed the request to the surgeon who was on another line. The surgeon left the phone but soon returned and gave Ferguson Dorothy's reply.

"I don't know what this means," Ferguson said, "But your wife says: 'Annie Laurie Kay'. "

Archer was ecstatic.

"Oh, my God," he roared. "My wife is alive!"

He embraced each hostage in turn and then stomped around the living room in elation crying out for joy. Stupefied by Archer's behaviour, his prisoners stood by and watched him prance about yelling over and over, "Now I have a reason to live! Now I have a reason to live!"

For the hostages this was the turning point that they had hoped for. From that time on, all of them felt there was a glimmer of hope they might get out of their nightmare alive. Their biggest fear now was that the police would lose their patience and rush the house in a hail of gunfire. When they discussed this possibility with Archer, he instructed them that in such an event, they should immediately run upstairs into the master bedroom and cover themselves with the mattresses that had been laid aside for this purpose.

"I don't want any of you being hurt," he cautioned.

In Brandon General Hospital, Candy Smith was still listed as critical but the doctors could see that she was stabilizing after her eight hours of surgery. Up on the surgical floor, Russ Hornseth was doing nicely. There was some concern that his left eye might have to be removed because a shotgun pellet had damaged it badly. Although his forehead was torn up, the doctors advised they were not going to remove a number of pellets that were imbedded under the skin. The surgeon told Russ that, in time, these would either work their way to the surface or, barring complications, remain there for the rest of his life.

Over at Bert Fuller's place, the grizzled old teamster was thoroughly exasperated with the police occupation of his home. Not only was he denied the comfort of sleeping in his own bed but now they wouldn't let him listen to the radio or watch TV. He became so frustrated, he told the police he wanted to put on a flack jacket and charge into the "Doc's place" with his own shotgun. The RCMP tried to placate him by telling him that his courage was admirable and his intentions were good but his plan was impractical.

"You're going to have to stay put and wait it out like the rest of us," a young corporal told him.

Then the phone rang. The Mountie who answered it told Bert that his son Donald was on the line and wanted to speak to him. Donald was a truck salesman in Brandon. He had come to Oak Lake to try to get his father to vacate the house. The police wouldn't let him penetrate the blockade so he was calling from J 'n A's Groceteria about six blocks away. Bert listened to Donald's argument for a very short period of time and then told him, "I'm not leaving. I'm OK and I'm going to stay right here."

When Donald persisted in his plea, Bert curtly interrupted him and said, "Mind your own business. I told you I'm staying, now leave me alone." Then he hung up.

The next call he got was from his daughter, Cheryll, in Oklahoma. She had finally come to realize from the news that the troubled little town in Canada was Oak Lake. Further she had come to suspect that the Doctor's house was the Scherz' place and the

211

RCMP snipers were manning their rifles in her very own bedroom.

When she talked to her father, he confirmed all of her suspicions.

"How are you?" she inquired.

"I'm OK but the cops are a damned nuisance."

Like her brother before her, Cheryll tried to talk her dad into moving out of the house but it was to no avail. He did admit to her that one of the reasons he wanted to stay was to keep an eye on all the antiques that he had collected through the years. Some of the police had already offered to buy some of his prized possessions.

Before he hung up, he confided to his daughter in a whisper, "You never know if you can trust these guys—even if they are cops."

If Bert Fuller had been allowed to watch his television set, he would have seen a number of news items pertaining to the siege of his little village. Some of those being interviewed were angry. The President of the Canadian Police Association told reporters that Dennis Onofrey was the fourth police officer to be killed that month across Canada. He blamed the increase in violence against the police on the recent abolition of the death penalty. In Saskatchewan, the Prince Albert Police Force concurred and ninety percent of its membership held a march to protest the new law and honour the memory of their fallen comrade, Dennis Onofrey.

Some of the pieces were political. John Diefenbaker, the sitting member for Prince Albert and leader of the Conservative opposition, reacted to the police march in his riding in his predictably bizarre manner. With jowls atremble he glared into the camera and pronounced that any complaints the city police had about the removal of the death penalty should be directed to the Liberal Party. Diefenbaker admitted that he favoured abolition of the death penalty but insisted he had voted to retain the death penalty until the end of 1978. In view of that, he proclaimed, "I cannot be blamed."

Equally shameful in his use of a personal tragedy for political gain was the announcement from Ron Basford, the Federal Justice Minister. He declared that he was now prepared to discuss the value of doubling the minimum penalty for hostage-taking to ten years in prison.

Along with these national items there were regular updates

from Oak Lake. Seldom was there any real progress to report.

Soon it was bedtime again and the three hostages trudged off to their rooms upstairs. Archer fortified himself with more amphetamines and followed close behind them. While the hostages slept, he would spend the second long night of the siege fighting his weariness and wistfully looking out into the darkness.

By contrast the Mounties who were off duty were tucked snugly in their army cots in the gym of the command centre. One of them slept so soundly, he snored like a baby hippopotamus and finally he and his sleeping bag had to be banished to one of the classrooms.

It was almost impossible for Archer to nod off because all through the night the phone rang intermittently. When Archer answered it, there was either no one there or an RCMP negotiator on the other end, doing his best to pester Archer with some mundane question or comment that was designed to interrupt his sleep and torment his nerves.

Outside the house, police cars took turns moving quickly from place to place with their roof lights flashing or their siren on. Every time this happened Archer jumped up to see what was going on. With his body a jangle of tension and alarm, he knew another long night lay ahead.

NEGOTIATIONS

For Archer and his hostages, Wednesday morning began much the same as it would in most other homes across the country. He and his captives greeted each other groggily and took their turns in the bathroom. Before long they were sitting down to breakfast in Stefanie Scherz' kitchen. With the exception of Archer, they all seemed to be well rested. The only indication of tension among them was the absence of idle chatter.

Archer, who brought his rifle to the table with him, looked awful. His eyes were glassy, his face was drawn, his clothes were rumpled and his hair unkempt. During the long night he had been able to take the odd cat nap but only when he was sure that Dave Penny was sound asleep. Any activity outside the house and the least movement from Penny in the bedroom jarred him awake. It was only the amphetamines that kept him going. Although the pills tended to make him edgy and irritable, he still managed to be reasonably polite and considerate with his captives at breakfast.

When the RCMP cut off the electricity so that Archer couldn't see or hear the 9:00 a.m. news, he was outraged. He stomped around the house, yelling about being treated in such an underhanded manner. Then he got on the phone and demanded the electricity be turned back on. The police said they would see what could be done. In thirty minutes the power was restored and Archer felt somewhat satisfied that he had been able to force them to do what he wanted. He didn't realize the police would turn off the power during all newscasts and any special reports about Oak Lake for the duration of the siege.

Archer had just began to settle down about the hydro problem when the police cut off the water supply to the house. Once again, he exploded, which is exactly what the authorities intended. What's more, the police were able to hear his childish behaviour. By means of an intricate process that cannot be divulged in this book, the Mounties, at this point, were able to monitor almost everything that went on inside the house. This gave them a tremendous advantage in dealing with him because they were constantly aware of what was taking place between him and the hostages.

215

From what the police could discern, it appeared the Stockholm Syndrome had taken hold. The atmosphere in the house was less tense and the authoritative distinction between Archer and his hostages was beginning to blur. On several occasions they heard Archer discuss his dire predicament with Stefanie Scherz and Dave Penny. Archer always did most of the talking but when his two captives got a chance, they did their best to buoy his spirits and keep him calm. Markus Scherz, on the other hand, barely talked to Archer at all. When he did, it was usually in a rather offhand manner.

On one occasion the doctor said, "Listen, I am going to my office."

"All right, Doc, you go where you want to go," Archer replied. "You know I don't worry about where you're going."

The police were also aware that Archer was playing a game with them. He was the consummate manipulator. To the police, he acted like a cold-hearted, vicious killer who would stop at nothing to get his freedom. To the hostages he showed himself as a benign and reasonable man who was simply caught up in a situation beyond his control. He told the hostages repeatedly he would never hurt them. And, almost every time he did that, the police heard what he was saying.

One time on the phone to negotiator Don McDonald, Archer said if a certain request wasn't met, he was going to "cut off the hostages' fingers and send them out piece by piece." But as soon as he got off the phone, he told his captives apologetically, "I was only saying that. You know I'd never hurt you." The police heard Archer say that too. Although it was some consolation that they knew he was playing the role, they could never discount the fact that Archer was dangerous. He was impulsive, with a hair-trigger temper and he could be totally irrational when things didn't go his way. After all, this was a man who had killed an RCMP officer at point-blank range. The police had to be careful with a man who would do such a hopelessly self-defeating thing. Now that he had nothing to lose, what would make him snap again? No matter how foolish or benign he sounded in the house, the police could not afford to let their guard down.

Occasionally Archer allowed the hostages to speak on the phone to assure the authorities they were unharmed. From these conversations the police felt reasonably confident that Archer and his captives were becoming comfortable with each other. These

216

instances and other kindly things he said to the hostages, helped the police determine their course of action. As explosive as Archer could be, they knew that in dealing with him time was their greatest asset. The longer Archer spent with his prisoners, the less likely he was to do them any harm.

The police negotiating team wanted to continue to bother him but they didn't want to get him as upset as they had before. At the same time, they didn't want Archer to relax and be comfortable. Cutting off the hydro and the water were inconveniences intended to frazzle his nerves They wanted him to know there were a lot of people outside who were watching him closely and waiting for him to surrender.

Every time a news report was due on the air, Archer would sit himself in front of the radio or television to listen. Then just as the announcer was about to read the latest flash about the Virden or Oak Lake incident, the power would go out. Each time this happened Archer would go ballistic and the police listened carefully as he stomped around ranting and raving. When he called the negotiators to complain about the power outage, they apologized and said it wasn't their fault. They made up stories about how they were trying to stop this from happening but they had to go through a lot of bureaucracy to get it all straightened out. According to them, it was always somebody else who did it and they promised to take care of it right away. But, of course, they never did.

Between disturbances, Archer would become almost a comical figure to the people inside the house. Sometimes he would busy himself reading from an encyclopedia with an old pair of Scherz' granny glasses. At one point he was trying to learn about Albania. One of the hostages had told him this was one of the few countries in the world to which he could escape and then avoid extradition. Albania and Cuba were suggested to him. But Archer claimed that Cuba was out of the question.

"I'd never go there," he said. "I hate communists."

When the police heard him say things like this, they had to chuckle. It was starting to dawn on them that they were not dealing with a mental giant.

Although there were odd moments of humour inside the house, things remained deadly serious outside among the police. Later in the morning, at the request of the RCMP, two explosives experts from Canadian Forces Base Winnipeg arrived in Oak Lake in a specialized army vehicle. They went directly to the command post and awaited further orders. The police refused to explain why they were called in with their specialized equipment.

In Calgary, the constant pressure from the media forced Police Chief Sawyer to call a press conference in the police station. When the reporters were assembled, the chief gave them the facts at his disposal. He said there had been a death in Calgary on Saturday night, a police officer murdered in Virden on Monday morning and there was a hostage-taking going on at the present time in Oak Lake. He told them he had a reason to believe that all three incidents were related. Then he made a request. The chief said the hostage taker was listening to news reports and the RCMP in Oak Lake were concerned. If the connection between Calgary and Oak Lake were made public, they knew the fugitive would hear it. This could upset the negotiations that were taking place and might endanger the lives of the hostages. Sawyer said he was relaying the request from the RCMP that none of this information be reported. Describing the gunman's behaviour as erratic, Sawyer told them, "What's at stake here, and I don't want to sound over-dramatic, is the lives of three people."

While he had their undivided attention, he added, "While we can only guess what the reaction would be on the part of the gunman, we have been advised not to do anything that will irritate the situation."

He said he had decided to give them this information and ask that it not be released rather than run the risk of them getting the story from another source and running it.

Sawyer added, "It would be very unwise at this stage to allow the hostage taker to be made aware of what the police suspect in connection with the homicide here.

"One can only speculate what may happen but we know the man has access to media broadcasts and their (the RCMP) option is that nothing should be released until the hostages are safe."

He finished by telling them if anyone released the information he had just given them and the hostages should suffer as a result of that, it would be "on your heads." The end result of the meeting was that the entire Calgary media present agreed to cooperate and not report the possible connection between the two events.

In Brandon, Gerry Coulter went back to the hospital for his second visit with Malette. Even though he reviled Malette for being involved in the murder of a fellow officer, even though he found her to be haughty and difficult, he knew he had to put his personal feelings aside. To be effective, he knew he had to remain pleasant, composed and gentle. His experience, training and instincts told him nothing could be gained by being harsh or abusive.

As soon as he entered the room, Malette looked up at the ceiling as she had done during their last session together. Gerry noticed there was an intravenous tube in her arm.

"How are you feeling?" he asked in his low-key manner.

"Not good."

"How long will you be on IV . . . before you can take any solids?"

"I don't know."

"Do you remember me?" Gerry asked.

"Yes," Dorothy sighed. "You were here yesterday."

"Do you mind if we talk?"

Now she looked at Gerry and showed some emotion. "I want a phone so I can talk to my husband. I won't talk to anybody until I talk to him."

"Why do you want to talk to him?" Gerry asked.

"Because!" Malette snapped, glaring at Coulter. "Because I want to know where he is and how he is. I want to make sure he's alive . . . and for him to tell me what to do."

Coulter could see she was aware that the only way out of her present predicament was through Archer and his hostage demands. Nevertheless, he continued.

"Would you consider asking your husband to give himself up and take his chances in court?"

"I'd have to talk to him first," Malette replied.

"Would you think about asking him to do that?"

"Maybe."

"Do you want me to get a hold of anyone for you?"

"No."

"Can I bring you any reading material?"

"I can't read under these conditions."

Coulter could see their conversation was going nowhere. Knowing that time was on his side and rather than irritate her further, he said good-bye and left. At the nurses' station, he learned that medically Malette was stable and on her way to a quick recovery. He also heard that she was becoming an irritation to the nurses with her abrasive behaviour and demanding ways. The nurses confided to him that this was a foolish ploy on her part because, the more she demanded and complained, the slower they responded. Gerry also determined that the two Virden police officers were both doing well. Hornseth was strong enough to go home but the doctors wouldn't allow it. Smith was heavily sedated but appeared to be out of danger.

When Coulter left the hospital he went to see Harold Scherz and asked him for a set of keys to his father's house. He explained that the police wanted the keys in case they had to get inside in a hurry. From there Gerry made a special trip into the optometrist in Virden. Archer's eye glasses had been left in the room at Countryside Inn and, considering the mayhem he had caused with his rifles at the motel, the RCMP wanted to see what Archer's eyesight was like without his glasses. Coulter was advised that Archer's eyesight was very good for distances; he only needed his glasses to read. Without them he was obviously still able to fire a gun at a distant target with deadly accuracy. This information was disseminated among all the police in Oak Lake.

Now the streets of the little hamlet were extremely quiet. Other than the policemen stationed at various posts, the only person allowed to move about was Elmer Gomph. Since he was responsible for delivering the Winnipeg and Brandon newspapers to his customers all over town, the RCMP felt there was no need to deprive them of their morning reading, especially when so much of the news was happening right in their own back yard. The Mounties let him drive down the streets and make his deliveries from door to door with the exception of Dr. Scherz' house. It was an eerie feeling for Elmer to be wandering around the village all by himself. Everywhere he went his customers wanted to know what was happening over at "the doc's place." His honest answer was that he didn't know. "The police don't tell me nothing," he would say as he handed them their paper and headed back to his car.

As Wednesday evening approached, Bert Fuller was more irascible than ever. He couldn't see any progress being made in this "damn-fool nonsense" and was not looking forward to another uncomfortable night on the couch. It only made things worse when the producers of the CBC radio show "As It Happens" managed to contact his house by phone. They wanted to interview him about the situation across the street but the RCMP wouldn't let Bert talk to them. This made him really angry because he wanted to go on the radio so that he could give them "a piece of my mind" about how he would handle the whole matter in an entirely different fashion.

That night at the Thompson Funeral Home in Winnipeg, the body of Dennis Onofrey lay in an open casket dressed in his red serge uniform. At 8:00 p.m. a large crowd of mourners gathered to offer prayers for the repose of his soul. At the front of the group Rose Onofrey sat crumpled and dazed in a chair staring into her son's coffin. As the priest intoned the rosary, the huge throng of friends and relatives that filled the room behind the broken woman murmured their response: "Holy Mary, Mother of God, pray for us sinners now and at the hour of our death. Amen."

Paula Onofrey was conspicuously absent. The young mother-to-be could not bring herself to see her husband like this and had decided to stay with her sisters and mother in Winnipeg. She wanted to remember Dennis as she last saw him, waving his flashlight to her, saying good night from his police car.

About this same time in the evening another prayer service was taking place in the Scherz' living room. Dave Penny suggested that they all take a few moments to pray together and Archer enthusiastically supported his suggestion. As all four of the occupants of the house stood in a circle holding hands with their eyes closed, Dave led them in a prayer for protection against the turmoil of the world outside. Then Archer said his own personal prayer for forgiveness and help in his present situation. He also professed sorrow for what he had done. It was a moving experience for all of them. As Archer wept, the hostages attempted to console him.

At the command headquarters the police were not inclined to be as sympathetic. They felt more progress should be taking place and more pressure had to be applied. At 6:50 p.m. they cut the hydro off again and informed Archer that they would no longer let him have any contact with Hersh Wolch. This was very disturbing to Archer. He had become accustomed to hearing from Wolch on a regular basis and looked forward to his calls because he found them informative and consoling. When Archer

221

discovered that he was being cut off from this, he became very distressed. He felt he was being deserted in a crucial situation by his only friend. This was exactly the effect the police had hoped for. Archer argued vehemently to have them change their decision but the police wouldn't budge. The only thing they agreed to do was turn the hydro back on.

Shortly after losing Wolch, Archer experienced another alarming event. Ever since the hostage ordeal began, Dr. Scherz had showed signs of strain. Sometime after dinner he began to have chest pain. Around 9:30 p.m. it got worse. Archer liked the old doctor and didn't want to cause him any harm. He was afraid the situation had become too much for Scherz and it would cause a heart attack or a stroke. At 10:40 p.m. Archer got on the phone and told his old nemesis, Staff Sergeant Don McDonald, that he was prepared to release the doctor. In return he demanded a telephone call from his lawyer, Hersh Wolch.

Sensing a major crack in Archer's armour, the police moved quickly to get the doctor out of the house. By 11:00 p.m. the negotiations for the doctor's release had reached the point where they were close to an agreement.

When Archer told the doctor he was going to be released, the old man was relieved and thankful.

"I want you to go and see my wife," Archer told him, "and tell me how she is."

"I will," the doctor said. "I will speak to her surgeon and get the information back to you. And I will try to arrange that you have constant communication with your lawyer."

"Good, Doc," Archer replied. "That's important to me. I trust him and I need to talk to him."

"I will try to see to it."

Twenty minutes later Dr. Scherz kissed his wife and walked out the side door of his house into the bright glare of the police floodlights. When Gerry Coulter met him at the intersection of Second Avenue and North Railway Street, he could see the old man was trembling and badly shaken. Gerry helped him into a waiting cruiser and off they went to the Virden Hospital to have him examined. As the car pulled away, the doctor began to cry. He said to Gerry, "What is my station?"

"What do you mean, Doctor?" Gerry asked.

"Well . . . am I free? Can I talk to a lawyer . . . or my daughter? Where am I allowed to stay?"

"You are a free man, Doctor," Gerry assured him. "You're a victim in this matter. You can talk to anyone you want and you can stay anywhere you want. We just want to take you to the hospital for a checkup, to make sure you're all right."

At the hospital, Dr. Scherz was examined by Dr. Nixon and found to be in good health, both physically and mentally. After Gerry took a brief statement from him, he drove him to the house where his daughter was staying in Virden. The relieved woman welcomed her father with open arms.

After the doctor's release, the negotiating team began to hope that a satisfactory conclusion to the hostage episode was now in sight. Archer's attitude seemed more stable now. It was obviously a relief for him to see the doctor taken away, knowing he would receive prompt medical attention. Repeatedly he assured the two remaining hostages that he didn't want to hurt them either. Although he never said this to them, he had to know his only hope was to use them to negotiate the best possible deal for his surrender.

Once Markus Scherz was safely out the door, the three remaining in the house headed for their beds. At the top of the stairs Stefanie went one way to her room, Dave and Archer went another direction to theirs. It had been another long day for all of them. Penny was asleep moments after his head touched the pillow. Archer envied him. He would have given anything for a good night's sleep but he knew he had to fight off that temptation.

In an attempt to think pleasant thoughts, he tried to conjure up images of his daughters but the mental pictures wouldn't hold. He was too preoccupied with the nagging thought that this time he was in very deep trouble. Rocking back and forth on the edge of the bed, he murmured, "Just one thing after another. Six god-damn years of trouble." The sound of his voice was amplified in the silence of the tiny room causing Penny to moan in his sleep and roll over. At this point Archer didn't care what Penny might do. He closed his eyes too and nodded off.

As dawn broke on Thursday morning, the negotiating process had gone on for more than seventy-two hours. With everyone's nerves frayed and their emotions strained, this could have been a dangerous time in the siege. But it wasn't too bad. Both Stefanie Scherz and Dave Penny could see that Archer was losing his resolve to go on. He was utterly fatigued and openly admitted the best he could hope for was a negotiated settlement that would give him some reasonable terms. He almost looked forward to getting it over with. The very idea of ending it gave him a feeling of peace.

But he was jarred back to the harsh reality of his situation when he watched Dennis Onofrey's funeral on the morning television news. This time, to make sure he saw it, the police did not disconnect the power to the Scherz' house.

St. Mary's Cathedral in Winnipeg was Dennis Onofrey's special place. It was where he had been baptized, confirmed and married. Now he would be eulogized there. As the service began, six of his detachment colleagues escorted his coffin to the front of the massive church: Ralph Mahar, Joe MacDougall and Clem MacInnis on one side, Steve Howell, Jake Cullins and John O'Ray on the other. Over 800 people, including Premier Sterling Lyon and Attorney General Gerry Mercier, were in attendance. Paula and Rose sat in the front pew beside the flag-draped coffin. Both suffered terribly throughout the service and cried during Ralph Mahar's moving eulogy for his fallen friend. After the mass both wife and mother broke down as they followed Dennis' casket out of the church into the bitter cold.

As the heavy bell tolled, hundreds of police officers from across Canada and the United States lining the curb snapped to attention and saluted as the hearse and its black entourage passed by on their solemn journey to Assumption Cemetery. Among the peace officers were eight of Dennis' troop mates from Depot Division, including Alex McLean and Derrick Reilly. It had only been three short years since they had all been together in Regina and it was difficult for them to conceive this had happened.

Russ Hornseth watched the funeral by himself in his room at Brandon General. It was the first day that Kim hadn't visited him. She was at St. Mary's cathedral sitting with the other detachment wives who had come as a group to help share a small part of Paula's pain.

Russ wasn't a man to show his emotions but as he watched in the privacy of his room, he cried uncontrollably and called out, "Oh Christ! Oh Christ!" He could only wonder if his world would ever be right again.

224

Archer's reaction was much different. Every time clips of the funeral were shown on television, he watched with riveted attention. Any reaction Archer had, he kept strictly to himself so no one could tell what he was thinking or feeling. The rest of the time, he either sat staring into space or wandering aimlessly about the house while waiting for his next phone call.

In the meanwhile, the Calgary police were gathering more evidence against him in the Crystal murder case. A witness was located who said she saw Archer and Malette going into Crystal's Real Estate office in the Mayfair Plaza late on Saturday morning. Fingerprints placed Archer but not Malette at the scene of the crime and further information disclosed that the surgical tape used on Crystal had been recently purchased by Archer at a nearby store in the plaza. Also the police had found Crystal's orange 1975 B210 Datsun hatchback on the second floor of the Calgary Place parking structure. Dusting for fingerprints was about to commence.

At noon Dr. Scherz was brought to the command centre in Oak Lake to speak to the commanding officer at Brandon, Superintendent J. R. Corley. This was primarily a gesture in public relations by the police. After this meeting, Dr. Scherz was brought before the Emergency Response Team members to brief them about the layout of his house and how Archer had rearranged the furniture and fortified the rooms. Then a psychologist interviewed the doctor in an attempt to ascertain Archer's mindset and the disposition of the two remaining hostages.

By now the press corps milling around the Oakland Hotel was thoroughly bored. No one would give them any information, so they sat around the lobby playing cards or leaned their chairs against the wall and dozed off. Occasionally photographers with nothing to do took pictures of each other.

Unknown to the press, as the day wore on, things were beginning to happen. Wolch had reestablished contact with Archer and it was becoming evident to him that his client was ready to give in. Sensing Archer's willingness to capitulate, Wolch nursed him along, assuaged his fears and offered him counsel. Together they tried to determine what might be acceptable as reasonable terms. Archer seemed to be resigned to his fate.

Nevertheless, his surrender was not a sure thing and the police had to continue to play for every advantage they could. At 7:30

225

p.m. Gerry Coulter took Dr. Scherz to dinner at the Suburban Restaurant in Brandon. He was going to take the doctor to see Dorothy in the hospital and he wanted to outline some things to be accomplished during the visit.

When Coulter and the doctor got to the hospital, Malette was sleeping and Scherz went over and stood by the bed. It wasn't long before she opened her eyes.

"Do you recognize me?" the doctor asked gently.

There was panic in Malette's response. "What have you done to him?" she asked.

"No, no," the doctor assured her. "He's fine. I came to say hello from your husband."

Malette didn't know what to make of this.

"Do you believe me?" Scherz asked.

"I've been shot. I'm worried my husband's been shot."

"No, he's not been shot. I'm the only one out. We have an agreement. I promised I would come and say hello. I've discussed your condition with your doctor. Your condition is good."

"I just want to make sure my husband is OK."

"He's fine."

Malette became more animated. "I want to talk to him."

The doctor told her not to get excited because it was not good for her. He explained there were certain regulations that had to be followed and she had to deal with Corporal Coulter in these matters. Malette turned to Gerry and suggested that if he would let her make a phone call to Archer, the police could monitor the call. Gerry told her that they were working on doing that but it was going to take more time.

Occasionally their discussion became heated. Coulter wanted a commitment from her that she would try to get Archer to surrender. At no time was she willing to offer this. Without it, Gerry wouldn't allow her to talk to him. He figured the only reason she wanted to talk to Archer was so she could find out about his plan to get the ransom money and an airplane to flee the country. Although Coulter knew this was nothing more than a pipe dream, he also realized it was the only hope she had of escaping custody.

Finally Coulter asked her to commit herself. "Will you talk to him and try to get him to give himself up?" he asked.

"I can't say," Malette replied.

"Well then, I can't go for what you want."

"You bastard," she said. "You come in here at this time of night and get me all upset . . . and here I am shot in the back."

As she continued her tirade, Coulter signalled for the doctor to follow him out of the room. Once outside, they headed back to Oak Lake. There was no use staying any longer. There was nothing to be accomplished by talking to Dorothy.

By 11:45 p.m. they were back at the command centre to find that negotiations were well under way for Archer's surrender. By the time the police got to their final position, Archer had been bargained down to a set of rather inconsequential conditions. He wanted all outstanding charges against him in British Columbia and Ontario dropped. These included fraud and assault. He wanted to meet and talk with his wife in the Brandon Hospital for at least one hour before he was taken away. Fearing angry police reprisal, he demanded that his personal safety be assured after his surrender. Finally, he asked that he and his wife would receive competent defense lawyers.

It took a while to contact the Attorneys General of British Columbia and Ontario and get them to agree to drop all outstanding charges against Archer. Once they had that assurance, the rest of the conditions were easy to guarantee. As soon as Archer received confirmation of the terms, he agreed to surrender. Then Staff Sergeant Ferguson gave him explicit instructions on how he and his hostages were to leave the house. Archer told him he would call back when he was ready to step out.

He asked Dave Penny to take all his guns and empty them of their bullets and put the ammunition in a large candy dish on the coffee table in the middle of the living room. Then Dave was to lay his guns on the floor beside the table. While Penny did that, Archer went up to the bathroom and had a bath and a shave. In the meantime Stefanie Scherz washed Malette's blood out of his clothes so he would be presentable when he surrendered.

When Archer came downstairs, he asked Stefanie to make him a trade. Suspecting that Dorothy would have no cosmetics in the hospital, he asked Mrs. Scherz for a small package of lipstick and make-up in exchange for a pair of gold-plated scissors that Dorothy always used to cut his hair. Stefanie agreed and they completed their transaction just before 3:00 a.m.

After that, Stefanie Scherz offered him a shot of brandy and some coffee. Both she and Dave Penny, to a certain extent, had bought Archer's explanation of what had happened in the shoot-out at the motel. While Archer drank his brandy, Stefanie consoled him, "What you did was an accident. You murdered, yes. You are going into a murder trial but it was an accident. What you do now is intentional."

Of course, neither Stefanie Scherz nor Dave Penny had any knowledge of Archer's involvement in the Crystal affair in Calgary. Had they known about that, she wouldn't have been so prepared to dismiss his actions as an accident and certainly wouldn't have made any attempt to support him or bolster his confidence.

Archer nodded his appreciation. He felt a little stronger with the warmth of the liquor coursing through his veins. As usual, Dave Penny had little to say. He was just glad to be getting out with his life and looked forward to seeing his wife and kids again.

Once Archer finished his brandy, he said it was time to go. As they were about to leave the house, Archer said he was afraid they would shoot him. He wanted to put a hood over his head so no one would be able to recognize him.

"You are not a hood," Stefanie insisted, "so don't put a hood on top of your face."

That seemed to set his thinking straight. He took a couple of deep breaths and then the three of them made their way out the side door into the glare of the police floodlights. As Ferguson had instructed, Stefanie went first. Behind her came Archer with his hands on her shoulders and his head bent down. Behind Archer came Dave Penny with his hands on Archer's shoulders.

Waiting to meet them on the side street were Hersh Wolch, Jerry Ferguson and Sergeant Howard Comba. A good distance behind these three stood a crowd of fifty accredited media observers. They had been alerted at the last minute by the police and were allowed to line up single file along the side street to witness the end of the ninety-six hour drama. It was 3:02 a.m.

Before Archer was taken into custody, Stefanie Scherz offered him a little goodie bag and then gave him a kiss on the cheek.

"Do the best with what you have," she said.

"Thank you, " Archer replied.

Then the police handcuffed him and led him away to a waiting unmarked cruiser. Not far down the road, one of the Mounties standing by his vehicle reached for the car's microphone and reported to Brandon: "Suspect in custody."

Across the street Bert Fuller smiled as he pulled on his pajamas and went to bed in his own room. One of the longest hostage-taking episodes in Canadian history had ended.

For Archer it was the beginning of his descent into doom.

BRANDON

O nce Archer was in custody, the police kept their promise and drove him to Brandon General for his one hour visit with Dorothy. During the trip he spoke endlessly and openly about his predicament. Constable Gary Harrison, one of his guard-escorts, paid particular attention so that he could make notes about what Archer said. Much of it was a repetition of what he had been telling Jerry Ferguson on the phone for the last four days.

Several times he professed how sorry he was that one of the RCMP members was killed. But he offered an explanation: "When the policeman kicked in the door . . . all the police had their guns drawn and one told my wife to come out from behind the screen . . . when the cop on the right pulled back the hammer of his gun, I fired."

Archer went on to tell how he spotted another figure kneeling against the motel wall and fired at it with his shotgun. He thought this shot had been deflected by a piece of wood or something so he grabbed his .308 rifle and fired with his left hand, aiming with his left eye. "Once the shooting stopped," he said, "I ran out of the motel and got into the police cruiser. Before long Dorothy followed me and I was then I heard her scream but didn't know if she was hit. Dorothy jumped in the car and told me to drive."

In his disjointed, rambling manner Archer went on to say, "I tried to be rough with the hostages but they got to me first. They were such nice people, I didn't want to harm them . . . sometimes the hostages were left in a room alone with the guns but they were afraid to touch them." Archer also told Harrison that during the hostage-taking he didn't always carry a gun and that he walked around a lot at night "afraid the RCMP would come through the windows."

When they got to the hospital it was 4:30 a.m. and Archer was taken directly to Dorothy's room. She had been sleeping lightly and was easily awakened by his presence. They were allowed a few brief kisses and then he was settled into a chair at her bedside. Their conversation was intense and relatively private with a police officer

231

stationed just outside the open door of her room.

Both of them were concerned about what would happen to them now. Archer told Dorothy that he had arranged to get all charges dropped that were pending against her in Ontario and British Columbia. He said he would get the best lawyer available to defend her and assured her that she would have little trouble getting off with a relatively minor sentence for her part in their latest escapade. "After all, honey," he said, "you didn't do anything. I'm the one who did all the shooting."

Then, in what seemed like a matter of moments to them, their hour together was up. Glancing back at her as he was led away, Archer called out, "I'll see you later." From there he was taken to a private room and given a brief physical check, after which he was happy to crawl into bed. Including the drive from Lethbridge to Virden, Archer had been awake for the best part of the last 115 hours. To monitor his vital signs, the doctor hooked him up to some electronic devices. Then, even with his ankles shackled uncomfortably to the bed, he fell asleep in minutes.

Two police guards were stationed in his room. At one point in the night, the alarm on one of the machines went off causing blinking lights and a loud warning noise inside the room. When the two guards, who were reading magazines, looked up at the monitor they saw that one of his vital signs had flat-lined. Even though no medical assistance seemed to be on the way, the two policemen glanced at each other for a moment then went back to reading. When medical help did arrive, they discovered it was a machine malfunction. The two policemen didn't care. To them, Archer was a "cop killer" and their reaction was an indication of their contempt for someone who had taken the life of one of their colleagues. It was the kind of disdain that would be directed at Archer daily for the rest of his life.

When Archer woke up it was Saturday. He had slept for over twenty-four hours. Once he finished his breakfast, Gerry Coulter came in and asked if he would care to make a statement. He was eager to do so.

It took him one entire hour to dictate a long, rambling statement that, when transcribed, went on for seventeen pages. In it Archer stated that he had been afraid of people getting at him (especially on his job) for a long time and he took some pills

232

at the Virden motel to help him relax before going to bed. The next thing he knew, there was some banging on the door and he didn't know who it was. When he realized it was the police, he was alarmed to see them with their guns drawn. Archer said he knew he was in some trouble with the truck and "what have you" and he didn't know what to do and panicked. He got his guns together and opened the door. Then, he told Coulter, "I remember I seen one officer, his face . . . and he had the gun put alongside his head and brought it down . . . and then he brought his gun out and pulled back the hammer and when he did, I thought he was going to kill her and I shot him . . . at him. I just pointed in his direction and squeezed the gun off . . . I was afraid he was going to kill us. And then all hell broke loose and there were bullets all over the place.

"My wife was screaming, 'they are going to kill us, they are going to kill us' and somebody out there was yelling 'kill the son of a bitch, kill the bastard' . . . it was not that I was killing anybody; it was like I was in a shooting gallery, shooting at little targets and the lights were going on and off. And that's all it was. It was not the idea of killing somebody. It was, I don't know, like a target practice . . . and the thing is, these targets were shooting back at me.

"I did not do anything until the hammer started to come back and that was it . . . if they had approached me differently . . . if they had maybe stood back with horns (loudhailers) and talked to me, I probably would have come out with no trouble. But to jump at me like that after taking my pills and having a long day and being nervous driving in that weather . . . but when I seen the guns, it just triggered me that's all, it just triggered me . . . I have been a hunter and it was just a hunter's instinct . . . I can equate it with the fact that my wife was going to be shot. That's the only thing."

Archer finished with his feelings of remorse: "It grieves me to know that I have done such a bad thing. It really does. I have nightmares every time I close my eyes, I see them and I am just sorry that it happened."

Coulter didn't ask any questions or respond in any way to what Archer told him. He simply copied down his statement without comment. But as he wrote, he found what Archer was saying to be distorted and very self-serving. Why was there no mention of the Crystal matter in his statement? Obviously he wanted to conceal that information. Why did he take his guns and his ammunition into the motel room? Coulter could only conclude that Archer wanted to be ready if the police came knocking at his door. He was prepared for a fight. He took his chances and fought it out with the police; now he was looking for a way to avoid the consequences.

Once he signed the statement and Coulter was gone, Archer began to feel a change in attitude from everyone who dealt with him. They were now less attentive, less communicative. Even the nurses had fewer words for him and, on the rare occasion when they looked at him, he could feel the chill of their cold stares. Moment by moment the harsh reality of what people thought of him was beginning to surface. He was no longer the omnipotent master over his frightened hostages.

Later that morning, he was shackled hand and foot, whisked out the back door of the hospital and taken to the Brandon RCMP detachment where he was mugged and fingerprinted. When Ken Bullock was filling out one of the administrative forms on Archer, as a matter of course, he asked him his occupation. Archer answered, "Killer." It was an admission of guilt that later would be used against him. After that Archer was shipped to Headingley Provincial Jail on the western outskirts of Winnipeg where he was warehoused prior to his trial. At Headingley, Archer got his first dismal taste of real, prolonged incarceration. He was locked in a small, dank, antiquated cell with one bare light bulb to read by. For security purposes, he was separated from the other inmates. For all intents and purposes, Archer was in solitary confinement. He complained about it but nobody listened.

By now the connection between Archer and Malette and the Crystal killing was being reported in the media. As soon as Archer was taken into custody, Calgary Police Chief Sawyer released the pertinent details of the Crystal case. These included: the advertisement in The Albertan that Crystal had answered and the fact that Crystal's credit card was used at the Virden motel and more credit cards and identification were discovered in the Virden motel room. Sawyer ordered two of his detectives to fly to Brandon to interrogate both Archer and Malette now that she was sufficiently recovered from her gunshot wound.

On Monday, January 30, Archer appeared in court in Brandon

and was served with a joint first degree murder charge. Because of Malette's isolation, she was not made aware of the fact that she was being jointly charged with him. For some reason, Dorothy was under the illusion that she wouldn't be charged with murder at all. In idle conversations with the police guard at her room, she said that Bruce had indicated she might get six months for her part in the house break-ins and hostage-taking. On another occasion she said a lawyer speculated to her that she might get somewhere around two years for her minor role in the recent series of incidents—the house break-ins and hostage taking. From one of the investigating police officers, she was led to believe she was looking at anywhere from five to twenty years for her part in these incidents. None of these opinions took into consideration that she might be charged for Onofrey's murder. Consequently, Malette was in for a very big surprise.

On the same day that Archer was charged with murder, he was taken to the Brandon City police station and put in a lineup with a dozen other men. For identification purposes arrangements had been made to bring in all the hostages as well as most of the other witnesses from the several farms Archer had raided. Asked individually to pick Archer out of the lineup, they all did so successfully.

On Thursday, February 2, two detectives from Calgary, Ray McBrien and Russ Bain arrived in Brandon and met with Gerry Coulter. He took them to see Malette in the Brandon General Hospital. When Coulter introduced them to her, she refused to talk. "I'm not answering any questions," she said in a pleasant but firm manner, "talk to my lawyer." Then she handed them a letter from Hersh Wolch that instructed the detectives that they were not to talk to his client, Dorothy Malette. When the same two Calgary investigators visited Archer in Headingley, he refused to talk and admitted nothing about having Crystal's credit cards in his possession.

The following Monday, Malette was well enough to leave the hospital. Gerry Coulter took her to the Brandon detachment where she was photographed and fingerprinted. When they advised her that she was being charged jointly for the first degree murder of Dennis Onofrey, her jaw dropped in disbelief. She asked Coulter how could they charge her with murder when, as Archer had told her, "she hadn't done anything."

After the initial shock wore off, Malette made a move that backfired on her. She knew the contents of the rental truck were stored in the basement of the detachment and asked Coulter, since they were in the building, if she could get something out of her personal effects. Gerry suspected she might want to retrieve some incriminating evidence from the pile of refuse from the truck that Ident were still processing. So he agreed to let her go down in the basement and lead him to what she was looking for.

Coulter followed her down to the rifle range and stood back while she went directly to one box that had as yet not been catalogued. As she started to open the box, Gerry told her, "Hang on for a minute." Looking at his watch, he said, "I've got to get you to the Remand Centre in Winnipeg right away. We're going to have to come back and do this another day."

Malette argued vigorously, trying to persuade him that it would only take her a few seconds to find her stuff. But Gerry stood firm and led her upstairs. From there, two other RCMP took her to the Winnipeg Public Safety Building, where she was locked up.

As soon as Malette left, Gerry went down to the box that she wanted to open and examined its contents. It didn't take him long to find something interesting. There, in one of the albums in the box, were a number of Polaroid pictures of an older, balding man sexual engaged with Malette on a couch. Although most of the pictures showed mostly him and only the torso of a woman wearing black-net panty hose, two of the photos clearly showed Malette's face. In the photos where you could see her face, the panty hose she was wearing indicated she was the headless woman in the other photographs. The police determined that the man in the photos was Maurice Crystal.

One of the Polaroid photos shows Crystal in the same clothing, same bonds and in the same position on the couch as he was in the photos taken by Calgary Ident at the time his body was discovered. Since the Polaroid photos were taken at a variety of angles and distances it seems clear they were not taken with the use of an automatic timer. Obviously a third person was present in the room using the camera and in all likelihood it was Bruce Archer who was taking the pictures.

The implications were obvious. Coulter advised Detectives

McBrien and Bain of his photographic discoveries just as they were boarding their plane back to Calgary. They took some of the photos back to Calgary with them as evidence. Two days later, Archer and Malette were charged with first degree murder in the death of Maurice Crystal. Although a warrant was issued for their arrest, it wasn't executed. A decision was made by the Chief Crown Prosecutor for Alberta to hold the murder charges in abeyance and await the outcome of their murder trial in Manitoba.

In the meanwhile things had not been going so well for Russ Hornseth and Candy Smith. Russ' wounded eye had been damaged beyond repair and its function was threatening to impair the vision in his good eye. On February 8, on the recommendation of his doctors, his left eye was removed. By then Candy Smith had already been told the bad news that her injuries were so severe they would make it virtually impossible for her ever to bear children.

Almost six months after Dennis Onofrey's murder, on June 19, Archer and Malette's preliminary hearing began in the Brandon Court House before Judge Rodney Mykle. The inquiry was to establish whether or not the crown had sufficient evidence to warrant holding Archer and Malette for trial. The results of the hearing were as expected. In addition to a charge of first degree murder, fifty-two charges were laid against Archer and forty against Dorothy on counts including theft of a police cruiser, kidnapping and possession of a restricted weapon and possession of a credit card obtained by the commission of an offense.

The host of charges were compiled under the instruction of Jack Montgomery, the Director of Prosecutions for the Province of Manitoba. He also presented the case for the Crown at the inquiry. Montgomery was a wily veteran of the courtroom. At fifty-one he had established a reputation for being bright, thorough, articulate and flamboyant. Not at all uncomfortable with the heat of the lights at centre stage, he was renowned for his dramatic flare and was affectionately know among his colleagues as "Hollywood Jack." His nickname aside, when it came to prosecuting criminals, Montgomery was also renowned for being deadly serious about his work. He very seldom lost a case.

Testimony was heard for a two week period at the end of which time the two accused were committed to trial on a joint charge of first degree murder. All the other charges were referred to a later hearing. Once the trial date was set for the fall, the Crown and two defense lawyers began to prepare their cases.

Besides the ample witnesses and the mounds of evidence at his disposal, Montgomery wanted a model of the motel as a visual aid to help make his case clear to the jury. He spoke to photographer/artist Bernie Sucharov at RCMP Headquarters in Winnipeg and asked him to construct a model of the Countryside Inn on a 4' x 8' sheet of plywood. Sucharov, in turn, worked with Ken Bullock of Brandon and Clem MacInnis of Virden to help construct the model exactly to scale. They spent one full month measuring and photographing everything at the Countryside Inn including the adjacent houses on Nelson Street. The Province of Manitoba mapping office assisted by providing aerial survey mapping photos of the area that helped to make their drawings of the buildings extremely accurate. The result was a detailed model that proved to be very effective. To this day it has been preserved under glass and is on display in the spacious lobby of RCMP Winnipeg Headquarters.

Hersh Wolch was retained to represent Archer at trial. At thirty-eight, Wolch had already acquired a wealth of experience in the criminal courtroom. Early in his career he had been an effective crown counsel but in the last several years he had justifiably established his credentials as one of Winnipeg's preeminent defense lawyers. Wolch's style was quiet and gentle but the substance of his legal thrusts was often brilliant and effective. He and high profile murder cases seemed to be mutually attracted to each other. Later Hersh Wolch would go on to national prominence in his representation of wrongfully convicted David Milgaard by getting him released from prison after Milgaard had served twenty-three years of his murder sentence.

Wolch recommended that Malette use a young, highly regarded Winnipeg lawyer named Jay Prober. At thirty-five, Prober had amassed extensive litigation experience in Winnipeg almost exclusively in the area of criminal law.

The trial of Regina vs Archer and Malette began in Brandon before Mr. Justice J. M. Hunt in the court of Queen's Bench on the morning of November 7, 1978. From then until the conclusion of the trial, queues formed every morning for seats in the crowded gallery. Many of those in attendance, both police and civilians alike, wore red lapel buttons that said, "Support the RCMP."

From the outset, Montgomery felt he had no real problem in prosecuting Archer. Clearly his crime was the unprovoked murder of a police officer killed in the performance of his duties. But Malette presented a more difficult challenge for him. He based his prosecution of her on the premise that she was a "party to the offense" and together with Archer formed a common intent in the act of murder. His contention was that she knew there were loaded guns in the motel room, didn't yell out or warn the police of the danger they faced and then, after the murder, fled the scene with Archer. To make his case against both parties, Montgomery called twenty-one police witnesses and forty-one civilian witnesses. He was greatly aided in his reenactment of the Onofrey murder by his use of the scale model of the motel.

Wolch knew he had problems in defending Archer. He considered using the defense of insanity and ordered a forensic psychological assessment of his client. But he rejected that approach when it was determined that Archer was not psychotic.

Once that was established, Wolch considered another option. He knew that Archer had a recent history of amphetamine abuse and realized the Valium and Darvon that he had taken the night of the shooting would probably have impaired his ability to think clearly and thus reduced his culpability. But Wolch rejected this defense as well. He knew from experience the jury would not buy this argument because most jurors are not inclined to be sympathetic to an accused who gets himself all "juiced up" and then commits murder.

The biggest difficulty Wolch had was that he couldn't let Archer take the witness stand. Nothing in Archer's recent past would endear him to a jury, especially Maurice Crystal's death and, although Wolch knew that this could not be entered directly against him, it was a spectre constantly hanging over Archer's head. Furthermore, Wolch knew the crown wanted Archer to take the stand because Montgomery had extensive knowledge of Archer's background and would have kept him in the witness box for days, literally boiling him in his own oil.

With all this against him, Wolch decided to build his case around the concept of self-defense. He knew it wasn't strong but it was the best he had, considering the circumstances.

Prober's defense of Malette was simple. His contention was she didn't do anything. She didn't fire a gun; she didn't load a gun; she did nothing to cause Onofrey's death. Furthermore, Prober felt there was no evidence that she was a party to the offense. He argued that "she committed to do nothing which would make her a party to the offense and there is no evidence of a common intention (on her part) prior to the shooting."

Contrary to Wolch's strategy with Archer, Prober wanted Malette to take the witness stand. He felt he needed to separate her from Archer on a number of levels—physically, psychologically, emotionally, and most of all legally. On the stand she could plead directly with the jury in her own words saying: "I didn't shoot; I didn't kill; I'm innocent." More importantly she could give the jury a reason to see her as a separate entity and thereby distance herself from the main culprit, Archer.

But Malette wouldn't listen to Prober; she refused to take the stand. She seemed to be taking her instructions from Archer. It was almost as if she was under his spell. Also she was probably very sensitive about having her past reviewed in newspapers across the country, especially if the sordid details of Crystal's death were somehow to surface at trial.

Once it was established that she would not take the witness stand, both Wolch and Prober agreed not to call any witnesses for the defense. That way they would be entitled to give the last summation to the jury. It was their way of playing for every advantage they could muster.

The only real surprise witness in the trial was Eldon Malette, Dorothy's thirty-seven-year-old husband, who testified he was still legally married to the accused. Eldon stated that he had married Dorothy when she was sixteen and said although she was pregnant at the time, her parents had consented to the marriage. He said he hadn't seen either Dorothy or Archer for six years, since 1972 in Peterborough. He stated that he had not been notified of any divorce proceedings at any time. This was Montgomery's way of establishing that her legal name was really Dorothy Lillian Malette.

Malette's behaviour during the trial was curious. At various times during the proceedings she fed Bruce chewing gum and candies. She treated him like a baby, patting his head, rubbing his arm and stroking his hair. Prober was unable to convince her to keep away from him in the court room. Besides that, she seemed haughty and unrepentant, almost as if she enjoyed her moment in the spotlight. To some observers her behaviour was dramatic to the point of being offensive. Occasionally she would glare at one of the young Virden RCMP wives who sat together in the court room. At other times she would fix a ferocious stare on someone in the crowd. Her actions did not go unnoticed by the spectators. It was very unwise of her.

By contrast, Archer sat like a big lump and looked pathetic and forlorn. He appeared to be remorseful, contrite and regretful of his terrible deeds.

In his closing argument, Jack Montgomery argued that Constable Onofrey's actions at the motel were in the performance of his duties as a police officer and that his death resulted from a single shotgun blast fired by Herbert Bruce Archer. He also submitted that Dorothy Lillian Malette was every bit as culpable and blameworthy for Onofrey's death as her co-accused. He claimed the evidence clearly established that Archer and Malette formed a common intention to carry out an unlawful purpose to escape arrest. In carrying out that purpose, Archer killed Onofrey and Malette knew, or ought to have known, that the commission of the offense would be a probable consequence of the common purpose. Holding the jury in rapt attention with his formidable dramatic flair, he argued that Malette was a party to the crime, a full partner and every bit as responsible as if she had pulled the trigger herself.

Montgomery turned his attention to Archer, saying the gunman killed deliberately and not accidentally. He pointed out that the police had identified themselves at the door and "of course Archer knew the police were there at his door." His contention was that Archer had sixty seconds to decide what he was going to do and because he abhorred the idea of going back to jail and because he hated the police, he decided to shoot his way out of that motel.

"This is not self-defense," Montgomery railed. "Archer was not acting under the reasonable apprehension that his so-called wife was going to be killed. If there ever was a case of an unlawful killing this is it."

After a twenty minute recess, Montgomery came back into

court and went after Malette: " . . . throughout this lengthy trial have you heard evidence of a ripple of remorse from the lips of the female accused? I think not. Did you hear a fragment of testimony that led you to the conclusion that the female accused wanted to disassociate herself from Archer's actions? I think not. Did she scream to high heaven that she was an innocent victim of a terrible mistake? I think not . . . You see, she was there with Herbert Bruce Archer assisting him in carrying out their common purpose of resisting arrest . . . the female accused gives an order "Drive!" to flee from the scene of a murder in a stolen police car . . . Oh, indeed, she is a party to this unlawful killing . . . "

After Wolch and Prober gave their closing arguments, which were strong and clear, Mr. Justice Hunt offered his instructions to the jury. During his charge, the judge said the police didn't know what they were dealing with when they went to the motel. "It might have been anything . . . it could have been a Bonnie and Clyde situation." This badly upset both lawyers for the defense and they asked the judge to recharge the jury. Mr. Justice Hunt refused to do that.

By 11:00 p.m. that Friday night, the jury was unable to reach a decision. Their indecision led to a great deal of consternation among local Manitobans who had been following the trial. They couldn't understand what was taking so long. Many callers to a local phone-in show were very vocal about the obvious guilt of the accused and couldn't comprehend the jury's problem.

The jury reconvened at 9:00 a.m. the next morning and shortly before noon reached a verdict. As the panel filed back into the courtroom, Archer and Malette kissed briefly and then sat expressionless as the jury foreman announced the verdict. Both were found guilty of first degree murder.

When Archer was asked if he had anything to say before being sentenced, he responded in a composed manner and told the court: "I would like to inform everyone here that I am not guilty. True, I took a life and I am very sorry but if I must spend the remainder of my life in prison to save the life of my wife, I will gladly do it."

Dorothy winced when she heard the guilty verdict read against her name. She was visibly shaken when she spoke, "It's not fair. I didn't do anything." Then Justice Hunt sentenced them both to life imprisonment with no eligibility for parole for twenty-five

years. Archer was led away with his head down. Dorothy cried
openly. Thus ended the month long trial, one of the longest and
most expensive in the history of Manitoba.

After Archer and Malette were convicted of the murder of
Dennis Onofrey, the Calgary murder charge against them was
stayed. This was done for a number of reasons. First of all, the
cost of the Calgary trial would exceed $150,000. Secondly, since
there is no such thing as serving consecutive life sentences in
Canada, a convicted murderer can only serve one life sentence.
So, even if Archer and Malette were found guilty of the Crystal
crime, they would receive no extra punishment. Thirdly, it can be
assumed that there was a great unwillingness on the part of the
Crown to put Maurice Crystal's family through the torture and
embarrassment of an unnecessary public trial.

As soon as the Brandon murder trial was over, both lawyers
announced they would appeal the convictions. Wolch said he had
"ten strong grounds" and ten other grounds on which to base an
appeal. Speaking on Archer's behalf, Wolch said his client felt the
jury had done the best they could and now, as Archer said, "God
will be my judge."

The Onofrey murder trial was followed a month later by a
second trial where Archer and Malette pleaded guilty to the
outstanding charges of kidnapping and unlawful confinement. At
this trial, Archer was sentenced to twelve years and Dorothy to
ten years. Both terms were to be served concurrently with their
life sentences.

Prior to sentencing, Archer revealed a facet of his sociopathic
personality, addressing the open court in a speech replete with self-
absorption. "First of all, I'm terribly sorry for the whole incident
. . . I never dreamed this would happen to me." At this juncture
he began to cry but continued, "I was scared for my wife and was
looking for a place to get help. The first place with lights happened
to be Penny's. I feel so bad for Dave Penny . . . I tried to be nice.
I had to get my wife to a hospital and took some people along
because I knew I was being chased by a multitude of police officers
who wanted to kill me. I've been made to look like a criminal . . .
I've been a hard worker all my life . . . I've been in solitary
confinement for almost a year now." He began crying again and
turned to the small group of spectators in the courtroom and said,

243

"I'm sorry all this happened." Then he sat down sobbing.

Dorothy was equally moved in her comments before the court: " . . . I was frightened . . . everything exploded out of nowhere and turned into disaster . . . I'm sorry for what happened."

When she looked at Archer, she began crying. "At times I didn't realize what I was doing," she said, " . . . people say I showed no remorse, but I do feel very much remorse. I feel sorry for the inconvenience and hardship to all concerned . . . If I had not been wounded, none of the other things would have happened."

Their appeal before the Manitoba Court of Appeal was heard on June 18, 1979. Jay Prober listed twenty-one grounds in his argument including his request for a change of venue which had not been granted. He also cited the trial judge's reference to "Bonnie and Clyde." Wolch cited nineteen grounds in his appeal for Archer. His argument was basically the same as Prober's and included the issue that the trial judge gave faulty instruction to members of the jury and failed to put the facts of the defense case properly to them.

The five man appeal court listened to the defense submissions, recessed and then came back to the bench after a few minutes. Chief Justice Samuel Freeman announced: "We are all of the view that the two appeals fail. The appeals are dismissed."

In his written opinion Mr. Justice Gordon Hall dismissed Wolch's contention that Archer killed Onofrey in self-defense as "hogwash" and stated, "If anything, the judge was overly fair to the accused." He went on to say "the Archers" showed a common intent to flee justice in connection with the stolen van and earlier false pretenses charges from British Columbia. He continued by saying they took an arsenal of weapons into the motel and loaded the firearms before Constable Onofrey was shot.

Mr. Justice Joseph O'Sullivan said of Malette: "If she hadn't run around the country telling people she shot two or three cops, she might not have been convicted." Other judges said it was hard to believe that she was an innocent bystander when she had been travelling in a repainted stolen truck loaded with weapons. They said it was significant she had not testified in her own defense.

Neither Archer nor Malette showed much emotion throughout the whole process. When their appeals were dismissed, it was the end of the line for them. Twenty-five dismal years lay ahead.

When they were taken from court that day, it was the last time they saw each other . . . forever.

EPILOGUE

Bruce Archer died from cardiac arrest complicated by diabetes while recovering from gall bladder surgery in Vancouver's Shaughnessy Hospital on December 22, 1991. His death, unlike his four infamous days in Virden and Oak Lake, was of no interest to the media. There was neither an obituary in a newspaper nor a ten second news clip on the radio or television to mark his passing.

His life in prison in many ways mirrored his chaotic life on the outside. He never accepted the fact that he was a criminal and was unhappy when he didn't receive special treatment. At Headingley, when he didn't get his way, he tore his cell apart and had to be restrained by a riot team that had to beat him up to get him under control. As a consequence of his belligerent behaviour, he was shipped to Stony Mountain Penitentiary north of Winnipeg and locked in solitary confinement.

Wherever he served his time, he thought of his fellow inmates as scum and couldn't fathom why he had to live among them. He didn't understand or accept their code of behaviour and made mistake after mistake in the way he did his time. After a few months in Stony Mountain, he was sent to the Saskatchewan Penitentiary in Prince Albert. Here he got into a chair-swinging battle with a native Canadian that put him in the hole for days.

The system put him there for his own protection. Prince Albert is a prison that houses a high percentage of Canadian aboriginals. Somehow it didn't register with Archer that once he made an enemy of one of them, he had made an enemy of all of them. From the day he fought the native, he was a marked man in Prince Albert. So to keep him alive, they transferred him to Kent, a maximum security penitentiary in British Columbia.

For a while he managed to maintain his relationship with Dorothy via correspondence. But when he became distrustful of her relationships in prison, she gradually grew weary of his accusations and abusive letters. After only a matter of months, she refused to accept any more mail from him. Everything he sent her was returned unopened. From that time on, they were totally estranged.

247

No matter the prison, he constantly complained to the guards and wardens about his placement and his treatment. He wrote letters to Correctional Services Canada and other government agencies or ministries to appeal one ruling or another he didn't like. At Kent he became close friends with another lifer who was despised by the other inmates. Thus, by extension, Archer became an object of their hatred. This was evidenced during a riot at the prison in 1981 where, in the midst of the wild melee, the inmates stabbed Archer's friend twenty-two times and Archer was stabbed twice, in the forehead and in the torso. Both of them were rushed to Shaughnessy Hospital in Vancouver; both survived their wounds.

As a consequence of that incident, Archer was shipped to Kingston Penitentiary which, at that time, was the primary protective custody institution in the Canadian penal system. The place was full of informers, debtors and problem prisoners who, for one reason or another, needed protection from the other inmates in the prison system, the so-called population. Even among this lot at Kingston, Archer maintained his unacceptable behaviour. To curry favour with the guards, he went to "the copper" (the guards) and ratted on other inmates, sometimes right in front of the inmate in question. On one occasion he went to the warden about some convicts who were planning an escape. Before long, no one trusted him, guard or prisoner. In a very short time, he was hated by his fellow inmates and this can be dangerous in any prison. It got so bad for Archer that he was afraid to spend his free time in the exercise yard. He kept to himself and stayed in his cell, seldom venturing out among the other convicts, even at exercise time.

It was at Kingston that he hatched his plan to get someone to write his life story. He wanted to have the book written in time for his fifteen-year review and use it to enhance his chances of getting early parole. Like most of his schemes, this one didn't work out either.

When Archer chose this author to write his book, his intention was to have me tell his side of the Virden gunfight, a version he felt was never adequately told at his trial since he hadn't taken the witness stand. He also hoped to gain public sympathy by having the book tell of his impoverished and deprived childhood and his years of honest labour. He wanted to illustrate his loving, responsible days as a husband and father. His idea was that such a book would impress the jury at his hearing and influence them to release him early from what he called "this terrible life."

In the months following our first meeting, he did everything in his power to impress me and the warden with the completeness of his rehabilitation. At Kingston he served as a reliable clerk in the stores. He joined the Mormon Church and claimed to have found God. At Warkworth, a medium security penitentiary in Ontario, he joined the Junior Chamber of Commerce and helped raise money for needy children. He wrote articles and poignant poetry in the prison newspaper. Most of these works professed his sorrow and anguish for his crimes. He played Santa Claus at the Christmas party for the inmates' children. In effect, he became a model prisoner.

At no time through my correspondence with him and all my visits with him at both Kingston and Warkworth, did he tell me about the Crystal incident in Calgary or the charges levied against him in that case. In the course of my research, when I discovered the incident on my own and brought it to his attention, he became livid, arguing that the Crystal case had nothing to do with the Virden gunfight and should not be included in a book about his life. When he saw that I wouldn't accept this argument and when he further realized that my manuscript was, on balance, more condemnatory of him than laudatory, he began to oppose the publication of the book.

After being transferred back to Kent, during a monitored phone call from another man in Ontario, he was overheard talking about a wild scheme to break out of prison and kidnap the children of a wealthy lawyer. His plan was to hold them for ransom and use the money to fly himself out of the country. As a result of this phone call, Archer was thrown in the hole again. When I asked why he was back in solitary, he balked at letting me know the details. He argued that this too had nothing to do with his life story. From that time on, our relationship deteriorated badly. He had always been infantile—obdurate and demanding—but then, seeing that he wasn't going to get his way, he became abusive and threatening. When I said I wouldn't submit a finished manuscript until I knew the story of this latest episode, he said he wanted nothing more

249

to do with me. The last time I heard from him was in June 1990.

In his later years in prison Archer developed diabetes. Because he didn't watch his diet or take his medication faithfully, the disease eventually started to cause him problems. In May 1990 he suffered a heart attack and was given nitro pills to ease his angina. Then in December, after several gall bladder attacks, he was taken to Shaughnessy Hospital for surgery. He survived the operation but, two days later in Intensive Care, died from another heart attack.

Thus all his best laid plans went for nothing. In 1978 he had been sentenced to life in prison and that's exactly what he served.

Dorothy spent the majority of her incarceration at the Prison for Women in Kingston, Ontario. In September 1993, under Section 745 (Sub 2) of the Criminal Code of Canada, she appeared before a jury in Winnipeg at her fifteen-year judicial review. This review is a controversial process in Canada whereby those who have been sentenced to prison for life with no parole for twenty-five years are allowed an appeal to have their sentence reduced. At her review, Malette's lawyer Hymie Weinstein argued, "There is not one person who says Dorothy Malette should not be released on parole—not one person."

This was not completely accurate. Victim impact statements are not allowed at these hearings. Only those who can shed light on Malette's character and her conduct while serving her sentence were permitted to give testimony. What Mr. Weinstein should have said was that there is not one among those *allowed to give evidence* who would say she should not be released. Rose Onofrey would certainly have argued that Malette should have completed her twenty-five years behind bars. So too would a legion of law enforcement officers across the country. But they weren't allowed to testify.

Weinstein told the jury, "The deputy warden of the prison says it's time for Miss Malette to be released on parole. Not only does she feel it's time but (she says) Miss Malette will be a positive member of the community."

A case management officer with Correctional Services pointed out that even if the jury agreed to lessen Malette's parole eligibility, she would still be on parole for the rest of her life because she was serving a life sentence. "If she breaches any of her conditions, she would find herself back in jail. She'll never be walking away. She'll always be under supervision."

On her own behalf Malette begged, "Give me a chance to show I'm a good person on my own . . . what happened fifteen years ago was a nightmare. I regret I was even there when it happened, but it was fifteen years ago.

"My kids and my grandchildren need me. If I could turn back the clock and make it go away I would.

"I still have nightmares about it. I can imagine what their (the Onofrey family) lives have been like."

The jury deliberated little more than an hour before granting Malette permission to apply for immediate parole, thus offering her the chance to leave prison ten full years before her time.

Rose Onofrey was not at all happy with the ruling. She left the courtroom seconds after their decision was announced. Outside she said bitterly, "I'm not surprised." Then she added, "I'll do what I can to persuade the National Parole Board not to let her out."

To the media, Hymie Weinstein said that in 1987 the Supreme Court of Canada had struck down provisions in the Criminal Code that had allowed an 1978 jury to find Malette guilty of being a party to first degree murder, even though she didn't know Archer would shoot Onofrey. He added, "There's no question in my mind that today, she wouldn't have been convicted. There's a very good chance she wouldn't even have been charged."

What he was forgetting was that if she hadn't been charged with first degree murder in Onofrey's death, she certainly would have been tried on the forty other counts against her that included theft of a police cruiser, kidnapping, possession of a restricted weapon and possession of a credit card obtained by the commission of an offense. She also might have been charged for at least manslaughter in the death of Maurice Crystal. And if she was found guilty of all these charges, her sentence might have run consecutively and sent her away for more than fifteen years.

Rose Onofrey wrote the Parole Board a lengthy letter about Malette that, in part, said, "She says she has changed and wants to visit her children. I have to go to the cemetery to see my son. She is responsible for him being there.

"Dennis left behind a wife, a one-and-a-half-year-old son and his daughter was born a month and a half after he was killed. His children had to grow up without a father because Dennis put his life on the line to protect you and the people that want to parole her now. The law protects the criminal and forgets about the victim.

"Dorothy Malette was not an innocent bystander. She chose to leave her children and go away with Archer . . . she knew Archer had an arsenal of weapons which had been taken into the motel room. She could have yelled out that Archer was coming out shooting. Perhaps my son would have been alive today."

Malette was granted immediate parole and is now living among us.

As for the Crystal murder case in Calgary, it will never proceed to court. Although the Statute of Limitations never runs out on a murder charge, too much time has lapsed since Crystal's death. Any attempt to bring this before the court would probably be interpreted by any reasonable judge as an abuse of due process and an attempt to seek vengeance rather than justice. As such, the case would be dismissed.

In a letter to Archer at Warkworth Penitentiary, an Assistant Crown for Alberta addressed some of Archer's questions regarding the Crystal case.

March 23, 1988

Mr. Archer:

In your letter dated December 30, 1987 you asked a number of questions regarding your future liability for the murder of Mr. Maurice Crystal, who was killed in Calgary in 1978. I have been asked to reply to your inquiries.

As you know, you and the woman you refer to as your "wife" were charged with first degree murder following the discovery of Mr. Crystal's body. Before you could be apprehended, you and your "wife" killed an RCMP officer and seriously wounded another near Brandon, Manitoba. The Calgary murder charge was then held in abeyance to wait the outcome of your trial in Manitoba. Following your conviction for the murder of the police officer, the Calgary charge against you and your "wife" were stayed. At this time we have no intention of recommencing those proceedings. Accordingly, to answer your question, "Are my wife and I still in fact in line to face these charges upon our release from prison?" The answer appears to be no.

You also asked what effect this charge may have on your "15 year judicial hearing in Manitoba". I don't know . . .

Peter Martin
Assistant Chief Crown Prosecutor

Nevertheless, it is a fact that in 1979 Archer was prepared to plead guilty to a manslaughter charge in the Crystal case and, in this regard, asked for legal assistance from Legal Aid Alberta.

A letter from this agency to Archer in the Saskatchewan Penitentiary reads as follows:

October 8, 1979

Dear Sir:

We have been advised that you are facing a murder charge in Calgary. It is also our understanding that it was your intention to plead guilty to the lesser charge of manslaughter, once the appeal to the Supreme Court of Canada on your murder charge in Manitoba has been completed.

Apparently, you have not yet appeared in Calgary on this charge and when you are ready to do so you may write to us and we will consider appointing an Alberta lawyer for you at that time.

Yours truly,
The Legal Aid Society of Alberta
Olga Dobrowney
Director, Southern Alberta

As to what really happened that night long ago in Maurice Crystal's real estate office, we'll probably never know.

After Dennis Onofrey's funeral, Paula Onofrey went back to Virden. Not knowing what to expect, she tried to block the incident of Dennis' death out of her mind and get back into some kind of normal routine. But it was difficult to live in the house alone so she moved in with Syd and Vivian Barrie until her baby daughter was born in March.

Over the next two years things began to change in Virden. Gradually many of the members and their wives were transferred out and Paula decided to move out too, to start her life anew. "I felt part of my life line was fading away," she says. "I thought it might be better for me to leave than keep watching them go one by one." She didn't know where to move but decided it wouldn't be back to Winnipeg. She knew too many people there. "I wanted to start fresh and meet new people," she says, "I decided to move west towards Vancouver."

First she moved to Port Moody, then to Port Coquitlam, British Columbia where she lived alone and raised her two children, Corey and Beckie, until they were almost teenagers. It was a very difficult time for her. There were problems with the children. Paula says, "It's tough raising kids as a single parent. My son, Corey, wanted a dad so bad. He had such a deep hurt inside him. When he was smaller he asked me why he didn't have a dad like the other kids. Sometimes I thought he blamed me for it."

Paula says when Corey was twelve-years-old he discovered there was a painting of Dennis in his RCMP red serge uniform and asked that it be hung in his bedroom. Paula agreed and put it up but very soon the young boy found that it upset him and she had to take it down.

In 1991 Paula remarried and since has had two children by her second husband. At this writing they are nine and five years of age. The older children are well on the way to establishing their own lives. Corey works with his stepfather and Beckie is enrolled at university.

The bad times are over for Paula. With the warmth of her family around her, the pain of that cold night in January has gradually begun to fade. Now she can look ahead rather than back on that life-shattering experience.

Rose Onofrey is seventy now. She's retired from her job as a secretary at Pioneer Feeds. Soft and gentle, still attractive and well-

255

groomed, she says she thinks of her son every day. She visits his grave as often as possible and has bought the plot next to Dennis so she can be buried beside him.

She says, "There's no greater sorrow than a mother's sorrow for a lost child. Every time I hear a police siren go today, I always say a prayer for those policemen so that they will get home safely.

"It's a terrible pain I carry everywhere, but you learn to live with it. I don't pity myself. Anyway, it's the next life that counts. We're only here for a little while. If I can put a smile on somebody's face, it makes my day."

Rose is still close to Paula and her grandchildren and has a very high regard for Paula's husband. "He's a wonderful man and so kind with the children," she says. Her modern apartment in downtown Winnipeg is bright and cheery with family pictures placed around the room. On one table there is a framed portrait of Dennis taken just before he died. Beside it is a photo of Beckie in her high school graduation gown. Rose says, "When Beckie sent me her picture she told me to put it beside her dad."

Rose says she doesn't hate Archer, she just constantly wonders why he had to do such a thing and wishes he had killed her instead. She never refers to him by name.

"I don't want to think about him. I hope he suffered one quarter the pain I feel. He wasn't sick; he was just bad . . . as long as he got his way." Then she concludes, "He didn't care; I don't want to forgive him."

She is angry about Malette's release. She says, "My life will never be the same but victims have no rights. Only the criminals have rights."

Russ Hornseth is retired from the RCMP and lives on a fifty acre farm near Chatsworth, Ontario with his wife, his young son, Richard, and three of his beloved horses. He spends a lot of his time riding with his boy or taking him to hockey tournaments in southern Ontario. An avid member of the Chatsworth Legion, Russ does a lot of volunteer maintenance work at the hall.

Still honest, straightforward and dependable, he's as well-liked there as he was in the west. Now in his fifties, he's no longer the party animal that he once was back in his Virden days. Today he has a glass eye and wears his brown hair combed low down on his forehead to cover up the eighteen shotgun pellets that are still imbedded under his skin. "They just told me there was no sense taking them out," he says.

Strangely enough he's not terribly disturbed about having a glass eye. It seems both his mother and his grandmother had to use a glass eye because of accidents they had as younger women. "There was always a couple of spare ones rattling around in a drawer so it was never a big deal to me," he insists.

What Russ found interesting was that the doctors didn't remove his eye right away, but only when his good eye began to deteriorate in sympathy with the one that had been so badly damaged by the shotgun pellets. When they told him they would have to take it out, his primary concern was that he wouldn't be forced to leave the field and take a desk job.

Before the operation he was assured by his superiors that he would not be forced to go inside and take an administrative position. The RCMP kept their promise to him, for a while. In July of 1982 he was transferred to the Indian Reserve at Norway House at the top of Lake Winnipeg. Russ loved it there but, because he only had one eye, the Force began to pressure him to move inside to a desk job. They were concerned about his driving and carrying out his general duties in the field. At his request they did give him a second extension to stay at Norway House but after that they began to block any transfer requests he made that would allow him to continue working in a police cruiser. Finally in July 1987 they brought him into Headquarters in Winnipeg. It was very much against his wishes. "I tried it and I didn't like it," he says.

Ever since Virden, he's harboured some regrets and he doesn't mind talking about them. "We should have phoned (the Archer's motel room) first. It was too damn routine and it blew up in our faces."

Then he talks about the one thing that bothers him most. It deals with his decision to leave the scene and go to the Virden hospital in the middle of the gunfight. "It doesn't sound good . . . that I left. I was in charge. I was responsible. It's bothered me all these years . . . my conscience."

Then he goes on to another topic of conversation among policemen. "We should have had a shotgun with us. If we had had a shotgun, I would have charged the room and I'd have got a piece of him. But the way it was, he had us outgunned. That's why he got away."

Other than that, he never thinks of the two culprits that ruined so many lives that night. He doesn't care that Archer died in prison and has no interest in what becomes of Malette.

John O'Ray is a corporal with the RCMP who has just been transferred to Dauphin, Manitoba. He has been with the Mounties for twenty-seven years and the gunfight with Archer was by far his biggest nightmare in all that time.

"I've been very bothered by this thing ever since it happened," John says. "It's had an effect on my nerves. It's been haunting me. The why, that why. Why didn't Dennis pull the trigger or get the hell out of the way?"

"This whole thing is full of whys. Why did Dennis die instead of Archer? If Archer had to raise his gun and pull the trigger and all Onofrey had to do was pull the trigger, why did Dennis die?"

John shakes his head and continues, "Why did he hesitate? Why did he hold off? Do members hold off because of our training? The RCMP have made us very aware of the consequences."

O'Ray thinks a bit and then goes on about Onofrey. "Dennis was methodical, deliberate. He didn't fly off the handle. He didn't do things quickly. He thought things out. He tried to weigh the pros and cons and this time he ran out of time.

"When I heard Hornseth yell, 'He's got a gun', I was gone. If he's got a gun, I figure he's going to use it. Everybody scrambled and ran like hell. I don't know why Dennis stood there. Sometimes we think too much. Maybe this was a time Dennis thought too much instead of letting his instincts take over.

"My instinct was to get the hell out of there. Move. Get under cover. I'm just so sorry it happened.

"I guess I was a little disappointed at the way we came down. We needed a person or a team to help us work our way through this.

"It really affected my wife. She's the one who stays at home and waits for the phone calls."

Marion O'Ray says people started calling her that day at 7:00 in the morning and were asking if it was John that was killed. "I couldn't believe it at first but when reality set in and I realized it easily could have been John, it started taking its toll."

Marion says she had to fight with herself to keep it out of her mind. "I used to think about the incident constantly," she says. "Especially when John was at work late and the phone rang. As I was walking to answer it, I kept saying to myself, 'No, no, no. Everything is all right.'"

Marion says, "At the trial, Archer told John he was going to get him for shooting his wife." Then she tells a disturbing anecdote. "Every time I used to see a white van, it took me back. Years ago I was travelling to Winnipeg on the Trans-Canada when I came up behind a car with a licence plate that said "Archer." I'm thinking maybe it's him, maybe he's out. Maybe he knows it's me. He turned off to the right. I accelerated but was watching in my rear view mirror all the way to Winnipeg.

"I hate them. I wish they were both dead for what they have done to my family. They have left behind a lot of damage. What they did was not right. They did it with a sane mind. They should suffer the consequences."

John has been watching his wife and listening to her. Angrily he says, "Look at the damage that ten minutes of craziness has caused . . . years of suffering and heartache . . . for everybody."

Candy Smith has had a long, agonizing recovery. She recently resigned from the Force and lives a rather secluded life in British Columbia. At first she was willing to assist in the writing of this book and submitted to a long interview with the author. But since then, she has been unwilling to participate any further and prefers not to dwell on the incident. Painful memories still sear her emotions and she needs to avoid bringing those feelings to the surface.

Prior to resigning Candy worked in recruiting—talking at schools, interviewing applicants and lecturing at Fairmount Academy. This is a small RCMP instructional school in Vancouver where she lectured to NCOs heading for their first command. One of her primary topics was post traumatic stress disorder, a term originally coined to describe the psychological difficulties experienced by combat veterans returning from Vietnam.

Candy went through a long bout of this disorder in the aftermath of the gun battle in Virden. After her surgery, there was a lengthy convalescence where she had to learn to walk again. Then she was assigned to a desk job in Brandon for three months until she was put back in a patrol car. All the while she felt the pain of guilt in not having pulled the trigger when she had Archer in her gun sight.

At the motel, she thought to herself, "If I'm going to kill him, I have to warn him." When she hesitated and warned him, he got away on her. She says, "I hated myself for a number of years for that. Those people were taken hostage because I hadn't done my job. Because I hadn't stopped him."

Her guilt was compounded by sly comments and insinuations from other members of various police organizations. "They liked to tell me how I should have done it. There was a lot of second guessing. I had to keep defending myself. After a while I wouldn't debate with them. I just pulled inside myself." She stops for a moment to collect her thoughts and then goes on, "All I wanted was for them to ask 'How are you doing? How are you handling it?' But I guess they wanted to feel superior. I could feel their hate."

The women's issue was also subtly involved in their comments and attitudes. Candy bristles at that. "I hesitated to shoot Archer because I'm human, not because I'm a woman. But for the longest time I couldn't shake the feeling that I kind of let my gender down."

After the incident, as she was transferred from Flin Flon to Ottawa to Vancouver, things got progressively worse. Candy was all right at a desk job but she was very nervous in the field, working in a cruiser. This filled her with guilt and shame and she began experiencing terrible mood swings. Feeling unsupported and alone, she gradually became more and more depressed and withdrawn. Eventually she became angry and resentful towards the impersonal and unfeeling bureaucracy of the RCMP. "I felt so isolated and frustrated with their lack of concern. Why didn't they see it?"

The turbulence she felt inside was compounded by her natural reluctance to demand help. She was on the horns of a dilemma. On one hand she was concerned that if she asked for help, everyone would know she was in trouble. She says, "The minute you ask for psychological help they remove you from the field." She didn't want her colleagues talking about her like she had heard them talking about others who had experienced problems. On the other hand, she was resentful: "Why do I have to beg?" After eight and a half years of torment, she'd had enough. She said to herself, "Hold it! I have not talked this out. I am not living the rest of my life like this."

When Candy finally did ask for help, she got it immediately. She spent twenty-four sessions with a psychologist who helped put her life and her job back in order. Although her experience was difficult, Candy is quick to explain that today the Force is much improved at recognizing and assisting members with these kinds of problems. At present, anyone experiencing a traumatic incident will receive psychological counselling immediately.

Candy Smith has some nice memories of the Virden incident. She remembers the thousands of cards, letters, poems, books and tapes she received from all over Canada. There were so many flowers, they wouldn't fit into her room so the nurses just showed them to her and then spread them all over the hospital. "It was simply wonderful. Things came from Nova Scotia to British Columbia—the majority from Manitoba, of course."

Candy also recalls a brief exchange she had with Archer at the trial in Brandon as they passed each other in the courtroom.

Archer said, "I hope you're OK."

Candy replied, "Yes, I've recovered quite well."

As he was being led away, Archer turned and said, "I'm sorry."

Candy says she somehow found God in the Virden incident and that has led her to forgive Archer for what he did.

Dave Penny is retired from the Virden Waterworks. He lives in a different house now but on the same 130 acres where the hostage incident began. He is a private person who reads a great deal and studies the Bible through courses offered by the Jimmy Swaggart Ministry. Still big and strong, he remains quiet and gentle as a lamb.

Dave found Jesus when he was twenty-seven and is constantly trying to make himself into a better person and help others to a better life. He has no rancour towards Archer. He says Archer was like a child and when Dave told him about Christ, the Lord seemed to help Archer and stabilize him. Penny is not sure about the Stockholm Syndrome taking hold but admits that to a point they did like each other throughout the ordeal.

"You get attached to a person," he says.

"I told Archer that I sympathized with the predicament he was in but he would eventually have to face his punishment."

Penny still feels that Archer wasn't a hardened criminal.

"He didn't have a bad attitude and he was very concerned that the lady police officer was going to die."

"I felt all along that he wouldn't hurt us except if he lost his mind and went berserk. We all tried to keep him stable." Dave feels everything worked out because "the Lord was watching over us."

At the time of the trial, people around Virden looked at him with suspicion because he spoke nicely about Archer in his testimony. But even today Penny has nothing against him. "I felt sorry for him," Dave says, "but he had to pay the penalty . . . capital punishment, hanged or shot, whatever the law requires. If I had done what he done, I would say the same for myself. It's nothing personal with Archer. The Bible supports capital punishment. The government is responsible to take appropriate measures."

Like a kind philosopher, Dave finishes by saying, "I feel terrible for the policeman's widow and children and for the lady who got hurt so bad. But I also feel for him. It could have been so different. I understand he had a lovely wife and beautiful children. His life went up in smoke."

Lloyd Hatch had suffered from stomach ulcers for years but in March of 1986 he had surgery to relieve his distress. When the doctors operated, they discovered cancer and they thought that the spread of the disease indicated he only had a few months to live. Being the tough old farmer he was, Lloyd outlived that prognosis by a number of years. In the summer of 1988 he was still so vital he played a major role in the 100th anniversary celebration of the Oak Lake United Church. After that, throughout the spring and summer of 1989, his health deteriorated rapidly and he died in September of that year.

Wilma Hatch still lives at the end of the same long lane that leads to the lovely spread at Pleasant Dawn Farms. She and Lloyd made a nice contrasting couple. Wilma is soft and gentle and guarded with her words; Lloyd was feisty and outspoken.

When I last interviewed Lloyd, he was ill. He and Wilma came out to meet me at the car. It was their way of being hospitable while making sure I didn't overstay my welcome.

"I should have jumped Archer," Lloyd said. "He wasn't that big. I should have jumped him." It seemed like a lingering regret.

When asked about Archer's punishment, Lloyd made his position perfectly clear. "I'm a great hanging man," he said. "Why spend $500,000 to keep him locked up?" Warming to the subject he continues, "And she was more dangerous than him . . . "

"Now Lloyd," Wilma cautioned, trying to temper his remarks. It was clear he wanted to talk more but he didn't want to be misquoted or say anything to discredit the RCMP with whom their son Fred still served. "Anyway," he said, "when you write your book don't knock the Mounties. They have had enough of that. And remember, every Mountie's got a father." The look in his eyes said he meant business.

Then Wilma touched his sleeve which was a signal to him. They both said good-bye and, hand in hand, headed back into the house. They were a beautiful couple, caring and interdependent. Lloyd lived more than a year beyond the time of that interview. Sadly, now Wilma is alone. She is comforted knowing that, just like the night Archer and Malette came calling, she still has her son Tully and his family living right next door.

The white house overlooking the railway tracks in Oak Lake still belongs to Stefanie Scherz. For many years it was a curiosity to outsiders who continued to ask townsfolk directions to it. She has lived there alone since 1991 when her husband died of a heart attack. Mrs. Scherz suffered a stroke in 1989 and fell and broke her hip in 1996. She is able to get around her house with the use of a walker but doesn't venture outside very much any more.

It wasn't long after the four day ordeal ended in 1978 that the doctor and his wife decided they didn't want to talk about the incident any more. In declining a later request for an interview with a Winnipeg newspaper reporter, Dr. Scherz advised, "Don't take it personally, but that was a long time ago. We just want to forget it."

Mrs. Scherz seems to be extremely sensitive and defensive about one facet of the decade-old hostage taking. To the same reporter she blurted out, "It was not the Stockholm Syndrome." And this was before that topic was even mentioned. Most observers of Archer's surrender would disagree with her. Hersh Wolch says that what he saw at the capitulation certainly looked like the residue of the Stockholm Syndrome.

"We didn't hate him," Mrs. Scherz admits. "But we didn't know those terrible things about Calgary at the time." Now the only comment she will make is, "It's over. I don't want to talk about it anymore."

Hersh Wolch is established as one of the most successful and accomplished criminal lawyers in all of Canada. There was little he could do for Archer. "The odds were enormously against Archer," he contends. "We couldn't get a change of venue and the negative publicity in Brandon made it extremely difficult."

When asked why he took this case he replies: "Well, I got a phone call from Mike Ward at the CBC and the guy (Archer) needed a lawyer. At least he was going to need a lawyer. Besides that, there were lives in danger and I couldn't say that I was too busy to get involved. That's what it's all about. How can you be a lawyer and not get involved? I must admit I didn't think the hostage-taking was going to last for five days."

Since that time Hersh has been involved in many other hostage cases. It's become somewhat of a mini-specialty with him. He says the negotiating strategy is relatively simple. "It's no big secret. You've got to keep them talking, play for time so that they wear down." After reflecting he adds, "You know, it doesn't take long before you kind of become the guy's friend." Then a broad smile comes over his face and he says, "The ironic thing in the Archer case was that after all the time I put in, Legal Aid wouldn't cover those days. They said that I needed an application completed. I guess I should have gone up to the house with all those policemen around it and Archer inside with his guns and yelled 'Time out everybody, I got to get this application filled out.'"

He laughs at his own anecdote until he thinks of a more serious topic. "Dorothy should not have been convicted on the murder charge. She should have got seven or eight years for the other crimes, but she wasn't guilty of murder. The problem was that everyone in the courtroom and especially the jury thought of her as the one behind it all, the power behind it. Archer looked somewhat sorry and sympathetic. She didn't appear that way."

Jay Prober is grayer now than he was at the time of the trial— he was only thirty-five then. But he's still dapper and compact, bright and dynamic. He maintains the opinion that her conviction for murder was unfair. "She was not an active participant in the murder," he says. "She had no plan to kill anybody.

"Oh sure, after the fact, she may have been guilty of those other crimes—kidnapping, unlawful confinement and so on—but she was not guilty of murder. Dorothy Malette was convicted simply because she was associated with Archer and I couldn't convince her to keep away from him in the courtroom.

"She just wouldn't do it," he concludes in exasperation.

Jack Montgomery, of course, doesn't see it that way. "You see she hadn't distanced herself from the conspiracy. She didn't disassociate herself from Archer, didn't warn anyone that he had a gun and they took off together in flight."

Although he's retired now, he clearly remembers Archer and Malette as loathsome and repugnant criminals whose offense was heinous. He savours a distant memory: "Archer was not a problem right from the beginning. But most of my colleagues didn't think I could convict Malette and I was concerned about that because she was guilty as a party to the offense."

That he was successful in convicting Malette only proves how good he was at his job. Modesty precludes him from saying so but as a prosecutor his conviction rate was exceptionally high. Down through the years, only one accused murderer has been acquitted in all the many trials where Jack has acted for the Crown.

Other than Paula and Rose Onofrey, the people who have suffered most from Bruce Archer's infamous behaviour are his own wife and daughters. All three of them live in constant fear that they will be discovered as members of his family. They have all distanced themselves from the places where Bruce lived or was known. Both of Archer's daughters were badly shaken when their identities and whereabouts were ascertained by the writer. They pleaded for anonymity. However, it was important to them that the reader should understand their father was not a totally bad person. They acknowledged full-well that what he did was wrong but they can't forget the many times their father was good to them. They wanted people to know about his gentle side.

One daughter says, "Still to this day there are songs I hear (that he sang) and it breaks my heart to hear them."

Even when Archer was alive in prison, the other daughter wrote to me and said: "I feel sick when I think about my father murdering someone else and being involved with those other things. I feel that the dad I grew up with is gone. We've undergone a similar grieving process as someone who has lost a family member to a physical death. It's been a long and painful process that we are still undertaking."

In the six months before Archer died, both his daughters refused to go and see him because, "he wanted to remarry and integrate his new wife with his old family." His daughters didn't want that. They were even concerned that he would have a successful fifteen year review and be allowed out on the street again. They were frightened he would "screw things up again" as he had before.

They worried how this would adversely affect their own little families. "We loved him," one daughter said, "but we had to distance ourselves from him." Because of the rift, Bruce Archer died without his daughters having a chance to say good-bye. "There was no farewell," she said, "and that was very painful for us."

When Bruce Archer was cremated, two parties asked for his ashes. The pastor at his funeral was torn between giving them to his estranged daughters who had known him all his life or to a new woman in Archer's world. Through his typical scheming, he had met her six months before and they had recently married. She was not a person his daughters had met or wanted to know.

Even in death he had managed to stir up a torturous dilemma.

ROBERT KNUCKLE

Robert Knuckle is an Actra award-winning writer for radio, television and the stage for his play I AM NOT A LEGEND, based on the life of the NFL's coaching immortal Vince Lombardi.

He is also the author of IN THE LINE OF DUTY (General Store Publishing, 1993) an epic that chronicles the lives and deaths of the 188 members of the Royal Canadian Mounted Police who have been killed in the performance of their duties and enshrined in the Honour Roll of the RCMP.

His last book THE FLYING BANDIT (General Store Publishing, 1995) tells the true story of an American escaped convict who flees to Canada, marries and has a family that he supports by robbing fifty-nine banks and jewellery stores for a total of over two million dollars.

Mr. Knuckle lives with his wife, Elizabeth in Dundas, Ontario. Their extended family includes Richard, Leanne, Laura, Bob, Mark, Scott and Kelly. Grandchildren are expected soon.